GRUNDLAGEN DER ANGLISTIK UND AMERIKANISTIK

Herausgegeben von Rüdiger Ahrens und Edgar W. Schneider

Band 36

Introduction to Cultural Studies

Topics, Concepts, Issues

Aleida Assmann

ERICH SCHMIDT VERLAG

Bibliografische Information der Deutschen Nationalbibliothek
Die Deutsche Nationalbibliothek verzeichnet diese Publikation in der Deutschen Nationalbibliografie; detaillierte bibliografische Daten sind im Internet über http://dnb.d-nb.de abrufbar.

Weitere Informationen zu diesem Titel finden Sie im Internet unter
ESV.info/978 3 503 13716 9

Umschlaggestaltung unter Verwendung
eines Motivs von Aby Warburgs Zettelkästen

ISBN 978 3 503 13716 9

www.ESV.info

Dieses Papier erfüllt die Frankfurter Forderungen
der Deutschen Bibliothek und der Gesellschaft für das Buch
bezüglich der Alterungsbeständigkeit
und entspricht sowohl den strengen Bestimmungen der US Norm
Ansi/Niso Z 39.48-1992 als auch der ISO-Norm 9706.

Satz: multitext, Berlin
Druck und Bindung: Danuvia Druckhaus, Neuburg a.d. Donau

Preface

The impetus for this English version of my Introduction to Cultural Studies originally came from my students, who told me that they preferred to read and learn about English texts and theories in the original language. I gladly accepted their suggestion that I should have the book translated and thus make it accessible not only to students of English but also to an Anglophone readership.

This book differs from other volumes of its kind in two ways. One is that it provides an introduction to concepts, questions and theories derived from the German Kulturwissenschaften, as well as from the very different British and American approaches to the subject. The second is that its structure is not dictated by various theoretical trends, schools and paradigms, but by seven major themes that have emerged as important and productive areas for cultural research: signs, media, body, time, place, memory, and identity. The subject of 'gender' does not have a chapter heading of its own, but is covered in various forms by the chapters on media, body and identity.

The aim of this book is not to instruct so much as to stimulate the interest and independent thinking of students from various backgrounds by providing them with a fund of general knowledge, texts, tools, ideas, questions and inspirations for their own readings and intellectual endeavors. Much care has been taken to introduce theories and concepts not in the abstract but within a concrete framework of texts and contexts which illustrate their potential in action. Theory and text, concept and example have therefore been woven together as closely as possible.

This volume has been translated from the third German edition and so profits from its improvements in terms of readability, corrections and updated bibliography, which now contains a slight preponderance of English titles. I am greatly indebted to David Henry Wilson, who has managed to smooth out my sometimes cumbersome German sentences, making the text much more lively and accessible. The dedicated support of Janine Firges has been a huge help. She has devoted a great deal of time and scrupulous attention to the details of this English edition, weeding out mistakes and inconsistencies. Last but not least, I would like to thank Dr. Carina Lehnen from the Erich Schmidt Verlag, who has supported this translation project from the start and seen it through every stage of the printing process.

September 2011 Aleida Assmann

Table of Content

Introduction

The purpose and structure of this book

In 2002, the German *Anglistenverband* issued an announcement on the Internet that cultural studies were now an integral element of *Anglistik*, and these transcended "the traditional borders of specialist disciplines", enabling us to prepare for "the challenges of the 21st century".[1] It was against this background that a conference was held in 2003 on the subject of "Cultural Studies in *Anglistik*. Where We Are Now", the proceedings of which were published on the Internet.[2] There can be no doubt that cultural studies have indeed established themselves as **integral to the study of English language and literature** in Germany. The initial, innovative phase is over, and there are now large numbers of works devoted to the restructuring of the whole subject.[3] The aim of this book, however, is not to go over what is already old ground, or to reinforce an argument that has already been accepted. Nor, in the face of the countless introductions and anthologies available on the subject, shall we be offering a survey of the various methods and approaches used in the study of British and American culture. This is neither an encyclopaedia nor a handbook, and you will find no lists of names, trends, or developments in the field. Our objective is to identify some basic themes which we will discuss from a cultural point of view, and link with literary texts. It goes without saying that the examples can only be selective. Our hope, though, is that they will stimulate interest in certain fascinating areas and will provide fresh approaches to complex questions. We will seek to delve into the basics of literature and to sharpen our awareness of its dependence on, and critical perception of, 'culture'.

Our introduction to cultural theories and methods will therefore be interwoven as tightly as possible with an introduction to British and American literature.

---

1 http://www.britcult.de/DOTagungInhalt.htm; (September 2011).

2 A documentary of the conference can be downloaded here: http://www.britcult.de/doKomplett.pdf; (September 2011).

3 Herewith a small selection of publications from a list that has rapidly become unmanageable: Toby Miller, ed. (2001): *A Companion to Cultural Studies,* (Blackwell Companions in Cultural Studies 3), Malden/Oxford: Blackwell; Ansgar Nünning/Vera Nünning, eds. (2003): *Konzepte der Kulturwissenschaften*, Stuttgart: Metzler; Ansgar Nünning/Roy Sommer, eds. (2004): *Kulturwissenschaftliche Literaturwissenschaft*, Tübingen: Narr; Chris Barker (2008): *Cultural Studies: Theory and Practice,* 3rd ed., London: Sage; Michael Ryan (2010): *Cultural Studies: A Practical Introduction.* Malden/Oxford: Blackwell; Harun Maye/Leander Scholz, eds. (2011): *Einführung in die Kulturwissenschaft,* München: Fink.

This will occasionally entail excursions into areas beyond the Anglo-American language and culture in order to clarify certain general contexts. We will also be linking cultural concepts to literary texts of different historical periods. With this combination of the old and the new I hope to show that a cultural approach should not be confined to contemporary texts but can also shed light on the literature of earlier epochs.

This volume is divided into seven chapters dealing with seven different fields, combining basic methodological concepts, theoretical approaches, and literary texts. Under the heading of **'signs'**, we shall deal with the smallest unit of cultural semantics, which forms the foundation of all processes of comprehension and interpretation. The following chapter on **'media'** develops this subject, investigating the material forms of presentation through which signs are 'mediated' and also tracing the history of these media and their constructive importance in the facilitation of artistic expression. The chapter on **'body'** deals with the physiological foundations of culture as well as with what is excluded from and undermines all abstractions, idealizations and virtualizations. The dimensions of **'time'** and **'space'** are each given a chapter of their own and cover the physical and mental coordinates of human existence that determine our actions and synchronize our ways of living within a social and political framework. The chapter on **'memory'** is concerned with the different forms and strategies we use to reach into both the individual and the collective past, and to bring the absent back into the present. This chapter leads to the subject of **'identity'**, which comprises forms of individual and collective self-awareness and self-presentation; in accordance with cultural preconditions, these may be construed as an ever evolving unit, a multiple self, or an ethnic-cultural individuality separate from and different to that of outsiders. The reader may note the absence of certain headings from this list, for example the theme of 'gender'. This theme would really need a volume of its own, but in fact it has not been ignored – it is subsumed under the chapters on 'media', 'body' and 'identity'.

Concepts of culture

Nowadays the term 'culture' is used in many different ways, which we will try to summarize here. Basically, one can distinguish between three concepts that involve value judgements and three that do not. The word derives from the Latin *colere*, which means to cultivate. Originally, this was applied to farming – hence the English word 'agriculture'. However, there is also a German word *Kulturbeutel* (sponge bag, i.e. for toiletries) which relates culture to the body. In laboratories we talk of culture when we mean the growth of organisms under specially controlled conditions. These basic meanings can be expanded to encompass all kinds of human activities and images: youth culture, drug culture, corporate culture.

The meaning is very different, however, when the term is applied to **geographical and political entities** such as nations, with their different histories and the unity conferred on them by their language, character, art, customs and traditions. 'Culture' is the term that is used to give all these variegated elements an all-embracing name and identity. In this sense we talk about British, American, German or Western culture, implying a more or less clear distinction between these entities. However, while they may appear to be homogeneous from the outside, this impression usually changes considerably if we look at each culture from within. In recent years, the concept of cultural unity has rightly come under attack; the assignment of unified national characteristics has been deconstructed as a piece of fiction and criticized as 'essentialization'. Nevertheless, this justified criticism does not mean that we can altogether reject the concept of culture as a basic orientation. Despite their acknowledged heterogeneous, hybrid and open-ended nature, we still tend to refer to cultures as unified entities in practice.

Besides cultivation and national character, there is another concept which has gained increasing prominence during the last twenty years. This is the view that culture constitutes everything that is related to **humans**. The philosopher Bernhard Waldenfels writes that culture comprises whatever humans make of themselves and of things, and whatever happens to them in the course of the process. This includes symbolic actions, collective rituals, styles of art, social institutions, and the ever-expanding world of media and technology. Like the soul in Aristotle, culture is "in a certain sense, everything".[4] Whatever people do and touch and look at turns into culture, just as everything King Midas touched turned into gold. This approach does not end at Nature but can be extended to the natural sciences, which use culturally determined technology to study Nature out of culturally motivated interests. If everything is culture, the positive methodological outcome is that all areas of human life and experience are open to cultural study – from gambling machines to teddy bears to waste. This all-inclusive concept has given new interest and value to things that had previously been regarded as peripheral and unimportant. An ethnographic approach leads us from the study of exotic foreign cultures back to our own and results in defamiliarizing our own perceptions of the world. However, the extreme expansion of the term 'culture' also has its problems. With the complete removal of all cultural boundaries and of all distinctions between major and minor, high and low, comes the danger of a complete levelling of value and relevance.[5] If everything is culture, the meaning of the term implodes and is reduced to a hollow tautology.

4 Waldenfels (2001), 98.

5 Bill Readings raised similar objections (1997): "Culture ceases to mean anything as such; it is dereferentialized. [...] If culture is everything, then the invocation of culture cannot have redemptive force, cannot lend meaning (unity and direction) to symbolic life." (99)

The three uses of culture as *cultivation, national distinction* and *universal* concept have one thing in common: they exclude value judgements. As soon as **values** come into play, culture ceases to embrace everything and becomes something very special that stands in opposition to something else. Concepts of cultural values are generally polemical terms. That does not necessarily mean that culture must always be something good – as we will see, it can also be bad. 'Good' and 'bad' are both, of course, expressions of value. The decisive premise that underlies the following concepts is that which makes culture into a social and political showground for the bestowal or withdrawal of value – an arena in which the high, the middling and the low compete with one another, and good does battle with evil.

A normative concept that held sway throughout the nineteenth century until the mid-twentieth was that of *Hochkultur* (high culture). The bearers of this banner were the middle classes, who since the eighteenth century had discovered the secular values of the 'aesthetic' as a cultivation and sublimation of the senses, and thus drew a sharp distinction between their own culture and the entertainment industry which formed that of the lower classes. *Hochkultur* implies a vertical structure, in which 'high' refers both to social status and to aesthetic value. The two meanings converge in the concept of the elite, which can be applied equally to aesthetic aspirations and to separation from other social strata – and indeed sociologically the former could be interpreted as a means of implementing the latter. There can be no doubt that the elite culture of the middle classes canonized their concept of art in such a way that outsiders who had not enjoyed the privileges of a suitable education could never gain access. This was a major factor in preserving the social status quo. However, since the 1960 **culture as a possession** of the elitist upper and middle classes has undergone a reversal. Cultural studies have played a significant role in undermining the barriers between upper and lower. In a dynamic society with high rates of immigration and social mobility, rigid scales of aesthetic value and fixed boundaries between social classes are called into question. In Britain it was the immigrants from the (former) colonies that helped erode the hierarchical concept of culture, while in the USA it was feminism and the self-assertion of ethnic minorities. In France and Germany, the 1968 revolutions brought about a break with middle-class traditions, alongside explorations of new values and ways of living.

A second normative concept of culture is contained in the notion of the progress of civilization. Civilization in this normative sense is what makes us human and thus separates us from other forms of life. In this respect, a person is not a person *eo ipso*, but only becomes one through reflection and correction of the self. The key to this is self-discipline, control over one's natural instincts, which is a basic anthropological structure. The opposite to this concept is savagery and barbarism – that pre-cultural state of the so-called primitives, of whom it is assumed that they have not even begun the process of self-discipline.[6] 'Primitive' in this context refers not only to foreign tribes but also to one's own history. The sociologist Norbert Elias tells us in two fascinating volumes how difficult it was for Europeans in early modern times to learn forms of etiquette which are taken for granted today in the training of 3–5-year-olds: things like eating with a knife and fork, suppressing body sounds, wiping one's nose etc. The key expression in such training programmes is **'civilization'**, which means long-term control over the body, or "mastering nature in man" (Rudolf zur Lippe, 1987). Despite the centuries of such disciplinary training, however, Elias sees civilization not as a stable achievement but as a still weak counterbalance to unbridled affects – rather like a thin layer of ice covering hidden and dangerous depths.[7] This was also Sigmund Freud's view in *Civilization and its Discontents*.[8] On the one hand, he placed great hope in what he called "Fortschritt in der Geistigkeit" which is translated into English both as 'progress in intellectuality' and 'progress in spirituality'. On the other hand, Freud, who in a period of rising anti-Semitism saved his own life only by emigrating from national socialist Vienna to London, also realized that the process of individual cultivation could never be guaranteed and might at any time turn into a reactionary, collective unleashing of regressive instincts.

While Freud and Elias stand for culture as civilization, a third normative concept – linked to philosophers like Theodor W. Adorno and Walter Benjamin – is defined by a **critical approach**. Adorno connects the sacrosanct concept of *Hochkultur* with that of civilization, which is given a new, pessimistic dimension. As a Jew (like Freud, Elias and Benjamin) he is sensitive to the delicate balance of civilization, which is constantly under threat from opposing forces. His famous term for this delicate balance is the 'dialectic of the Enlightenment', because Enlightenment itself, from the very beginning, was permeated with mythical aspirations and stirred irrational countermovements. Adorno is also interested in culture as an ensemble of the peak achievements of artistic expression. His evaluations endow the works of particular poets, artists and musicians with a quasi-religious status. Culture for him is a form of transcendence. Like religion, it is the otherness, which comes to us from a different world; it is "air from other planets

6 This is the view that underlies, for instance, Joseph Conrad's *Heart of Darkness*, which we will return to in the chapter on space. In the generation that preceded Conrad, however, there was already opposition to such a perspective. The pioneering anthropologist Edward Burnett Tylor wrote a study with the provocative title *Primitive Culture*, which combined two words that were mutually exclusive according to opinions at the time. Tylor (1958) is commonly regarded as the founder of a relativistic, descriptive concept of culture.

7 Elias (1977, 1978).

8 Freud (2002).

blowing", as Herbert Marcuse once phrased it.[9] This auratic culture stands in total contrast to the mundane products of the 'culture industry', whose aim is to entertain the masses. For Adorno, this other form of culture reduces art to the level of consumer goods. The products of the culture or entertainment industry are worlds away from the elevated and genuine aura of true art. The culture-critical discourse of the so-called 'Frankfurt School' is anchored in this duality, and it has a distinctly melancholy tone engendered by the apparently unstoppable triumph of popular, mass culture.[10]

The terms **'aura'** and 'auratic' go back to Walter Benjamin. He championed the religious qualities of great art, which were irretrievably lost in the technological age of mass reproductions.[11] As a Jew he fled first from Germany and then from Nazi-occupied France to Spain, but unlike Freud, Elias and Adorno, he did not reach safety, and rather than be repatriated to Germany, he killed himself in 1940. His "Thesen über den Begriff der Geschichte" [On the Concept of History] – written when he was on the run in 1940 – contain the sharpest and most fundamental form of culture criticism.[12] This was launched not only at the products of mass culture, but also at liberal, middle-class *Hochkultur*, which capitulated to the rise of fascism. In the name of ethical responsibility, Benjamin stood up for history's oppressed people against the culture of the conquerors. From this perspective, against the tide of history, he looked on all products of culture with equal suspicion: "There is no document of culture which is not at the same time a document of barbarism"[13].

Six concepts of culture

- Cultivation in the sense of optimizing and upgrading a thing or an act (e.g. fitness culture)
- Geographical or political entities (e.g. French culture, Western culture)
- Ethnographic concept: inclusive term for everything done by or connected with humans
- Elitist concept: a 'high culture'
- Civilization: domestication of physical nature, instincts and drives
- Critical or auratic counter-concept to everyday reality (Frankfurt School)

9 Marcuse (1964), 61. 'Ich fühle luft von anderem planeten' is the first line of a poem by Stefan George, which Arnold Schönberg set to music in his second string quartet. This new use of the expression endowed it with special significance for the Frankfurt School (represented by Adorno, among others).

10 Another representative of this theory of culture is the literary critic Francis George Steiner (1997), who also entertains a Gnostic (in the sense of opposed to a false world) concept of art and therefore describes great works as 'counter-creations'.

11 Benjamin (1968).

12 Benjamin (2006).

13 Benjamin (2006), 392.

Why study culture?

200 years ago, at the beginning of the nineteenth century and the Industrial Revolution in England, the English poet Percy B. Shelley wrote the following analysis of the intellectual situation at that time:

> [...] our calculations have outrun conception; we have eaten more than we can digest. The cultivation of those sciences which have enlarged the limits of the empire of man over the external world, has, for want of the poetical faculty, proportionally circumscribed those of the internal world; and man, having enslaved the elements, remains himself a slave.[14]

He speaks here not of culture but of cultivation, which harks back to the basic meaning of *colere* in terms of maintenance, development and systematic extension. For Shelley, exclusive investment in the sciences and technology is a danger to culture, as it has brought about a one-sided cultivation of our faculty of reason, which has extended our dominance over Nature to an enormous degree, but which has also led to the atrophy of our other faculties. Man, according to Shelley, has not grown proportionately to the growth of his reason, and that is why he has become increasingly subservient to it.[15]

In 1821 Shelley was reacting to a dramatic change in humankind's view of the world and itself, brought about by the impact of science and technology on human life. It seemed to him that scientific rationality and poetic imagination were irreconcilable. Today, it is no longer possible to see the problem as merely a clash between two opposites, because **science and technology** have become just as integral to our culture as **poetry and imagination**. However, Shelley's alarm signal is no less relevant now than it was then. We are currently living through equally dramatic revolutions in physics and the biological sciences, whose new discoveries about the structure of the atom and of the genome have been a powerful influence in changing our culture. No less radical are the consequences of the electronics revolution that has created a communications network to encompass the globe and reach out into space. Together with all these scientific and technological advances, there have been social instruments of change, such as a redefining of gender relations, which have drastically altered the make-up of western society within just one or two generations. And of course one should not forget the impact of history and politics on culture: we are living in a world still reeling from the ongoing consequences of historical traumas – a world of mass expulsions and genocide, a postcolonial search for identity, and in Europe new transnational structures of organization.

14 Shelley (1968), 249.
15 His wife Mary Shelley's novel, *Frankenstein*, can certainly be regarded as a variation on this theme; see also Chapter 7.

It is my contention that cultural studies have not come about because of any new modes or methods or theoretical innovations, but that they are an answer to the radical changes in our society and our world (dis)order. This would explain why on the one hand cultural studies have developed in different places all over the world, and why on the other they have never produced a single uniform paradigm for research. Their emergence has been due not to the influence of any school of theory or to the dominance of any new method, but to changes in cultures themselves, and to the new questions and challenges that have arisen from these changes, with a concomitant effect on the study of literature as well as the other arts.

What, then, has been the impact of cultural studies on the individual disciplines? First and foremost, the **boundaries between these disciplines have become blurred**. The culture critic Raymond Williams writes: "The work which this book records has been done in an area where several disciplines converge but in general do not meet."[16] Art and literature are perceived as part of the overall culture, which relates them to political, economic, historical and social conditions and developments. This had been foreshadowed by the art historian Aby Warburg, who back in 1912 was already bemoaning the "border policing of disciplinary boundaries" of art history, and pleaded for a more comprehensive and contextualized concept of culture.[17] *Kulturwissenschaften* as he conceived of them proceed from the premise that the meaning of images and texts can no longer be confined within the borders of the work, but must also be related to its cultural environment and traditions, without denying its aesthetic status. The need for contextualization makes reference to related disciplines essential. Thus art historians, for instance, are made to discover language, writings and texts as complementary elements of their subject, while literary critics find that images and media are becoming increasingly important in their own field. This blurring of the borders, however, should not be mistaken for their complete disappearance. Indeed the different perspectives, whose foundations lie in the particular traditions of each discipline, should not be allowed to fade away in the course of this cultural restructuring. But the individual art subjects can no longer remain shut off within their self-referential, hermetic forms of discourse. Crossing disciplinary boundaries requires a common language which will be understood in all fields, and which will facilitate points of contact as well as the active integration of insights and discoveries from other fields into one's own.

Some critics see this **border-crossing as a threat** which will lead to an endless expansion of their subject. Cultural studies – and this is both their positive and their negative character – do not have any clear-cut definitions. They simply deal with culture. Culture is everything that is made or done by humans. As the Marx-

16 Williams (1976), 15.
17 Warburg (1980), 185.

ist literary critic Terry Eagleton once remarked ironically, this includes hairdressing, drinking habits, modes of address, the lifestyle of Turkish psychotherapists, a string quartet by Brahms, and the Divine Comedy.[18] While the objects under investigation are in principle boundless, the perspectives and the questions raised by cultural studies are relatively clear. The focus is always on how the man-made things that we call 'culture' are actually fabricated within a framework of specific conditions, methods, functions and consequences. At the end of the 20th century, this perspective of 'culturalization' engendered a view of cultural relativism that was similar to that of historicization in the middle of the 19th century. According to Nietzsche, its most scathing critic, the problem of historicization was also that the concept of culture had been dramatically enlarged and had lost all of its contours. Eagleton, too, complains about the postmodern randomness, which applies to a percentage of uninspired studies that sail under the banner of the new paradigm, but hardly represent the potential inherent in the new concept. Its aim is to illuminate an historical life-world in its context, to gain a better understanding of the mysterious processes of cultural transmission, and to contribute to a clearer and more comprehensive insight into the symbolic construction and contestation of our reality.

Cultural Studies and *Kulturwissenschaften* – two genealogies

Cultural studies as an academic subject have no clearly defined boundaries or unified programme, because they have developed out of a wide variety of approaches. This is due especially to the particular historical and sociocultural conditions from which they emerged. The genealogy of German *Kulturwissenschaften* is quite different from that of British and American 'cultural studies', as both are a product of the cultures from which they have emerged. It would therefore be useful to say a few words here about the difference between them. Only then will we gain a better understanding of why different local and historical situations have led to different problems, themes and methods.

Cultural Studies

Cultural studies emerged in the USA in the 1980s. Before that, they had an important antecedent in Birmingham, England, in the 1950s. In this industrial town with a high percentage of migrants and a new university, they arose from a **crisis in the humanities**. This at least is the thesis contained in the title of an essay by Stuart Hall, who played a major part in this new approach: "The Emergence of Cultural Studies and the Crisis of the Humanities".[19] Together with Raymond Wil-

18 On the inflation of the term 'culture', see Eagleton (2000), Chapter 2.
19 Hall (1990).

liams,[20] Edward Thompson and Richard Hoggart he belonged to a group of young Marxist literary critics who had studied under F. R. Leavis at Cambridge University. Leavis represented an elitist concept of bourgeois 'high culture' in which this younger generation (Hall came from the former colonies, Williams from a working-class Welsh family) could find no relevance to their own interests, experiences and aspirations. They left Cambridge for Birmingham where they developed a new concept of culture that contrasted sharply with that of their former mentor. Leavis had become a sort of pope who represented a sanctifying policy of canonization which formed the basis of the humanities; his magnum opus, significantly entitled *The Great Tradition*, had prescribed a new and binding evaluation of nineteenth-century English literature. At a time of increasing rationalization and technology, Leavis fought for culture as an indispensable source of energy for human life. His cultural-pedagogical model was founded on a clear opposition between the mindless, apathetic masses on the one hand, and on the other those few whose calling it was to be the conscious bearers of culture. This was the province of the elite, and it was their task to preserve the power of culture and cultural life.[21] The **Birmingham School** distanced themselves completely from this narrow, elitist concept and turned their attention instead to the study of industrialized mass culture. For this new generation, who like Williams had learned their lessons not only in Cambridge but also from the Second World War and later from Marx, Foucault and Gramsci, culture was not the embalmed heritage of a national tradition but the arena in which social groups fought for power, money, recognition and prestige. The momentum created by the Birmingham School, with its expansion **from high to popular culture**, was taken up with great enthusiasm during the 1970s and 1980s by all those who had found themselves excluded by the bourgeois, elitist concept, such as the working classes, immigrants, women and ethnic minorities. As Stuart Hall puts it, the canon – the idea of a shared and binding high cultural tradition – "was blown apart by world migration, by fragmentation, by the rise of margins, by the struggle of the margins to come into representation, by the contestation of the margins for cultural power, by the pluralization of ethnicity itself in English society."[22]

20 In his book *Culture and Society* (1958), Williams introduced a social dimension into the concept of culture by using terms such as 'class', 'industry' and 'democracy'. In the context of cultural studies, this book was far ahead of its time, as can be seen from the fact that it was assigned to a wide variety of categories, including cultural history, historical semantics, history of ideas, social criticism, literary history and sociology. Through this very resistance to classification, it undermined the disciplinary borders that were in force at the time. Even today the idea that culture encompasses both art and society does not seem to have found general acceptance. Ute Daniel's informative and instructive essay (1993) does not devote one syllable to art as a component of culture.

21 In addition to Leavis (1948), Matthew Arnold (1960) and T. S. Eliot (1962) were prominent advocates of 'art as elite high culture'.

22 Hall (1990), 21.

Cultural studies as developed by the Birmingham School were thus seen as a direct response to current social change.[23] In retrospect, Hall summarized this new vision as follows:

> The vocation of cultural studies has been to enable people to understand what is going on, and especially to provide ways of thinking, strategies of survival, and resources for resistance to all those who are now – in economic, political, and cultural terms – excluded from anything that could be called access to the national culture of the national community.[24]

This concept, with its close connection between **culture and politics** and its strategic incorporation of social and ethnic minorities, also found great resonance in the immigrant societies of the USA and Canada. The driving force was to help multiethnic societies with a history of colonial oppression to achieve multicultural recognition and equality of opportunity.[25] Its most important themes were youth and working-class culture, old and new media, women and ethnic minorities.

An important aspect of Birmingham's cultural studies was the expansion of the definition of culture. This was linked to a programmatic levelling out of the distinction between canonical literature and that produced for the masses. This approach was reinforced towards the end of the 1960s by postmodern theorists and critics from America. One of the most prominent was Leslie Fiedler, who became famous through his slogan **'Cross the Border, Close the Gap!'**[26] He was among those who announced the end of modern literature. By this he meant not that the masterpieces of Proust, Eliot and Joyce had lost their importance, but that

---

23 "They are themselves focused by, organized through and constitute responses to the immediate pressures of the time and society in which they arose", writes Stuart Hall (1986), 34.

24 Hall (1990), 22.

25 The man who has most consistently followed the approach of the Birmingham School through into a second generation in the USA is Lawrence Grossberg, himself a student of Stuart Hall's. His form of cultural studies is Marxist orientated, and focuses on an analysis of cultures as frameworks for economic and political action. Some critics, however, have already consigned this approach to the past: "Old-fashioned oppositions between centre and margin, power and resistance, mainstream and subculture, hegemony and subversion, which among others have established themselves in the reception of British cultural studies, continue to be sent out into the field as if nothing in Germany had changed socially or culturally since the 1960s." Mayer (1999), 235.

26 In 1968, Leslie Fiedler gave an impromptu lecture in Freiburg that was published shortly afterwards in the journal *Christ und Welt* before appearing the following year in English in *Playboy Magazine*. In the online *Oxford English Dictionary*, Fiedler is named as the man who in 1965 first introduced the term 'postmodern' – previously confined to architecture – into the study of literature. The text is published in: Fiedler (1971).

an end had come to the dominance of a restrictive system of aesthetic values promulgated and preserved by critics – a system that had honed itself on these works and had developed more and more into a defensive weapon against contemporary culture as shaped by modern media. His appeal was directed at teachers and critics, who should adapt to a new era in which the great gulf between high art and mass culture had to be bridged, emphasizing the need to study popular culture as a new and serious subject for investigation.

If we consider the subsequent history of cultural studies in the USA, we may note that not only was Fiedler's call to transcend borders and balance out differences not heeded, but in fact what happened was the exact opposite. In the 1970s, a feminist movement established itself in the universities, followed by ethnic and post-colonial movements which set up studies of such subjects as American-Indian, African-American and Jewish-American identities, traditions, literatures and cultures. These new categories show that it became more and more important actually to create a **consciousness of borders and gaps** which could no longer be ignored in the cultural context of social and political power struggles. New boundaries such as gender and ethnicity were established, which the white male power elite had tried to ignore or cover up in order to minimize their subversive potential. Thus, the 1980s and 1990s were a period of unrest, in which the national consensus was challenged: the fiction of unity came under fire and new internal borders were established.

A different, less activist and more academic branch of American cultural studies founded its own journal and regularly promoted its programme in a number of publications. This was **'New Historicism'**, which came about on the initiative of a group at Berkeley University, whose mouthpiece was the journal *Representations*. The most famous member of this school – though it still resists being called a school – is Stephen Greenblatt, whose speciality is Shakespeare and the English Renaissance. His particular inspiration came from the ethnologist Clifford Geertz, who saw cultures as texts. As an active observer and researcher, Geertz himself turned cultures into texts by developing his own form of **'thick description'** for specific cultural practices.[27] The New Historians radically extended the textual basis of their field. The texts they introduced into their literary studies came from historical archives in which they led a somewhat shadowy existence. The challenge raised by the New Historians consists in the fact that they cancel out traditional criteria of literary values by demanding just as much care and attention for archival texts as for the canonical texts of great literature. If culture is really summed up and manifested by texts, then all texts have an equal claim to importance and analysis. New Historicism focused on dismantling the 'aura' that had been imposed on the literary work by its bourgeois reception. By embedding literature in the historical context that gave rise to it, the New His-

27 Geertz (1999).

torians sought to undo the effects of canonization. The new focus was not only on what had been marginalized but also on what had been ignored or excluded during the process of canonization. This programme of the New Historians was promoted by Stephen Greenblatt as follows:

> The risk, from a culturally conservative point of view, is that we will lose sight of what is uniquely precious about high art: new historicism, in this account, fosters the weakening of the aesthetic object. [...] When the literary text ceases to be a sacred, self-enclosed, and self-justifying miracle, when in the sceptical mood we foster it begins to lose some of the special power ascribed to it, its boundaries begin to seem less secure and it loses exclusive rights to the experience of wonder.[28]

Kulturwissenschaften

In Germany, *Kulturwissenschaften* go right back to the beginning of the twentieth century. At that time a few individual critics, such as Georg Simmel, Karl Lamprecht, Aby Warburg, Walter Benjamin and Ernst Cassirer began to break away from the established arts and sociological disciplines and to develop new lines of inquiry, forms of perception and methods of work. These separate ventures by predominantly Jewish scholars were not able, however, to make any inroads into the existing, institutionalized structures, and in fact in the 1930s they were brutally extinguished through the persecution and expulsion of these pioneers by the Nazi regime. The abandoned fragments of such programmes were not taken up again immediately after the Second World War, but only began gradually to re-emerge during the 1970s and 1980s. Since the 1990s, this renaissance has flourished to the extent that *Kulturwissenschaften* have become institutionalized at many German universities.

Here we will give just a brief account of the intellectual changes that brought about the rise of the new paradigm in Germany. One striking change through which the traditional *Geisteswissenschaften* [humanities] gave way to *Kulturwissenschaften* is the replacement of the key term Geist [mind, spirit, intellect] by new headings such as **'symbol'**, **'medium'** and **'culture'**. Scholars like Wilhelm Dilthey, Heinrich Rickert and Hans-Georg Gadamer had set the tone for the humanities paradigm, which was based on certain fundamental oppositions like mind vs. matter, subject vs. object, history vs. Nature, and understanding vs. explanation. All of these equated the realm of the human with living consciousness, subjective intentionality, and historic forms of expression. This kept them distinct and separate from non-human spheres such as materials, Nature or tech-

28 Gallagher/Greenblatt (2000), 11 f. Other focal points of New Historicism are: the importance of the body and the limits to which it can be textualized and represented, the forms and media of representation and their relationship to actions and events, and a preference for selective case studies more anecdotal than exemplary in character.

nology. Within this framework it was essential to show "how all the content of culture [...] has as its precondition an original act of the mind."[29] The central and unifying concept of 'Geist', however, remained a purely internal and mysterious spiritual energy, which – even though it expressed itself in material forms – could never be equated with its external manifestations.

The most essential strategic element of modern *Kulturwissenschaften* is their undermining of the above-mentioned nineteenth-century oppositions that remained in force until the 1970s. While the concept of 'Geist' aimed to identify, isolate and reaffirm an all-important factor in the making of culture, *Kulturwissenschaften* focus their attention on structures, processes and practices in a context which from the very outset is seen as technomorphic. At the centre of this new paradigm is the axiomatic **constructiveness of the media**, which are no longer regarded only as forms of representation but also as genuine ways of 'world-making'. The philosopher Ernst Cassirer based his philosophy of culture on a theory of symbolic forms, which in diverse areas such as myth, art, science, technology, religion and law constituted the essential cognitive and creative power that fashioned the work. For him the terms 'symbol' and 'medium' were interchangeable. His central thesis was that 'symbol' and 'medium' were the prime elements of culture, and with them he shifted the focus of cultural research from the black box of 'Geist' to forms and media of representation.[30]

In the course of this switch from 'Geist' to media, the technical media have increasingly become the subject of attention, and instead of being seen as intermediaries they are viewed more and more as genuine organizational forms of the worldly human experience. However, these forms, which have come to be regarded as a kind of 'second nature', have their own history. A glance at this history will show us its flexibility and its contingency, and thus help prevent us from reifying or naturalizing it.

The Germanist Friedrich Kittler played a decisive role in the movement from *Geisteswissenschaften* to *Kulturwissenschaften* when in 1980 he published his book with the provocative title *Exorcising the spirit from the humanities* [Austreibung des Geistes aus den Geisteswissenschaften].[31] This is not a detached report of something factual but denotes direct action – the title itself announces an agenda, and as such uses 'performative' language (see Chapter 1). The author makes his views plain straight away in the Introduction: the mind must be 'exorcised' from the humanities very much like a demon inhabiting a living being. Kittler shows that the 'Geist' itself is a historical construct which, together with the academic institution of the humanities, was invented between 1770–1800 – the years which the historian Reinhart Koselleck identified as an important

29 Cassirer (1988), 11.
30 Cassirer (1983), 176.
31 Kittler/Turk/Nassen (1980).

juncture in western history and which he called the **'saddle period'**. During this period, three new terms were coined that were to form the basis of the humanities in Germany, and each of these concepts arose in the same manner: by reducing earlier multiples to singularities. *Mind* replaced *minds*, *history* replaced *histories*, and *man* replaced *men*. One must also add the replacement of *arts* by *art*. These new collective singulars, according to Kittler, were the bases of new disciplines for which the nineteenth century created the first professorial chairs: history, literature, aesthetics, anthropology, linguistics, and art history. Together these disciplines form the nucleus of the humanities, with their own culture of learning, as distinct from the sciences subsumed under the heading 'Natural'.

Kittler replaced the exorcised mind with a plural term which was also the title of his book *Discourse Networks* [Aufschreibesysteme][32] – we might call these **media**, another term only used in the plural. Under Kittler's influence, cultural studies now concentrated on the concrete, technical history of communication, so that his study of literature at times bordered on the field of engineering.

A more philosophical though no less media-conscious approach is the French, **post-structuralist** philosophy of writing associated with Foucault, Lacan and especially Derrida. Here too, the concept of 'mind' came under attack, this time in the form of **'logos'**, which also defies any concretization. Derrida's analysis deals with the phantasm of originality, immediacy and pure present, which he regarded as the basis of western philosophy. He opposed the consequential neglect of the media by foregrounding his analyses of writing, difference and suspension which lead to the irreducible dynamism of uncertainty, mediation and delay.

During the 1960s, international media-orientated cultural studies were linked to a more historical and comparative perspective. Of particular note were the studies of oral and written culture carried out by the **Toronto School** in Canada, with Harold Innis, Eric Havelock and Marshall McLuhan among the most prominent names. Eric Havelock, for instance, classical philologist and expert on the 'cultural revolution of the alphabet', regarded his work as a continuation of empirical studies on the rules governing oral epics in the living traditions of the Balkans.[33] His research focused on the dramatic influence of the alphabet on the hitherto oral nature of Ancient Greek culture, and he described how this media revolution changed ways of thinking and indeed the entire culture.[34] His central thesis was that cultures are defined by the capacity of their media, i. e. by the technologies used to record, store and communicate information. This argument gave high priority to what had long been regarded as subsidiary factors such as writing systems, forms of communication, the dissemination of news, and methods of storing knowledge.[35]

32 Kittler (1990).
33 Havelock (1982).
34 Havelock (1986).
35 Assmann, A./Assmann, J./Hardmeier (1998).

This view of the manner in which culture is shaped by its media has proved to be startlingly relevant in an age of dramatic technological evolution. It is one of the various roots that lead to the **study of cultural memory**, which is also historically orientated and embraces both ancient and non-European cultures. In this field, the study of media is closely linked to that of cultural memory, the importance of which as a central factor in the construction of identity and the self-image of societies right through to the present has become more and more evident, and is currently rapidly expanding as an independent branch of international cultural studies.[36]

As we have seen, cultural studies came into being in England during the 1950s as a response to a crisis in the humanities, and in Germany during the early 1990s the *Kulturwissenschaften* arose from a **crisis in the *Geisteswissenschaften***. In 1995, the philosopher Jürgen Mittelstraß added fuel to the fire. He claimed that the humanities had brought this crisis on themselves through their esoteric self-referentiality and by separating areas of study that belonged together.[37] While the Natural sciences and technology were up with the times and were actively reshaping our modern world, the humanities were losing out in the whole process of modernization. Instead of shaping the world and helping to fashion its future, they had allowed their conservative retrogressiveness and soft values to push them out into the margins, where at most they might fulfil some kind of compensatory function. Mittelstraß called on the humanities to cut their obsolete ties with subjectivism, historicism, text authentication and hermeneutics, and to concentrate instead on an objective standard for truth and on problems related to reality. They should face up to their actual task of fulfilling a normative and social educational function. Then and only then could they take on a role comparable to that of the Natural sciences and technology by providing means of orientation, thereby actively helping to shape the modern world.[38]

Mittelstraß's solution to the problem of the humanities was to endow them with a powerful, normative impetus. Such a radical change of direction, breaking with all the historical traditions of the arts, is easy enough to decree but (fortunately) not so easy to accomplish. What is much easier, though, is to change the termi-

36 Assmann, A. (1999a); Assmann, J. (1997).

37 Mittelstraß (1996). I discussed Mittelstraß's arguments in a correspondence with him that was printed as an appendix in: Assmann, A. (2004).

38 This was also the conclusion reached in a memorial paper entitled *Geisteswissenschaften heute*, in which a research team set out a framework for the new *Kulturwissenschaften*. These should "as an instrument of intercultural education and anthropological knowledge make a genuine contribution to the problem of reintegrating technological civilization into the social culture of the future." Frühwald (1991), 11. Clearly what underlies this formulation is the old contrast between the contemplative culture of the Germans and the modern civilization of the French. See Elias (1978), 1–42.

nology. And so in the early 1990s, from the ashes of the crisis-ridden *Geisteswissenschaften*, arose almost spontaneously the radiant phoenix of *Kulturwissenschaften*. Was this merely false labelling or a genuine change of paradigm? In an essay written in 1997, the Germanist Uwe Steiner analysed this change more closely.[39] He did so in response to a well-known German journal that had published a call for answers to the following question: 'Can cultural studies lay claim to a new moral function?' Steiner's prize-winning essay begins with the substitution of 'culture' for 'Geist'. While the unified concept of 'mind' is inaccessible to empirical study, 'culture' is always a pluralistic concept whose internal differences allow for a multitude of new questions. Steiner analyses cultures as self-organizing systems of symbols. In this respect, he distances himself from the then current crisis rhetoric, which he replaces with Niklas Luhmann's systems theory and its constructivist language and concepts. In a world of change, contingency and transience, the task of cultures is to fashion recognizable forms while at the same time reacting to those changes with flexibility. In this context, the main role is played by symbolic processes. The debate about the humanities which had begun with (the lack of) values, is countered by Steiner with a discussion on the meaning of symbols. He argues that while cultural studies do not have a claim to normative orientation, they do claim a special **competence in symbols** – including their irreducible potency, their structure and functional mechanisms, as well as their effects on everyday issues of communication and identity-building under the pressures of politics and social conflict. At a stroke, with their new claim to mastery of the symbol, German cultural studies were able to throw off the yoke of apologetics which had lain so heavily on the shoulders of the humanities. As for the prime question concerning a moral function, Steiner's answer was negative. As regards the increasingly moral, political and fundamentalist trend in British and American cultural studies, he saw this as part of the problem and not the solution. It was not the task of *Kulturwissenschaften* to inject direction and stable values into the normative vacuum of society – this was the job of other institutions. Their competence consisted in critical analysis and exploration, not in laying foundations. On the contrary, they must ensure that the balance in modern society between possibility and reality, between potential and fulfilment, was preserved and not destroyed by the imposition of specific values or by restrictions on authoritarian discourse.

This brief survey shows very clearly the underlying differences between German *Kulturwissenschaften* and Anglo-American cultural studies. In general, we can say that the latter set out mainly to abolish the elitist concept of 'high culture' and to make way for a new understanding of mass culture in its technological context, thereby readjusting the literary canon to the demands of social and cultural minorities which had been oppressed and marginalized and were now increasingly demanding access. Culture viewed in this perspective is an arena in which

39 Steiner, U. (1997).

values, re-evaluations and the politics of identity fight for recognition – a battle in which cultural studies themselves play an active part. The German *Kulturwissenschaften*, on the other hand, regard culture as primarily a subject for academic investigation. Their main aim is to build a wider interdisciplinary frame for the study of cultural artefacts and practices, reconstructing the contexts and conditions from which they arose. Important questions relate to the use of media, the role of symbols in the process of cultural transmission and the anthropological roots of the term 'culture'. This frequently extends the investigations to historical and ethnographic contexts, which direct the attention to the unfamiliar in the self and the other.[40] The most important distinction, though, between cultural studies and *Kulturwissenschaften* is probably the fact that the latter are based exclusively in academic institutions, whereas the former are also directly connected to social movements and new cultural practices. Perhaps this may also explain why the German variety is more reflective and analytical, while the Anglo-American thrives on action and conflict.

Cultural Studies	***Kulturwissenschaften***
• Culture as a battlefield of identity politics	• Culture as a subject of academic research
• Extension of the concept of culture from high to popular culture	• Historical (re)contextualization of art
• Reconstruction of the literary canon	• Interest in cultural memory
• Claim of social and cultural minorities to increased participation	• Reflective and critical analysis of symbolic representations

Select bibliography

Barker, Chris (2007) *Cultural Studies: Theory and Practice.* 3rd ed., London: Sage.

Collins, Richard, ed. (1986) *Media, Culture and Society. A Critical Reader.* London: Sage.

During, Simon (2005) *Cultural Studies: A Critical Introduction.* London (et al.): Routledge.

Leistyna, Pepi (2005) *Cultural Studies. From Theory to Action.* Malden/Oxford: Blackwell.

Miller, Toby, ed. (2001) *A Companion to Cultural Studies.* (Blackwell Companions in Cultural Studies 3). Malden/Oxford: Blackwell.

Ryan, Michael (2010) *Cultural Studies: A Practical Introduction.* Malden/Oxford: Blackwell.

40 Assmann, A. et al. (2004).

1. SIGNS

1.1 The use of signs as an anthropological basis

Friedrich Nietzsche once defined man as an animal that can remember. It is this faculty that enables us to position ourselves in time, to look back into the past, and to plan for the future. We are not at the mercy of the present, but we can create a time frame for ourselves in which we can move around, remember, build expectations and set ourselves goals. This time frame, however, would not be possible without the use of **signs** and **symbols**, and so if we are to study culture it makes sense to begin by explaining these basic concepts.

We can gauge the anthropological significance of symbols with the aid of certain observations made by the American literary theorist Kenneth Burke. In an essay entitled "The Definition of Man", he made a list of various attributes that distinguish humans from other forms of life.[1] First of all, he says that man is a **'symbol-using animal'**. As an example he takes a wren which he watched nesting and breeding. He saw the young birds learning to fly and then leaving the nest, apart from one which kept putting off the scary moment of its first flight and so finished up as the only fledgeling left. The mother wren devised a clever ruse: she brought him a worm, but kept fluttering around with her prey so far from the nest that the fledgeling had to lean out in order to get a bite. Immediately, the mother darted away, and the little bird tumbled out of the nest, involuntarily spread his wings, and off he flew. Burke comments on his observation in the following way:

> Surely this was an 'act' of genius. This wren had discovered how to use the principle of leverage as a way of getting a young bird off the nest. Had the exceptionally brilliant wren been able to conceptualize this discovery in such terms as come easy to symbol-systems, we can imagine him giving a dissertation on "The Use of the Principle of Leverage as an Improved Method for Unnesting Birds or Debirding a Nest." And within a few years the invention would spread throughout all birddom, with an incalculable saving in bird-hours as compared with the traditional turbulent and inefficient method still in general practice. (4)

In the animal world, such discoveries and experiences can only be transmitted and used through mimesis. Each generation of birds therefore has to start again from scratch. Animals are perfectly capable of doing this, because their genome is programmed with instinctive knowledge of what they need. This is not the case with humans. They have no adequate biological equipment that gives them

1 Burke (1966).

direct instructions on how to act and how to make themselves safe. Instead, they use symbols with which they create their own environment.

Burke acknowledges, however, that the use of symbols is not an exclusively human privilege but also occurs among different species in the animal world. There are abundant studies to show that many species of animal use sometimes highly complex sign systems in order to communicate vital information. Bees, for instance, perform dances that communicate exact details of where lush supplies of nectar are to be found, and ants too have systematic ways of passing on information about complex routes. Animals, then, are certainly able to devise sounds, movements and other interactive signs through which they can communicate with their own species in space and time, but what they cannot do is store these signs externally in order to recall them later at another time or place. In this respect animal language comes up against an insurmountable barrier. They use signs as **means of communication**, but not as a **storage medium**. In their language information cannot be used for a new application in another context or for transmission to future generations. They have no access to the **mnemotechnical function** of retaining images and signs for actions beyond the present moment, so it is also impossible for them to build up a shared memory and thus expand their horizons in time and space. As Nietzsche put it so succinctly, animals are "tethered [...] to the stake of the moment"[2]. The deliberate use of symbols, on the other hand, allows humans to prolong these ties by recalling information from the past and projecting it into the future.

Symbols are never identical to what they represent or refer to. You cannot sit on the picture of a chair, and you cannot eat the word bread. The Belgium artist Magritte reminded us of the necessary difference between an object and its representation when he captioned his painting of a pipe: 'Ceci n'est pas une pipe'. This basic differentiation opens up an amazing range of mental and symbolic operations – abstraction, substitution, abbreviation, negation, generalization, condensation, and displacement. For Burke there is a prime energy inherent in all sign usage, which he calls **'transcendence'**. In this sense, every symbol contains an energy that enables us to transcend the limitations imposed on us by our bodies. The symbol or sign (we still use these terms synonymously) carries its user from me to you, from here to there, from now to then, from the literal to the figurative, from matter to mind. This consistent exploitation of the power of symbols frees humans from the narrow confines of their immediate lives so that they can move out into an open world which they themselves help to shape.

Language, then, is what makes us humans human. This organ of historical growth and change, this medium of long-term, trans-generational communication simply does not exist in the animal kingdom. Nor will you find there any genetic apparatus for the acquisition of language or for the principle of **'double**

2 Nietzsche (1874), 125.

articulation', which combines the phonetic and semantic distinctions without which it would be impossible to organize this limitless store of signs. Of course the cultural creation of language has emerged from certain natural preconditions. However, it reaches far beyond these, and is distinguished from other cultural creations in so far as it is not only a product of human creativity but is also the most important **tool in man's self-creation**. Language is the medium through which we shape our world, our culture and ourselves, and everything we do depends on it. Even so, it is far from being a fixed and closed-off system. Just like cultures, history and ourselves, it is in a continual state of flux, and as a central resource for collective and individual self-creation, it requires constant care and attention.

1.1.1 Language scepticism and 'linguistic turn' around 1900

In 1952, the linguist and literary theorist Roman Jakobson delivered to an international symposium a lecture on anthropology in which he referred to two publications from the year 1916.[3] One of them was Albert Einstein's Theory of Relativity, the other was called *Cours*, and contained the transcript of a lecture given by Ferdinand de Saussure a few years earlier in Geneva.[4] With this combined reference to the works of Einstein and Saussure, Jakobson pointed to the principle of relativity in both physics and language as one of the central discoveries of the twentieth century. A generation after Jakobson, the term **'linguistic turn'** came into use, reinforcing the idea of Saussure's works as a landmark in language and sign theory.

The meaning of this 'turn' can be derived from a literary work which was written at the beginning of the twentieth century and in its own unique way encapsulates the linguistic scepticism (in two senses) of its time. The work is a fictional letter purported to have been sent in 1603 by a Lord Chandos to Francis Bacon, in which he reports his withdrawal from language and hence from the social world. The text comes from the pen of Hugo von Hofmannsthal, who with this piece overcame his own writer's block from which he had suffered for several years. The insight that paralyses the fictional letter-writer to his innermost soul is his knowledge of the **disconnectedness of words and things**. Without an unquestioned link between language and reality, words lose their referential function. Because of this awareness, Chandos feels utterly alienated from his environment. In his most famous utterance he feels the abstract words disintegrating in his mouth "like rotten mushrooms"[5]. The consequence is that he abstains from communication and retires into silence.

3 Falk (1995).
4 Saussure (1916).
5 Hofmannsthal (2005), 121.

The Chandos option in favour of silence and against language is, however, only one side of the coin. The other is a completely new view of language, which was part of the radical change to which writers and critics, philosophers and linguists all contributed at the turn of the century, and which was later to be called the 'linguistic turn'. The dislocation between linguistic signs and reality, which caused Chandos's deep pessimism, is also the root of modern **constructivism**. This too was based on the insight that language is not congruent with the world. A positive way to describe this phenomenon is to say that humans can create or 'construct' their own world. They do not live in *the* world but in *a* world, which is the product of their terminology and their ability to give it linguistic expression. It is to the Genevan linguist Ferdinand de Saussure, founding father of French **Structuralism**[6] and the linguistic turn, that we owe the modern definition of the sign, which he described as a complex of the signifier and the signified. The signifier (Fr. *signifiant*) is the external, material side of the sign which can be perceived by the senses – e. g. the articulated sound of a word or its visual shape in writing; the signified (Fr. *signifié*), on the other hand, is the cognitive, internal side of the sign that contains its meaning which has to be learned along with the language. The signs are part of a code (i. e. a system of rules for the production and interpretation of signs), thanks to which humans are able to understand one another. In contradiction to Chandos's scepticism, then, words have by no means lost their content and meaning, but their content is no longer to be identified as a reference to the outside world. Instead, the concept that underlies the word is now part of the language system which functions through internal correspondences that are independent of direct links to external reality.[7] Words carry meaning because they relate to concepts and not to given facts and objects. In other words: Signs separate and mediate: they create a **gulf between language and the world**, but at the same time they provide a bridge between the two.

According to Umberto Eco, signifieds are 'cultural units' – i. e. concepts formulated within specific cultures – in which they function as shared images.[8] This language theory is relativistic in so far as words are no longer seen as names for things but as signs with a double, phonetic-semantic structure. Its starting point is the fact that the world is never directly accessible, but can only be mediated through language, which makes it a human creation and a cultural construction.

---

6 Saussure himself did not use the term 'structure', but preferred 'system'.

7 In the history of semiotics, the signifier was traditionally seen as being beyond language. St Augustine, for instance, saw it as a pre-linguistic, internal word or as universal knowledge anchored within human beings. "The thought formed from the known object is therefore the word which we speak in our heart. This is not Greek, not Latin, and does not belong to any other language." Quoted from Todorov (1995), 34.

8 Eco (1972); Eco (1985). This book has never been translated completely into English.

It was this insight into the 'arbitrariness' of the sign that drove Chandos into silence and isolation. The same insight had the opposite effect for Saussure: he embraced the social and conventional character of language which opened up to him a totally new, **constructivist perspective** on the world. And so the consequences of the linguistic turn were not the loss of self and world but a new awareness of what humans have made, what they live in and on, and what they are responsible for. Saussure stands in the tradition of great philologists like Herder and Humboldt. His legacy lies in a consistent, constructivist concept of language as a sign system which does not reflect the world but actually produces it. This view is summed up in the following statement by the American sociologist George Herbert Mead:

> Language does not just symbolize situations or objects which are given, on the contrary, it makes the existence and the emergence of situations or objects possible because it is part of the mechanism through which these situations or objects are being created.[9]

1.1.2 The basic structure of the sign: aliquid stat pro aliquo

It has been repeatedly pointed out that there is nothing in the world that cannot be made into a sign, in the sense that it is perceived and interpreted by humans "as referring to something else or standing for something else."[10] We not only produce signs, but we also see ourselves surrounded by them. In Nature we study coded messages from transcendental powers in order to extrapolate clues about our destiny, or we follow tracks in order to gain access to events that have happened before we arrived on the scene. Thus there are signs beyond those of human communication and the written text, but not beyond a culturally conditioned point of view. The discipline that deals with the structure and use of signs in this general sense is **semiotics**, which has developed from structuralism though its roots reach far back into Antiquity.[11]

---

9 Mead (1993), 117.
10 Trabant (1999a), 33.
11 Semiotics embraces sign processes and communications of all kinds, regardless of whether they are produced by humans or animals. See Posner (1997). Literary semiotics, however, covers a more restricted field, because as an essentially scholarly exercise it refrains from any interpretation of the text. Jürgen Trabant wittily summed up the essence of literary semiotics: "'Against Interpretation' was the motto, even before Susan Sontag was writing this on her polemic proofs. In his 'microscopic' views of poems, Roman Jakobson showed how such semiotics might appear: it observed phonemic recurrences, analysed syllabic structures, related grammatical categories to one another and to the phonemic structure etc. Ultimately, the poetry was a projection of the principle of equivalence from the axis of selection to the axis of combination (you know what I mean?). And what was explicitly excluded from all this was what it all meant, because working out meanings was not the business of the scholar." Trabant (1999b), 271.

The basic structure of the sign was succinctly summed up by a phrase used in medieval semiotics: ***'aliquid stat pro aliquo'*** – something (x) stands for something else (y). Between the sound of the word 'chair' (x') or the picture of a chair on the one hand (y'), and an actual chair on the other (z'), there is an obvious **ontic difference**. By using coded, concise, economical signs in language and image, we can easily convey the idea of something that is absent. But of course this substitution of signs for absent realities can also open the way to misunderstanding or deception. In an episode of *Gulliver's Travels* Jonathan Swift offers us a vivid example.[12] Here, the language and sign sceptics, who are not prepared to take any risks, carry a sack of objects over their shoulders. Whenever they meet to have a chat or pass on information, they do so not with words but with items they pull out of their bags to show one another. When the silent conversation is over, they repack, help each other to hoist the heavy bags back onto their shoulders, and depart.

Swift's sign sceptics renounce what Werner Stegmeier has called the *Weltabkürzungskunst* [the art of abbreviating the world][13] of the signs and communicate through the unwieldy medium of objects. Like words and gestures, **objects can become signs** too, on condition that they are first stripped of their practical function. A hammer in a toolbox is simply a hammer, but a hammer forming a cross with a sickle inside a garland and painted on a flag signifies a 'Workers' and Farmers' State'. As objects taken out of their normal context, exhibits in a museum also become signs of a bygone era and past ways of living. A seven-armed candelabra, removed from its religious setting, may stand for a lost Jewish culture; a Volkswagen car in Berlin's History Museum represents the economic boom that West Germany enjoyed after the Second World War.

Language and sign philosophers have drawn attention to the fact that Saussure's clear distinction between the two components of the linguistic sign into signifier and signified is not without its problems. The second element, which must be understood without use of the senses, cannot really be grasped unless we put it back into words (lexemes), thus transferring it back into signifiers.[14] The French philosopher Jacques Derrida used this insight to undermine the whole edifice of

12 Swift (1965), 185: "Since words are only names for *Things*, it would be more convenient for all Men to carry about them, such Things as were necessary to express the particular Business they are to discourse on. [...] if a Man's Business be very great, and of various Kinds, he must be obliged in Proportion to carry a great Bundle of *Things* upon his Back, unless he can afford one or two strong Servants to attend him. I have often beheld two of those Sages almost sinking under the Weight of their Packs, like Pedlars among us; who when they met in the Streets would lay down their Loads, open their Sacks, and hold Conversation for an Hour together; then put up their Implements, help each other to resume their Burthens, and take their Leave."

13 Stegmeier (1994).

14 Cf. Simon (1989); Flasch (1992).

structuralism, thereby ushering in the approach known as **post-structuralism**. He criticized the static sign architecture of a signified that was detachable from but firmly dependent on the signifier as being 'essentialist', and he pointed out that the sign process **(semiosis)** could only take place within an endless chain of signifiers. Consequently communication was not a transfer of messages, but a game of signifiers that could only be stopped by means of an arbitrary interruption, because otherwise it would have to go on forever. An example of this chain is the fantastic etymology for the name 'Kashmir' that we find in one of Salman Rushdie's novels:

> As the light failed, they passed a sign that had originally read WELCOME TO K; but somebody had daubed it with crude, irregular letters, so that it now said WELCOME TO KOSH-MAR. 'What's Kosh-Mar?' Haroun wanted to know. '[...] It's a word from the ancient tongue of Franj, which is no longer spoken in these parts,' Rashid explained.
> 'In those long-gone days the Valley, which is now simply K., had other names. One, if I remember correctly, was "KACHE-MER". [...] 'Do those names mean anything?' Haroun asked. 'All names mean something', Rashid replied. 'Let me think. Yes. That was it. "Kache-Mer" can be translated as "the place that hides a Sea." But "Kosh-Mar" is a ruder name. [...] In the old tongue', Rashid admitted, 'it was the word for "nightmare"'.[15]

Following on from Derrida, the linguist Ludwig Jäger also took a close look at the sign process of meaning construction (semiosis) and put the status of the signifier under his microscope.[16] For him it was a black box, because in the reality of the communication and comprehension process, it had no fixed position from which we could objectively view, control and calibrate the meaning of our words. Jäger argues that meaning is not a stable unit (as is suggested by the fixed definition we find in dictionaries) but a mental and cultural projection which the speaker introduces into communication. Since there is no meta-linguistic agency to control this projection, communication occurs as a continuous process of reciprocal adaptation by all participants. It develops, according to Jäger, through the continuous interplay of **reciprocal semantic projections**. Thus meaning can never really be assumed and simply passed on, but it has to be constantly renewed, renegotiated and cooperatively created by those involved. Signs and words therefore have no permanent, static meaning but take on their meaning through this process of assumption, testing, confirmation, correction etc. in real-life situations of communication.

1.1.3 Functions of signs

From these critical observations let us now turn once more to the basis of linguistic practice, the (more or less) everyday business of communication, in

15 Rushdie (1990), 40.
16 Jäger (1997).

which for the most part we can say that despite all the obstacles and dangers, understanding is eventually reached. This will be between two conscious people with shared social and cultural attributes, whom we can call the **sender** and the **receiver**. The action of communicating (i. e. sending and receiving) takes place between these two poles in face-to-face situations, during which of course the roles may be continually exchanged. The linguist Karl Bühler started from this paradigmatic communication situation to develop a schema illustrating the **three basic functions of language**: one is **representative**, connected to a shared reality which is being referred to; one is **expressive** and refers back to the speaking subject (sender); and one is **appellative**, i. e. directed towards the perceiving subject (receiver).

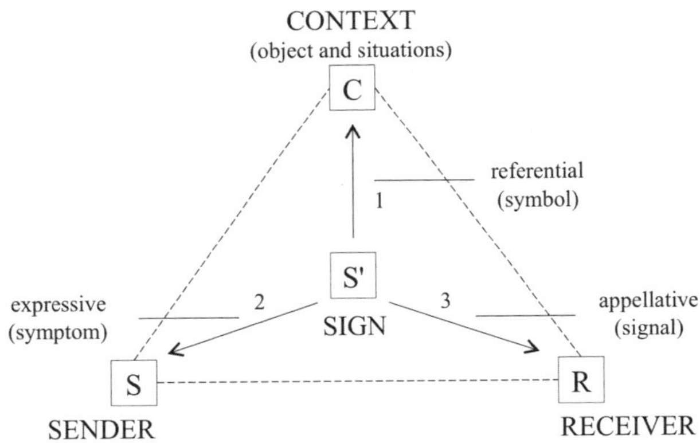

Three sign functions formulated by Karl Bühler (Organon model)

This three-part schema (which the linguist Klaus Heger later condensed into a simple triad of symptom function / symbol function / signal function[17]) was expanded by the Prague structuralist Jan Mukařovský during the 1930s. His important addition to Bühler's model was the '**aesthetic function** of language'. By this Mukařovský meant a use of language in which attention is drawn not only to what is represented but also, and at the same time, to the sign itself. This aesthetic function is to be found wherever the purely communicative function is transcended and the use of the sign becomes 'self-conscious'. Mukařovský called this linguistic self-consciousness 'autonomy', referring to a mental operation in which attention is shifted from the external object to the sign itself. He emphasized that the aesthetic function is in no way confined to literary artistic con-

17 Heger (1976).

texts but is also to be found in everyday contexts. The boundary, he wrote, "separating the aesthetic function from the practical functions is not always distinct; in particular, it does not coincide with the dividing line between art and other human activities."[18] We can see, for instance, that the aesthetic function frequently comes into play when one wishes to attract the attention of the observer, e.g. in advertising. In a logo, the name is transformed into an immediately recognizable image, so that it will catch the eye. On a duty-free carrier bag, you might see the slogan SEE – BUY – FLY, with the final Y transformed into a soaring seagull.

The aesthetic function of the sign, then, is to focus the receiver's perception on the representation itself. A similar effect is created by nursery rhymes, which thereby gain a mnemotechnical, almost magical quality. Political slogans also make use of the aesthetic function: In 1953 Dwight Eisenhower's progress to the White House was greatly assisted by the catchy slogan 'I LIKE IKE'. Mukařovský therefore quite rightly emphasizes the fact that: "The aesthetic function is omnipresent; not even linguistics can deny it a place among the basic linguistic functions." (69) If we incorporate it "as one of the four main functions [that are] potentially present in every utterance" (72 f), our expanded schema will look as follows:

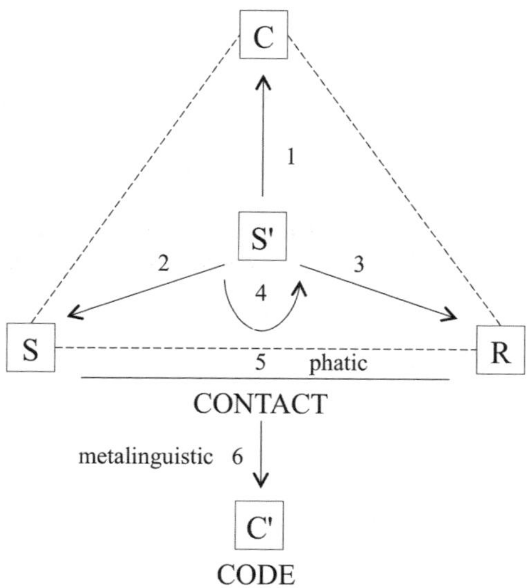

Four sign functions (extended by Jan Mukařovský)

18 Mukařovský (1977), 68.

Roman Jakobson later expanded this schema still further.[19] His aim was to transcend a form of linguistics that restricted itself to the referential function of language. He contended that "we cannot restrict the notion of information to the cognitive aspect of language." (354) His extension augmented Bühler's model of communication to **six factors** and **functions**:

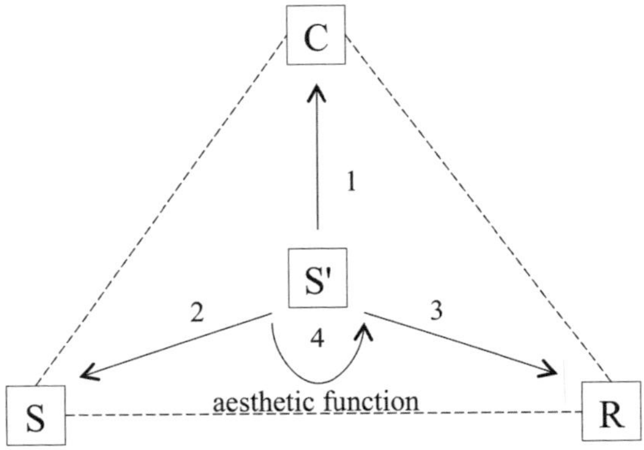

Six sign functions (extended by Roman Jakobson)

Jakobson introduces two new functions that constitute and frame the communication: one referring to the situational context (6), the other referring to the sign system involved (5). Jakobson took over the interesting concept of 'phatic communication' from the anthropologist Bronislaw Malinowski. This refers to empty forms of speech that have the sole function of establishing and maintaining the channel between the sender and the receiver. Metalinguistic references relate to the medium involved, e. g. in questioning and probing the meaning of words.

19 Jakobson (1960).

1.2 Problems of communication in literature

Nothing exposes the immanent **rules of communication** so well as misunderstandings and breakdowns. Beckett's absurdist plays, which empty the dialogue of meaning and reduce it to the formulaic exchanges that expose the rules of 'language games' (L. Wittgenstein), often do so by deviating from expected norms:

ESTRAGON:	(*chewing*). I asked you a question.
VLADIMIR:	Ah.
ESTRAGON:	Did you reply?
VLADIMIR:	How's the carrot?
ESTRAGON:	It's a carrot.
VLADIMIR:	So much the better, so much the better.[20]

Instead of answering the question, the receiver Vladimir responds with a counter question. Then instead of answering this, the new receiver Estragon replies with a tautological statement. Harold Pinter's *The Birthday Party*, another play in the absurdist tradition, is full of phatic communication. In the opening scene, a couple converse – one in the kitchen, the other at the breakfast table:

MEG:	Is that you, Petey? *Pause.* Petey, is that you? *Pause.* Petey?
PETEY:	What?
MEG:	Is that you?
PETEY:	Yes, it's me.
MEG:	What? Are you back?
PETEY:	Yes.
MEG:	I've got your cornflakes ready. [...] Are they nice?
PETEY:	Very nice.
MEG:	I thought they'd be nice. [...] You got your paper?
PETEY:	Yes.
MEG:	Is it good?
PETEY:	Not bad.
MEG:	What does it say?
PETEY:	Nothing much.[21]

Language seems to have been hollowed out here; redundancies and repetitions dominate a conversation that scarcely deserves the name. The sparse content dilutes itself in tautologies, and communication is reduced simply to maintaining

20 Beckett (1967), 20.
21 Pinter (1971), 9 f.

contact by means of words. However, it would be wrong to dismiss such forms of interaction merely as semantic nothingness, although generally this plays a significant role in absurdist drama. Anthropologically, the phatic function is that which children learn first and which is also practised with animals. As the basis and indeed the backbone of communication, it is irreplaceable as a social bond and as a precondition for the continuity of relationships in the routines and rituals of everyday life.

In Shakespeare's *Hamlet*, communication between the characters frequently breaks down, though for very different reasons. There is a high degree of **self-reflexive language** in this play, demonstrating an awareness of the difference between signifier and signified, which in successful communication should actually disappear. In *Hamlet*, attention is constantly being drawn to the gap between words and their meanings. Polonius, the Lord Chamberlain, who loves to make long speeches full of long words, is admonished by the Queen: "More matter with less art" (II, 2, 97). Hamlet's typical refusal to communicate expresses itself in his way of pretending not to understand the obvious intentions of the speaker (the signifier) and insisting on the literal meaning of the signs. With this act of linguistic sabotage, which one might call **literalism**, he confuses his partners by stubbornly switching from the level of the message (i. e. the signifier) to that of representation (i. e. the signified):

> Enter HAMLET, reading on a book.
> POLONIUS: What do you read, my lord?
> HAMLET: Words, words, words.
> POLONIUS: What is the matter, my lord?
> HAMLET: Between who?
> POLONIUS: I mean the matter that you read, my lord.[22]

Hamlet has no intention of cooperating in this verbal exchange, and so he uses linguistic means to irritate his partner. What happens here is just one example of many in the play. Instead of making the necessary leap to the meaning implied by the signifier, he concentrates on the signified (i. e. the words themselves), and so comprehension (or what Hans-Georg Gadamer would call *Horizontverschmelzung* – the merging of horizons) becomes impossible. With this strategy of evasive, **indirect communication** he prevents his partner from 'reading' him, his object being to remove all 'expressiveness' from signs that might otherwise allow insight into his real thoughts. Throughout the play he is constantly on his guard against revealing his true self to others.

Hamlet's use of signs here has a paranoid, hyper-reflective quality, but sometimes it is also playful and aesthetic. This is evident from the very first words that he speaks:

22 Shakespeare (1997a), II, 2, 167; 191–195.

KING:	But now, my cousin Hamlet, and my son –
HAMLET:	(*Aside*). A little more than kin and less than kind.
KING:	How is it that the clouds still hang on you?
HAMLET:	Not so, my lord. I am too much in the sun.[23]

The first reaction is not a reply to the opening gambit but an aside comment on the words 'cousin' and 'son'. He immediately focuses on the problematical relationship which, after his uncle's sudden ascent to power and marriage to his mother, has changed his status from that of nephew to that of stepson. He is evidently extremely reluctant to play the role of son, and resists the intrusive approach of the new king, who will soon be revealed as an usurper. All this is expressed in a single line of five stresses, which includes a play on words. 'Kin' as in 'kinship' denotes a family relationship, while 'kind' has a double meaning: the more modern one is in the sense of friendly and generous, while the older meaning, going right back to Chaucer, is that of species or nature. Hamlet here implies that the unnatural new family situation is marked by too much kinship connected with too little friendliness. Hamlet's second sentence is a direct response to a question, but this answer too is evasive. Here he takes the cloud metaphor literally. The question is supposed to mean: why do you continue to mourn? But his cryptic reply suggests that perhaps too much attention is being paid to him at court, while of course 'sun' is also a play on the word 'son', i. e. he does not wish to have Claudius as a father.

A pun is a play on words that is based on ambiguity, and once again we can see the aesthetic function of everyday language. This form of word play highlights the slippery or **gliding signifier** in its most perfect form. Minimal differences made on the level of the signified lead to semantic shifts that can open up new, surprising meanings. The pleasure is similar to the playing of pure associations, in which the conscious mind withdraws control and allows a free flow of thought. In puns, language takes over, not in the (sublime) etymological German tradition of Heidegger, but in the subversively playful tradition that leads from Shakespeare to Lewis Carroll right through to James Joyce.

One final example of literary misunderstanding is from an autobiographical novel by the Caribbean author Jamaica Kincaid, who recounts the following experience at Queen Victoria Girls' School on the island of Antigua. The 10-year-old first person narrator was told to learn Wordsworth's famous poem *The Daffodils* by heart and then recite it in front of a full assembly. The recitation was a great success, but for the girl herself, who had no idea what a daffodil was like, it was humiliating. The gap between signifier and signified resulted in a disastrous personality split: "I was then at the height of my two-facedness: that is, outside I seemed one way, inside I was another; outside false, inside true." The unknown flowers which she tried to forget kept returning to haunt her in her

23 Shakespeare (1997a), I, 2, 64–67.

dreams. Nine years later, when she was in the United States and went for a walk, she saw narcissi in flower for the first time in her life, and her first instinct was to grab a sickle and cut them down.

> Mariah said, "These are daffodils. I'm sorry about the poem, but I'm hoping you'll find them lovely all the same." [...]
> "Mariah, do you realize that at ten years of age I had to learn by heart a long poem about some flowers I would not see in real life until I was nineteen?"
> As soon as I said this, I felt that I had cast her beloved daffodils in a scene she had never considered, a scene of conquered and conquest; a scene of brutes masquerading as angels and angels as brutes. [...] It wasn't her fault. It wasn't my fault. But nothing could change the fact that where she saw beautiful flowers I saw sorrow and bitterness.[24]

1.3 Types of signs

1.3.1 Performative language

The philosopher J. L. Austin became aware that his colleagues had an extremely restricted concept of language, because they focused solely on its representative function. Language, however, does not only describe things, or represent them and point them out, but – according to Austin – it also creates a mode of action. Speech and action are therefore not necessarily mutually exclusive, but in some circumstances they can even be identical. Austin examines such cases in his book *How to Do Things with Words*[25], which provided the foundations for philosophical and linguistic **pragmatics**. Here the focus is not on the meaning (semantics) or accuracy of a statement, but on the efficiency of language as a genuine form of action. This is what Austin terms 'performative', as distinct from the mode he calls 'constative'.

Austin uncovered **performative language** on many different levels. It can be highly formal, as in institutional contexts and rituals, for example when a child is baptized, the bride says yes at the wedding ceremony, or a judge passes sentence in court. A less stylized form is to be observed in everyday situations, when for instance we make promises to each other, welcome somebody, place a bet, express disapproval, swear or apologize. Formalized performative language only functions when the necessary authority underpins the words and the action takes place within the right institutional framework. In everyday use, it only works if the speaker's intention is actually fulfilled by the utterance – otherwise the formulaic expressions remain hollow. Harold Pinter's *The Birthday Party* offers us another striking example:

24 Kincaid (1991), 18; 30.
25 Austin (1992).

MEG:	Do you want some tea?
	(STANLEY *reads the paper.*)
	Say please.
STANLEY:	Please.
MEG:	Say sorry first.
STANLEY:	Sorry first.
MEG:	No. Just sorry.
STANLEY:	Just sorry!
MEG:	You deserve the strap.[26]

Stanley breaks the rules of the common courtesy language game, because he does not fulfil the performative actions correctly.

1.3.2 Three types of sign: symbolic, iconic, indexical

In addition to Saussure's theory of sign *structure* and Bühler's theory of sign *functions* (together with the extensions brought in by Mukařovský, Jakobson and Austin), there is a third theory of sign *types* that we must look at. The American semiotician Charles Sanders Peirce distinguished three basic categories: the **'symbol'**, the **'icon'**, and the **'index'**[27] (as we have used the terms sign and symbol so far interchangeably, it should be noted that Peirce uses 'sign' as the general term while 'symbol' is restricted to one of its three types). The question underlying these distinctions is as simple as it is fundamental: what is the nature of the link that joins a material sign to what it denotes? According to Peirce there are three different answers: If the link is *arbitrary* and depends only on social conventions, he calls it symbolic; if it expresses a *similarity* between signifier and signified, it is iconic; if there is a *material contact* between the two, he calls it indexical.

Let us deal first with the distinction between symbolic and iconic. One of the oldest problems in semiotics is the question whether the signs through which people communicate with one another are **arbitrary**, i. e. random and interchangeable, or inherently and mysteriously **motivated**, i. e. meaningful in themselves?[28] Is there any plausible reason why a word should be what it is? Or can anything stand for anything else, and the links are simply due to human agreement and convention? This fundamental question is posed by Shakespeare's Juliet, when she starts pondering over Romeo's family name of Montague. This is a hated name for her, because it means that her beloved is one of the enemy:

JULIET:	'Tis but thy name that is my enemy;
	Thou art thyself though, not a Montague.
	What's Montague? It is nor hand, nor foot,

26 Pinter (1971), 17 f.

27 Peirce (1903).

28 This question is discussed in detail in Plato's dialogue *Kratylos*, in which Socrates adopts the position of arbitrariness, and Kratylos that of similarity and meaningfulness.

Nor arm, nor face, nor any other part
Belonging to a man. O! be some other name:
What's in a name? that which we call a rose
By any other name would smell as sweet.[29]

The name which Juliet talks about in such detail has no likeness whatsoever to the person she loves.[30] If the name is such an external thing, then why should it be so important? Why should it decide the identity of a person, and thus have jurisdiction over love, life and death? Where does this power come from to enable a name to govern people and their destiny? Juliet cannot answer such difficult questions, and simply wishes that in this case the name could be changed. But can a change of name do away with an identity and prevent prejudice and persecution? As many a migrant may well have asked, does a new name guarantee a new beginning? Juliet ends her reflections with an emphatic plea for the arbitrary quality of the sign, when she moves from *names* to *words*: "What's in a name? that which we call a rose / By any other name would smell as sweet." There is a lot going for this viewpoint, especially when one thinks of all the different languages and how they are translated. What the English call 'bread', Germans call 'Brot', and the French call 'pain', each of them just as precise as the other. The opposite theory is that of an 'original language' charged with intrinsic meaning because it consists, like the language that Adam found to name all the creatures, of only 'right' words. This episode in the biblical book of Genesis nourished the idea of such an inherently meaningful, **universal tongue**, and it was the subject of much theoretical speculation, not only during the Renaissance and the Romantic era, but also well into the twentieth century.[31]

The following poem by George Herbert is a meditation on the name Jesu, which is split up into its component parts to reveal a second, subliminal message almost like a secret code. For the speaker in the poem, the signifier becomes transparent and reveals a rich texture of unexpected meanings, which teach the reader that the name of God is far from being an arbitrary, non-motivated sign:

IESU is in my heart, his sacred name
Is deeply carved there. But th'other week
A great affliction broke the little frame
Ev'n all to pieces, which I went to seek.
And first I found the corner where was I,

29 Shakespeare (1997e), I, 1, 80–86.

30 The theory of names has a branch of its own in language philosophy; Saul Kripke sees the name as a 'rigid designator', Kripke (1980); Avishai Margalit (2003) talks of the metonymic quality of the name, which is a part of the person, i. e. the part through which a person lives on after death.

31 Assmann, A. (1991a). A late contribution to this theory came from Walter Benjamin, with his early language theory and his important essays on translation and the faculty of mimesis.

After where ES, and next where U was graved.
When I had got these parcels, instantly
I sat me down to spell them, and perceived
That to my broken heart he was *I ease you*,
And to my whole is *IESU*.[32]

To come back to Peirce's triad of sign types: he defines **symbolic signs** as those which, like proper names and the lexemes of individual languages, have an arbitrary quality. This means that they could be substituted by others which serve the purpose just as well, and it is only tradition and convention that make us adhere to the established designation. **Iconic signs**, on the other hand, are those that show a similarity between signifier and signified. This is most obvious with images that copy reality in their form and colour. On this level we can see precisely why – thinking in terms of Juliet's image – the picture of a dog is *not* interchangeable with that of a rose. While arbitrary signs of speech and writing can only be understood by way of a code that has to be learned, iconic signs or pictures are generally more accessible. Illustrations in the history of bookmaking were not just accessories for decoration, but also offered a more direct access to meaning, for instance the *biblia pauperum*, the Bible for the illiterate. When the silent movie emerged at the start of the twentieth century as a new medium of moving pictures, the film theorist Bela Balázs believed that humanity had rediscovered its universal language, and the confusion of tongues had been lifted for ever: "the art of film seems to hold out the promise of redemption from the curse of Babel. The screens of the entire world are now starting to project the *first international language* ... the language of gestures which has become standardized in film."[33]

We should not assume that the difference between symbolic and iconic signs is restricted to that between image and language. In writing too there are basic iconic elements, for instance in the layout of the page, where paragraphs indicate a change of direction, or where bold headings announce something general or important. The actual **typeface** can also contain additional information that emerges from a similarity to what is being represented. In a scene from Pinter's *Birthday Party*, Stanley is ordered by one of his tormentors to sit down. This instruction is printed in block capitals: 'SIT DOWN' clearly indicates that the order is not merely spoken but shouted. The similarity in this case consists in the common denominator of size, transferred from the letters to the volume of the voice.

Peirce's third category of the sign is called **'indexical'**. With our index finger we can point directly to something concrete that is co-present with us in space. Deictic words such as 'here' or 'there' perform a similar function. When Polonius says: "Take this from this if this be otherwise"[34], the sentence is incomprehensi-

32 Herbert (2002a), 220.
33 Balázs (1924), 98.
34 Shakespeare (1997a), II, 2, 156.

ble without the hand pointing first to the head and then to the chest. Deictic and indexical signs are 'empty' until they are filled with concrete references to specific real-life objects and facts. They convey meaning only in a particular situation. Peirce's three categories can be easily distinguished if we look at the example of a gravestone. This is a symbolic sign in that it represents a deceased person through engraved names, inscriptions and numbers. If in addition to the name, a cross or a comforting angel is engraved into the stone, it incorporates an iconic sign. We may argue that the material itself, be it stone or brass, is also iconic, as it promises a lasting memory that will resist forgetting. Finally the gravestone itself is an indexical sign because, independently of its coded information, it points to the place where the body or urn is buried. We can see from this example that the three categories do not have to be strictly separated but can actually support and overlap one another.

The paradigmatic indexical sign is the **track** that a person or animal leaves behind in the sand or earth. As Carlo Ginzburg has shown, reading tracks is one of the oldest forms of human thought, common to the hunter and the collector, the historian and the detective.[35] All of them follow the same basic, logical rule by extrapolating from the given indexical sign what has produced it and has now disappeared from the scene. When Defoe's Robinson Crusoe finds a human footprint in the sand, it marks the beginning of a new chapter in his life, because even though he has not seen another human yet, he knows he is no longer alone on the island. The footprint which informs him of this other person's presence fills him with fear: "I stood like one thunder-struck, or as if I had seen an apparition [...] after innumerable fluttering thoughts, like a man perfectly confused and out of my self, I came home to my fortification, not feeling, as we say the ground I went on, but terrify'd to the last degree."[36]

Another important example of indexical signs is **photography**. The prototype of this is the *vera icon*, the cloth with which St Veronica is said to have wiped the face of Jesus on his way to Calvary, and on which the imprint of his face remained like a photographic negative. This figured veil is kept in the Vatican, and is regarded as the most valuable of all relics because it has preserved a physical trace of the Redeemer. In photography, reality also leaves its traces or tracks. A photograph produces not just an image but also an impression of reality, which spontaneously inscribes itself as a sort of shadow writing in the silver bromide of the magnetic plate.[37] In Antiquity, *acheiripoeieton* (not made by human hand) was an expression for works of art that fell from heaven or were found on the ground. Photography replaces the human hand with an apparatus which itself, however, has been made by and is used by humans.

35 Ginzburg (1983).
36 Defoe (1972), 162.
37 On photography as traces, see Barthes (1981).

Another form of indexical sign is the **symptom**. Smoke, for instance, is a symptom of fire, with which it is linked in a causal relationship; we use the same word for physical signs of illness – outbreaks of sweat, red blotches, yellow skin are all produced by diseases which the doctor can identify from the symptoms. These are complex systems of signs and deciphering, and are based on thousands of years of observation and experience. The diagnostic process is a specialized variation on the much more general process of deciphering the physiognomy, of extrapolating the invisible from the visible, i. e. reading expressions and gestures in order to 'diagnose' the hidden intentions and thoughts of another person.

Once again, Hamlet's first appearance on stage offers us a vivid example of indexical signs. He stands to one side, a melancholy figure dressed in black, thus signalling his close bond with his late father and his detachment from his uncle and mother, who have got married with unseemly haste after his father's death. His mother asks him to join in the celebrations and adapt to the new situation at court: "Good Hamlet, cast thy nightly colour off" (I, 2, 68). This appeal spurs him into reflecting on the authenticity and (in)expressibility of human emotions.[38] He begins, typically, by seizing on the literal meaning of a single word:

QUEEN: Thou know'st 'tis common, all that lives must die,
Passing through nature to eternity.
HAMLET: Ay madam, it is common.
QUEEN: If it be,
Why seems it so particular with thee?
HAMLET: Seems, madam? Nay, it is. I know not 'seems'.
'Tis not alone my inky cloak, good mother,
Nor customary suits of solemn black,
Nor windy suspiration of forced breath,
No, nor the fruitful river in the eye,
Nor the dejected haviour of the visage,
Together with all forms, moods, shapes of grief,
That can denote me truly. These indeed seem,
For they are actions that a man might play,
But I have that within which passes show –
These but the trappings and the suits of woe. (I, 2, 72–86)

The 'signals' or 'symptoms' of mourning which Hamlet lists here are far from unmistakable. Seven times in a row he negates the very idea that from such **external signs** his **inward feelings** can be deduced,[39] as all these signs can be deliberately produced through disguise or acting. Anyone who knows anything about the theatre knows that all these actions are the result of signs that have been intentionally staged. But Hamlet goes one paradoxical step further, in so far as

38 Cf. Plett (1975).
39 Presumably, Shakespeare had read Montaigne's essay on physiognomy.

he stages the fact that his inner being is free from such signs. With this metatheatrical argument he both unmasks and transcends the signs of the theatre.

1.4 Language, culture and violence

We owe one important insight into the cultural dimension of language to the ancient tradition of **rhetoric**. This sets out to form people through use of language – or as Socrates put it so succinctly, "Speak, so that I may see you!" If the other person is to reveal himself, he must do so by speaking, because as long as he remains silent – even if his physical appearance is visually present – he remains invisible. We reveal ourselves, whether in a good or bad way, through our speech. Another Latin saying goes: 'If you had kept your silence, you would have stayed a philosopher.' If our own speech helps us to make ourselves visible, then we need to pay just as much attention to it as to our outer appearance reflected in the mirror. In this respect, rhetoric is linguistic cosmetics; it imposes on the existing form a new layer which is not given by Nature but comes solely from our acquired mastery of language. In history and literature there are many examples of such virtuosi, whose language skills more than made up for their physical defects. The stunted, hunchbacked poet Alexander Pope, for instance, was the shining star of eighteenth-century English society thanks to his brilliant, biting wit. The fictitious long-nosed Cyrano de Bergerac was far better at finding the right words to woo the fair lady than her handsome but none too bright cavalier. Training in rhetoric teaches one how to externalize one's interior. Whoever masters the art of fixing thoughts and beliefs in apt verbal expressions and conveying them effectively can establish relations and build bridges between himself and others. The rhetorical training programme is essentially social; the formation of a person follows on from the formation of his language, and this is always related to other people. As Herder once put it, language is a "bond between man and man."[40]

Language is what makes us **human** and distinguishes us from **animals**. This is the view Shakespeare puts forward very clearly in *The Tempest*. The all-powerful magician Prospero, who has also mastered the language of the spirits, has taught human language to his part-human, part-monster servant Caliban:

> PROSPERO[41]: I pitied thee,
> Took pains to make thee speak, taught thee each hour
> One thing or other. When thou didst not, savage,
> Know thine own meaning, but wouldst gabble like
> A thing most brutish, I endowed thy purposes
> With words that made them known[42]

40 Herder (1803), 421.
41 In some editions (e. g. the *Norton Shakespeare*) this passage is assigned to Miranda.
42 Shakespeare (1997g), I, 2, 356–361.

Language should help the speaker to get to know himself, and he can use it not only to understand his own desires and motives, but also to convey these to others. Self-knowledge and interaction with others are interdependent, and so reflection and sociability evolve together in the medium of language.

With this particular pupil, however, Prospero's efforts appear to have been unsuccessful. Caliban has completely different needs, and uses language as an act of revolt and self-assertion against his hated master.

> CALIBAN: You taught me language, and my profit on't
> Is I know how to curse. The red plague rid you
> For learning me your language![43]

This performative utterance proves his point. Cursing is one of many ways to use language, not as a means of informing or communicating, but as a form of action. One curse is as effective as another when it comes to frightening, intimidating, threatening, rebelling or repelling. One might couple this scene with one in Defoe's *Robinson Crusoe,* where the protagonist teaches his freed companion Friday to speak so that he can convert him. One of the first words he teaches him is 'master'.[44]

In the context of postcolonial theory, the character of Caliban has taken on new dimensions. We have come to see that this repulsive figure, who has remained halfway between man and beast, represents the colonized through the eyes of the colonizer. Today, one can therefore discern the subtext of **linguistic colonial politics**. All over the world, colonial rulers have forced their own language on the native inhabitants. In doing so, not only have they devalued existing local languages, but at the same time they have dismissed and destroyed the language-related traditions, cultural systems and oral practices of the vanquished. A language that has never been written down has no chance of surviving in competition with one that is written. It yields to the pressure of the colonial tongue, which spreads and perpetuates itself through complex bureaucracy, legal procedures and educational programmes. A female Caribbean author, M. NourbeSe Philip, has drawn attention to this tension between the native 'mother language' and the colonial 'father language' in the following poem:

> English is
> my mother tongue.
> A mother tongue is not
> not a foreign lan lan lang
> language
> l/anguish

43 Shakespeare (1997g), I, 2, 366-369. Stephen Greenblatt used Caliban's statement for the title of his book *Learning to Curse: Essays in Early Modern Culture* (1992).

44 Defoe (1972), Chapter 14, "A Dream Realised".

anguish
– a foreign anguish.

English is
my father tongue.
A father-tongue is
A foreign language,
Therefore English is
A foreign language
not a mother tongue.[45]

Language is ambivalent: it can be used as a means of hegemonic force and discipline, but it is also the basic instrument of human civilization. As Jean Paul Sartre wrote after the Second World War: "The failure of communication is the beginning of all violence. Once communication ceases, all that is left is beating, burning, hanging."[46] In the first act of *King Lear*[47], Shakespeare makes a profound statement on the subject of language and violence. Cordelia is unwilling to obey her father's demand that she participates in a competition with her sisters to show who loves him most; she feels unable to package her emotions in superficial clichés, and so she prefers to stay silent. She renounces language, because the order given to her is irreconcilable with the content to which it refers. Love cannot be commanded to express itself, and it cannot be measured by means of a public competition. She refuses to play the rhetorical language game because its basis is force, and force is what follows on from her refusal. She has offended her father's vanity, he loses his temper, and she becomes the object of his hatred. Later in the play, we see how Lear's violence brings about a breakdown in his own language, which coincides with his increasing social isolation.

Of course the idea that 'language = civilization' is an over-simplification. **Violence** is not confined to where language breaks down, but – for instance in the context of propaganda – language may even pave the way; or in the case of inquisition, interrogation and torture, **language** can actually be the **medium of the violence**. It can be used to whip up hatred, enrage the masses, or exert pressure on people. The latter is clearly demonstrated in Act Two of Pinter's *Birthday Party*, when Stanley is subjected by his two tormentors to a fierce cross-examination which will lead to his complete breakdown in Act Three. Loss of language makes such a breakdown all too obvious. The only answer he can give to the staccato sequence of painful questions is a scream, after which he kicks one of his interrogators and utters a few incomprehensible grunts. The inquisition is a form of brainwashing in which the victim's identity is totally demolished, to be afterwards reassembled in a new shape. All aspects of individuality and unmis-

45 Philip (1991), XI–XII; I am grateful to Monika Reif-Hülser for this reference. Cf. Wilentz (1992).
46 Sartre (1964), 167.
47 Shakespeare (1997k).

takableness (see Chapter 7) are expunged from this new construction of his social identity. Stanley, ultimately silent and immobile, stripped of his consciousness, his desires and his memories, is to become the embodiment of the smoothly functioning, properly adjusted new man:

GOLDBERG: We'll make a man of you.
MCCANN: And a woman.
GOLDBERG: You'll be re-orientated.
MCCANN: You'll be rich.
GOLDBERG: You'll be adjusted.
MCCANN: You'll be our pride and joy.
GOLDBERG: You'll be a mensch.
MCCANN: You'll be a success.
GOLDBERG: You'll be integrated.[48]

Pinter's play is not just a commentary on twentieth-century totalitarianism, but it also showcases those more subtle forms of structural violence with which society forces its members to conform. The theorist of this latent form of violence, whose writings might have influenced Pinter, is the French historian and sociologist Michel Foucault. It is he who introduced into historical research the 'body' disciplined and ravaged by power, but we shall return to this later.

The manner in which force can be introduced and stabilized is analysed in great detail by George Orwell in *1984*. He not only shows that indoctrination, threats, rabble-rousing and propaganda are actively violent forms of language, but he also delves into the more subtle forms of linguistic manipulation within totalitarian systems. He uses the example of a fictitious language project, **'Newspeak'**, to demonstrate how a natural language can be transformed into an artificial one. 'Natural' languages, which have evolved over centuries or even millennia, contain a rich historical archive of human experience and adaptation to a changing world, which is accessible through etymology. This dynamic process is always open to future influences. In addition to this historicity, natural language offers **multiple meanings**. The meanings of words can never be definitively laid down; they are 'overdetermined'. One word can have several meanings, and one meaning can be explained in several words; together with every denotation goes a diffuse collection of connotations. The 'Newspeak' project consists in eliminating these features, and changing natural into artificial language along the lines of scientific, mathematical and technical terminology. Such languages are closed systems with a rigid code in which there can be only one meaning per lexeme. Another vital principle governing the artificial language is economy: When it comes to signs and grammar, the more concise, the better.

"We are getting the language into its final shape – the shape it's going to have when nobody speaks anything else. [...] We're destroying words – scores of them,

48 Pinter (1971), 83 f.

hundreds of them, every day. We're cutting the language down to the bone."[49] This is how a government-employed linguist describes his work. The radical reduction of signs is meant not only to rob language of its history, but also to shrink the community's consciousness to the confines of the regime's ideology. While conciseness and precision are important and indeed essential in scientific language, for purposes of communication they represent a huge reduction of cognitive possibilities and an exclusion of human sensibilities. Language is the most important resource for reflection and contact – without it, there can be no thought, no self-awareness, no criticism. It is precisely these individual abilities which are to be brought under political control by the regime's new language:

> The whole aim of Newspeak is to narrow the range of thought. In the end we shall make thoughtcrime literally impossible, because there will be no words in which to express it. Every concept that can ever be needed will be expressed by exactly *one* word, with its meaning rigidly defined and all its subsidiary meanings rubbed out and forgotten. [...] Every year fewer and fewer words, and the range of consciousness always a little smaller. [...] The Revolution will be complete when the language is perfect. [...] By the year 2050, at the very latest, not a single human being will be alive who could understand such a conversation as we are having now. [...] The whole literature of the past will have been destroyed. Chaucer, Shakespeare, Milton, Byron – they'll exist only in Newspeak versions, not merely changed into something different, but actually changed into something contradictory of what they used to be. [...] The whole climate of thought will be different. In fact, there will *be* no thought, as we understand it now. Orthodoxy means not thinking – not needing to think. Orthodoxy is unconsciousness.[50]

In this negative reflection, we can read Orwell's high estimation of language as the foundation of culture and humanity. It is both an individual and a collective process, and just like history, culture and the human race itself, it is constantly evolving. We use it, but at the same time we are used by it. As a medium for reflection, identity formation and cultural memory it forms the basis of mental growth, a demanding and precarious process which can never be taken for granted. Language enables culture, but it also depends on culture, drawing our attention to it and forcing us to refine and nurture it. Literature, in which language is not only at its virtuoso best but is also always under close observation, is the paradigmatic medium for such attention and refinement.

49 Orwell (1961), 45.
50 Orwell (1961), 46 f.

Summary

One of the main distinctions between humans and animals is the use of signs for storing and passing on information.

Already in medieval semiotics, the basic structure of the sign was summed up by the sentence *aliquid stat pro aliquo* (something stands for something else). The modern definition of the linguistic sign as signifier and signified goes back to the structuralist Ferdinand de Saussure. In his model, the signifier is the material exterior of the sign, as perceived by the senses, while the signified is the cognitive interior, i.e. the mental concept that is symbolized by the sign. His insight into the arbitrariness of the link between signifier and signified marks the birth of constructivism (within the framework of the 'linguistic turn' around 1900). The central thesis of this is that humans do not copy their own world through language, but actually construct it.

Post-structuralist theories criticize the static architecture of Saussure's model, and argue that meaning should not be regarded as a stable entity but as a mental and cultural projection, which must be continually renegotiated between interlocutors.

Karl Bühler devised a communication model which distinguished three basic functions of language: representative, expressive and appellative. This was expanded by Jan Mukařovský and Roman Jakobson to create a model with six factors and functions: sender/expressive, communication/aesthetic, context/referential, contact/phatic, code/metalinguistic, and receiver/appellative. This model can be applied to a wide variety of linguistic contexts.

With his theory of sign types, the American semiotician Charles Sanders Peirce distinguished between 'symbol', 'icon' and 'index', each depending on the nature of the link between the sign and the signified.

Everyday communication, literature and culture are contexts for the use and interpretation of language and signs. Language is a fundamental means of civilizing humans, but it can also be used for hegemonic and violent purposes.

Select bibliography

Barthes, Roland (1982) Empire of Signs. Trans. Richard Howard. New York: Hill and Wang.

Butler, Judith (1997) Excitable Speech. A Politics of the Performative. New York (et al.): Routledge.

Eco, Umberto (1976) A Theory of Semiotics. London: Macmillan.

Hess-Lüttich, Ernest W. B./Müller, Jürgen E./Van Zoest, Aart J. A., eds. (1998) Signs & Space. Tübingen: Gunter Narr.

Loxley, James (2007) Performativity. The New Critical Idiom. New York (et al.): Routledge.

2. MEDIA

2.1 Media as mediators?

According to the philosopher Hans Blumenberg, human contact with reality is "indirect, clumsy, slow, selective and, above all, metaphorical."[1] The indirectness is the home territory of the media. With their assistance, humans sharpen their senses, expand their means of expression, and vastly extend their range of communication and storage.

The word 'media' is the plural of **'medium'**, and from its spiritualist associations right through to the most advanced technological apparatus, the function is always to provide access to something that is otherwise inaccessible. In this sense, the medium is a mediator. However, this definition is not only inadequate, but also misleading. For although the media mediate between us and the world, at the same time they actually produce the world, and us as well. This insight into their constructive character, which today is common to all the many books on the subject, already applies to signs and images, as the philosopher Ernst Cassirer has pointed out: they all "come between us and objects; but in doing so, they not only indicate the negative fact that the object is detached from us, but they also create the only possible and adequate mediation, as being the medium through which some kind of mental existence becomes graspable and comprehensible."[2] A more recent description runs as follows:

> Media do not simply deliver messages, but they create an effect that shapes the modalities of our thought, perception, memory and communication. [...] 'Modality' expresses the fact that our contact with the world, and hence all our actions and experiences that function by opening up the world, is shaped by the possibilities of differentiation offered by the media and by the limitations that these impose on us.[3]

Its ethereal amorphousness, what Cassirer calls 'mental existence' is impossible to grasp, and so if humans are to latch onto anything at all, first it has to be given a material prop and a sensory form. Anything mental that is to be communicated needs some kind of media: speech needs sound waves; thoughts need writing, print, books; images need paint, canvas and frame; music can't be made without vocal chords or instruments, films without celluloid or cameras. The *Geisteswissenschaften* [humanities] derived their fundamental unity from the col-

1 Blumenberg (1981), 115.
2 Cassirer (1983), 176.
3 Krämer (1998), 14 f.

lective, metaphysical concept of the *Geist* [mind, spirit], from which cultures emerged just as creation is said to have emerged from the breath of God. Cultural studies – and of course especially media studies – inquire into the nature and role of media as material preconditions for each and every form of artistic production and representation.

Media are the material bearers of sign systems, and the more modern they are, the more technological they become. It is clear that for us it is no longer enough to describe signs as a combination of signifiers and signifieds. If they are to be perceived, they require a **material exterior**, and that is what we mean by a medium.

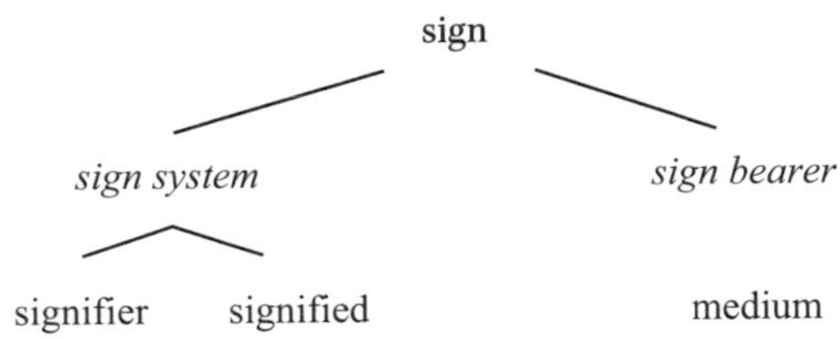

For a long time, little attention was paid to these material bearers. They were regarded as trivial, or were taken for granted, and to a certain degree that was understandable. As a tacit dimension of our communication processes, their very function is to be overlooked. This is not only because they have become so familiar – like the black letters on a printed page, or the flickering beam that projects the film onto the screen. We are culturally programmed to disregard the materiality of our media, because if we become aware of them, we shall no longer see what they are showing us: coded information on the page of a book, or the picture on the screen. The media and their mediated objects cannot both be perceived at the same time; just like the images psychologists sometimes use – at one moment you see a rabbit's head, the next a duck's – you can only observe one at a time. In other words, media are there to focus and not to be focused on.

2.1.1 Components of the compact concept of media

Cassirer blurred the distinction between 'symbolic forms' and media, i. e. between ways of perceiving and ways of recording, because he wasn't particularly interested in the material aspects of presentation. Today we take the distinction more seriously. We therefore differentiate **symbolic representation** from **medial presentation**. For example, one genre of painting requires a canvas and a frame; one genre of literature is drama, which requires a script and a stage; for a feature film you need the film itself, a projector and a screen. The borders between the arts are to a certain degree identical to the borders between the senses: music and poetry are for the ear; painting, photography and silent films are for the eye; sculpture is for eye and touch. The respective materials are voice, sound and letters, paint and canvas, paper and celluloid, wood, metal or marble. Thus senses, signs, arts and media are all interconnected. In the course of media history, initially one can detect a tendency towards separation and purity, but then the arts begin to interweave and overlap. The cinema, for instance, combines image, sound and music, thereby developing a synaesthetic art form, affecting different senses at the same time. Computers use the same digital writing to codify speech, image and sound.

Kenneth Burke distinguishes between four **stages of sign usage**, each of which builds on the others: *coding, communicating, storing* and *transmitting*. One can extend this list with *duplicating* and *distributing*, which were the hallmarks of the great breakthrough brought about by the printing press. In respect of these different technical stages and functions, the media theorist Siegfried J. Schmidt has rightly called the word 'medium' a 'compact concept', in so far as generally it incorporates and combines several different dimensions. If we now try to identify these elements individually, we will find the following:

1. *sign systems* and forms of expression, like verbal, visual, acoustic, numerical codes (e. g. English grammar, the alphabet, or a musical scale)
2. *forms of representation* within the different arts and their genres (e. g. painting, still life, novel, short story, documentary film)
3. *sign bearers*, relating to the various materials that preserve the recording and presentation (e. g. paint, wood, canvas, marble, voice, ink)
4. *media of encoding and distribution*, relating to forms of storage, multiplication and distribution by way of technical reproduction and channels of communication (e. g. book, newspaper, film, TV, video, internet)
5. *social forms of communication*, in the sense of contexts in which the media are embedded, such as institutions and places of performance, exhibition or sale (e. g. library, bookshop, marketplace, theatre, concert hall, cinema, festival)[4]

Artworks are generated through interaction with these different dimensions – semiotic (1), aesthetic (2), material (3), technical (4) and social (5) – and they vary according to the respective potentials and limits. We shall now take a closer look at the mediality of literature, and in particular at the significance of writing, its historical evolution, and the related social institutions. We shall also be considering images and imagery as the 'other' of writing and speech, and we will glance at the complex interplay between these different media.

4 I have based this schema on S. J. Schmidt's triad, proposed in his book *Kalte Faszination: Medien, Kultur, Wissenschaft in der Mediengesellschaft* (2000), 93 f. He distinguishes four components in the concept of media, which can be easily transferred to the above system: semiotic instruments of communication (= my level 1), the technical media with their appropriate technologies (= my level 3), the systematic socialization of a medium (= my level 5), and the concrete products of the media, i. e. books, films, musical compositions (my level 4).

2.2 Oral and written

2.2.1 Arts of memory: forms of repetition and forms of storage

According to Freud, there are two basic modes by which something is kept in the memory: frequency of repetition and intensity of impression.[5] These can be illustrated by two images: the **path** and the **track**. A path is only recognizable so long as it is in constant use. If people are no longer walking on it, grass will grow over it and very soon it will be indistinguishable from the land around it. Something very similar happens when we have forgotten an original event. In other words, when particular links between neurons cease to be activated, they will disappear. **Repetition** and renewal correspond to a dynamic storage technique, whereas engraving or **imprinting** are static. Unlike the path, the track leaves the impression of a single movement. Under certain conditions, tracks can be preserved over very long periods – a footprint permanently hardened in clay, for instance (even dinosaur prints have been discovered in this manner), a mark burned in wood, a scar or tattoo on the skin.

Path and track stand for two contrasting models of storage, which I would like to term *material impressions* and *inscriptions*. In simple terms, the storage techniques of oral societies depend on **repetition**, whereas written cultures depend on **preservation**. Societies without writing must store the knowledge they need for the future within living memories, and these will have to be periodically refreshed. The remarkable survival potential of written records consists in the fact that they can fix a particular content once and for all – thus providing a means of preservation that is independent of performance and repetition. Writing thus constitutes relief for the memory. In order to gauge the enormous advantage of this new invention, we need only imagine a book whose letters, if not constantly read, will gradually fade away; if that were so, our bookshelves would eventually be full of books with nothing but blank pages. We take it for granted that writing will retain its preservative power independent of memory.

In **oral societies**, the poets themselves are the physical media of cultural memory; they preserve important knowledge for the group, concerning its origins, its history and prehistory, its gods and its heroes. Being a medium in this context does not mean saying something of your own invention, but making knowledge available to the group. Oral poets and story tellers – be they minstrels, shamans, medicine men, rhapsodes, griots or whoever – are not expected to come up with

5 Freud (1966), 300: "According to psych[ological] knowledge, the memory of an experience (that is, its continuing operative power) depends on a factor which is called the magnitude of the impression and on the frequency with which the same impression is repeated. Translated into theory: Facilitation depends on the *Q* [quantity] which passes through the neurone in the excitatory process and on the number of repetitions of the process."

new ideas; their talents are for memory and performance. They must be able to improvise and provide variations on their themes, but they are bound to do this only in order to renew the tradition and not to change it. Poets who leave the service of the group in order to work for an individual patron, as happened in Greek and Roman times and indeed in Shakespeare's too, detach themselves from this communal bond of cultural memory, and instead become instruments for the personal glory of the patron, or their work becomes the medium for their own immortalization.

The oral staging of poetry is always **multimedial**. This is due to the (ceremonial) nature of the occasion, and also to mnemotechnical necessity. Music, rhythm, dance and voice are physical media that help to support the memory. This rich ensemble of embodied mnemotechnology, which the Greeks called *mousiké* and attributed to the Muses, is replaced by writing. All that remains of these different sign systems then is a single strand – language. But this too becomes separated from the voice, stripped of its sonant articulation, and reduced to a non-sensory chain of letters. There is another factor which is equally far-reaching: the wording is fixed. While oral literature only exists as the sum of its variations, for which there is no set original or so-called *Urtext*, writing gives the wording a single, final form.

Oral	*Written*
Performance as medium	Book as medium
Active interaction with audience	Absence of both author and reader
Collective experience	Individual experience
Improvisation, variation	Wording fixed by text
Set formulae, schemata	Freedom of imagination
Anonymous artists	Famous authors

2.2.2 Oral poetry – written literature

The German language distinguishes between ***Dichtung*** [poetry] and ***Literatur*** [literature]. The former is unmarked by pen or press, and like the word *Poesie* evokes the idea of an established, unwritten tradition. How is *Dichtung* handed down to succeeding generations without the preservative medium of writing? The answer is, with the aid of memory. How does memory achieve this? *Dichtung* stored in the memory, as opposed to on paper, contains certain elements that distinguish it from *Literatur* (derived from the Latin *litteratus*, which means 'lettered'). Some of these elements are:

- The principles of physical mnemotechnology are not external to *Dichtung* but are incorporated in the linguistic composition. **Rhythm, alliteration, rhyme** are not just decorative features in oral cultures but are always mnemonic strategies.

- Apart from sacred texts which have to be memorized word for word, with secular narratives it is the **underlying structures** and storylines that must be adhered to, while the **surface forms** can be freely varied at each repetition. The medievalist Paul Zumthor coined the expression *mouvence* for this[6]: oral compositions do not exist in any fixed form, but remain flexible in the 'stream of tradition'. In this context, a major role is played by the range of set phrases available in the repertoire of usable expressions. This repertoire functions as the memory's relay stations in order to keep the process of poetic reproduction going.
- What is preserved in the memory needs to be regularly reactivated by repetition so that it will not be forgotten. In memory cultures, a vital outlet for repetition is the **festival**. This offers a framework for the ceremonial staging of traditions through virtuoso performances. The crucial protection of oral tradition therefore comes not only from memory but also from performance. Oral poetry, like pop culture and slam poetry, lives through performance.

Against this background, writing presents itself as external, bodiless memory. In a remarkable narrative at the end of his dialogue *Phaidros*, Plato has Thot, the Egyptian god of invention, hail writing as a universal remedy against memory loss. However, this *pharmakon* (panacea) reveals itself – as such remedies often do – to be both a medicine and a poison. Therefore the proud inventor is finally given an answer which to this day is still stunning: "You have invented a means not of strengthening but of destroying the faculty of memory!"[7]

What **writing** can and cannot do becomes evident when we consider it against the background of traditional memory cultures:

- Instead of physical mnemotechnics, we have recording methods that have nothing to do with memory. Literary works can be as long as they like, because their volume will no longer depend on memory capacity or conditions of performance, but simply on writing materials. Elements of composition which rely on the body (the structure of sounds and rhythms, not to mention music and dance) are replaced by **non-sensory language**.
- The flow of *mouvence* is frozen by the text. As we shall see in the next chapter, whatever is to be communicated is fixed by its signs or wording, so that it can be reused or reread any number of times.
- Poets are individualized; they come up with their own aspirations for innovation, and detach themselves from the anonymous, communal tradition in order to establish their own distinctive identity as **authors** (see the comparison between performance and authorship in this chapter).

6 Zumthor (1983).
7 Plato (2009), 273c–274d.

- The survival of written texts does not require regular **performances**, or interaction with a partner. Even things that have long since gone out of use and memory can be recovered – if they are materially preserved – from obscurity and enjoy a second life.

Of course orality has not been totally replaced and has even found its way into the written text in various forms. For instance, the 'staging of orality' can become a particular feature of written texts.[8]

2.2.3 Text as repeatable communication

Use of the term **'text'** can generally range from written records and sign combinations through to extended metaphorical expressions like 'culture as text'. However, we shall now consider a different concept, which is the equation of text with a particular wording. Fixed wording need not automatically mean writing: oral statements can be learned by heart so that they can later be reproduced, for instance, as a messenger's report. In this limited sense, a text is **repeated** or **repeatable** information. Konrad Ehlich has defined text as a "communication taken up again in the framework of an extended communication."[9] An **'extended' communication** is one in which sender and receiver are not present at the same time or in the same place. Contact can then only be made if the information is held in some sort of intermediate storage, thereby transcending its original place and time of origin. The messenger may bring news that he was given three days ago in another town. The written text is an **'immutable mobile'** (Bruno Latour)[10] which can convey the message much more accurately than a messenger across time and space, but that is not all. As repeatable information, it can be used again in many other communication situations. The basic quality of the written text, then, is its potential for reiteration. This word contains the Latin *iter*, which means 'way'. Language signs that have been fixed in memory or text provide a track that can be followed as often as required. The text which is written on transportable material (as opposed to inscriptions on a gravestone or temple wall), is **mobile** but also **stable** because of its fixed signs, and yet at the same time it is basically open as far as communication is concerned, because the manner of its reception is bound to be indeterminate. Jacques Derrida focused particularly on this point when he distinguished the concept of **iterability** from that of repetition.[11] Acts of repetition and technical reproduction can be one and the same thing, but modes of reading are never identical. Even though the text offers a network of fixed signs that will always constitute the same path, no matter how often one treads it, the experience and aim of the movement can never be fixed.

8 For example, cf. Erzgräber (1998).
9 Ehlich (1983), 31 f.
10 Latour (1986).
11 On the concept of iterability, cf. Derrida (1988).

No-one can ever predetermine the interpretive direction that the receiver will take.

The **messenger** is an interesting figure, because he represents the principle of intermediate storage in human form; as a go-between he ensures communication but can also cause disruption to the message and its signs. This is indeed what happens in L. P. Hartley's novel *The Go-Between*, in which the boy who takes messages to and from the secret lovers begins to interfere and actually make changes according to his limited understanding.[12] In contrast to the reliable, fixed written text there are dangers of misrepresentation for the oral message when the communication situation is 'extended'. There is another instance of this in Laurence Sterne's *Tristram Shandy*. The problem here revolves around the name with which the none too lively newborn baby is immediately to be christened. The father, who is not yet dressed, can't attend to such matters at the appropriate speed, and therefore tells the maid Susannah to hurry downstairs with the information, which would not in itself be a problem except that the name the father has chosen is horribly difficult and unfamiliar: "But stay, – thou art a leaky vessel, Susannah, added my father; canst thou carry Trismegistus in thy head the length of the gallery without scattering?"[13] Of course she can't. ('Trismegistus' – literally 'the three times great' – is an Egyptian variation of the god Hermes, and refers to a legendary sage who is regarded as being the author of age-old 'hermetic' revelatory texts.) What enters the leaky vessel on the top floor of the Shandy household is "Tis Tris-something", which in his haste the priest turns into 'Tristram'.

The function fulfilled by the living messenger memorizing the message is the equivalent of that performed by the written, material version. In both forms we are dealing with texts in the sense of repeatable messages, and these make it possible for the separated sender and receiver to communicate with one another. But the messenger can only achieve this on a small scale, whereas writing has an almost unlimited ability to store information and to convey it over vast distances of space and time.

In a text entitled *Distant Correspondents*, Charles Lamb contemplates the problem of extended communication. One Sunday in 1823 he wrote to a friend in Australia. In those days he had to reckon with a time lag of about ten months. Little wonder, then, that he felt frustrated by the time and space separating him from his friend: "The weary world of waters between us oppresses my imagination. It is difficult to conceive how a scrawl of mine should ever stretch across it. It is a sort of presumption to expect that one's thoughts should live so far. It is like writing for posterity ..."[14] He almost lost the urge to write any more, because

12 Hartley (2002).
13 Sterne (2004), IV, xiv.
14 Lamb (1964), 150.

how could he guarantee that what was true at the moment of writing would still be true when his friend read it? Lamb felt that "not only does truth, in these long intervals, unessence herself", but he also feared the opposite – that a pure fiction could, during the long journey, ripen into a fact. Lamb's problem with his Australian letter is revealing because it clearly shows the borderline between **correspondence** and **literature**. Letters are one-way communications and are generally not geared to repeatability – in other words, they are not 'texts' in the sense we have been discussing. Unlike the letter, literature is perfectly adapted to the conditions of extended communication. Right from the start, its truths are insubstantial, in the sense that they are not restricted by reference to any outside reality, and so what it communicates can always be taken up again even when historical circumstances have changed.

2.2.4 Bearers of writing and book formats

The form of the book seems to have been permanent and stable, but in reality it has undergone radical changes over the centuries. Its history can be divided into at least six different stages:

1. **Tablets of clay** on which signs can be carved while they are soft and which can then be hardened by fire.
2. **Rolls of papyrus** (also called volumes or scrolls), made from papyrus leaves whose panicles are laid over one another in alternating perpendicular and horizontal layers, then pressed and stuck together. As the 'pages' can be stuck onto one another, there is no limit to the potential length; the writing is done in columns, and finally the whole thing is rolled up. These rolls are held in two hands, with the left rolling the text open, and the right rolling it closed until one comes to the required passage. With this book form, it is only possible to pick out individual passages by running through the whole thing, which is a feature it has in common with tape recorders and computer files, which also require 'scrolling'.
3. The **codex** is made of more stable material and forms the prototype of the modern book. It consists of **parchment** which is stuck together and bound in wood. Parchment comes from animal skins which have been shaved, dried and defatted in an expensive process.[15] A longer text would not fit onto a single cowhide but would require a whole herd of calves or sheep. Plato's *Timaios*, for example, used 16 skins, and an Anglo-Saxon Bible used no less than 520.[16] This type of book, which was introduced between the second and fourth century, was no longer scrolled but leafed. It became the medium of the future when the Chris-

15 HAMLET: Is not parchment made of sheepskins?
HORATIO: Ay, my lord, and of calves too.
(Shakespeare (1997a), V, 1, 102 f)

16 Jochum (1999), 61.

tians discovered the codex for their texts and thus set themselves apart from the papyrus medium used by heathen authors. Apart from a few isolated papyruses found in deserts, all that remains from the Ancient World's stock of books is those that have lain uncopied in Christian scriptoria, i. e. those rooms in monasteries where manuscripts were stored and copied. The Christians increasingly incorporated the classical canon, and "what was not copied in the course of this restructuring disappeared from the canon and was consigned to oblivion."[17] During the Middle Ages, the Church had a monopoly on writing; before the universities were founded, monasteries remained the centres of education and the seat of libraries. The production of codices was expensive and labour-intensive, and they became valuable objects, while a book with religious content was regarded as a sacred object in itself. Books were not yet used as tools for academic discourse.

4. That was to change after the twelfth century, when **paper** began to take the place of the expensive parchment. The technique of papermaking was imported to Europe from China, via the Arabs. The first paper mill in Germany was built in the fourteenth century. Paper was the material used in the newly founded universities, which joined the monasteries as centres for reading and writing. The practice of writing spread with the introduction of paper, and it was no longer confined to professional scribes. Authors like Thomas Aquinas began to write their own texts. With this expansion came a new discovery which Ivan Illich considers to have been an even more important technical innovation than the printing press. This was the layout of the **page**. Texts were now set out with a view to readability, and this was linked to a new technique of reading. The beautifully illuminated, continuous texts produced in the monasteries were designed for slow, contemplative, reverential reading, whereas the new, easy-to-follow layout aimed at accessibility and communication of information. Texts were given headings, and they were divided up into lines and paragraphs. The individual page, with a clear separation between text and commentary, became an optical aid in structuring thought. The use of paper and page were major achievements by the universities, as were the professional, commercial writing offices with their paid scribes, setting up business as a secular parallel to the monastic scriptoria.
5. In 1440 Johannes **Gutenberg** came up with the invention that made it possible to print texts on paper with movable letters, using a type case with different types. Now for the first time it became possible to have identical reproductions of a written text. From the handicraft of writing emerged the first branch of industrial production.
6. Currently, the latest book format is the **data file,** or storage devices such as the CD-ROM. After stone, clay, grass, skin and cloth, this bearer is almost immaterial. In contrast to the book, the stored data here have lost their sensory solidity,

17 Jochum (1999), 53.

and in order to read or write them, one needs technical apparatus. These devices are subject to rapid technological change. As the perpetuity of the data bearer is no longer ensured, institutions like libraries and archives have to preserve their material in a complex process of periodical re-copying through the latest storage system. In 2002, the E-Book appeared on the market with a reading device called 'Kindle', which brought with it a new form of competition, new legal problems and new reading possibilities. Today books "can also be bought chapterwise, in periodical updates or in wholesale classics editions that would otherwise fill many shelves."[18] Although more and more books are appearing today in digital form on the internet, the book as a material object, with the advantages of its tangibility, is in no way endangered, and it looks as though for pragmatic reasons it will maintain its place in the new competition between the media as well as in its new versions.

2.3 Writing and authorship as reflected in media history

In this chapter we will be looking at the historical dimension of literary mediality, using authorship as our example. We shall be mainly concerned with material modes of presentation (changes in techniques of writing) and social forms of communication (changes in literary institutions).

2.3.1 Stabilizing texts through writing and print

As we have seen, the introduction of writing led to a radical change in the conditions and status of oral literature. Written literature is less dependent on the ear and body, but more dependent on the reading eye, with the loss of sensory stimulation being replaced by greater semantic and structural complexity. Its production is freed from the collective, social framework of performance, and takes place in isolation.

The change from **oral** to **written culture** was not a sudden leap from one to the other. A transitional state is to be found in writings of the oral culture – which is also called **'recitation culture'**.[19] Geoffrey Chaucer, the great English poet of the Late Middle Ages, provides a clear illustration of this. There is a picture of him reading from his works to an attentive audience of aristocrats at the court of Richard II – a vivid illustration of a recitation culture halfway between the oral and the written tradition. The fact that his work is considered to be 'literature', in the sense of a new concept of text, is also neatly demonstrated by a short poem addressed to his scribe Adam:

18 Tagesspiegel, 4. 1. 2009.
19 Pearsall (1985); Müller (1996).

Adam scriveyn, if ever it thee bifalle
Boece or Troilus to wryten newe,
Under thy lokkes thou most have the scalle,
But after my making thou wryte trewe.
So ofte a daye I mot thy work renewe,
Hit to correcte and eek to rubbe and scrape;
And al is through thy negligence and rape.[20]

The talk of "rubbe and scrape" relates to writing on expensive, time-resistant parchment. Chaucer's *Canterbury Tales*, in which an oral narrative situation provides the frame for the actual story, clearly address a readership, since anyone who doesn't enjoy one story is directly encouraged to turn the page and try another:

who – so list it nat y – here
Turne over the leef, and chese another tale.[21]

Another example to show how the written text gradually penetrated a still mainly oral culture is the ban on improvisation which Hamlet imposes on the players: "And let those that play your clowns speak no more than is set down for them!"[22] These instructions run counter to the then common practice whereby comic roles were tailored to the talents of the actors in such a way that a clown could pursue his own personal glory at the expense of the play and its dramatic coherence.

Chaucer still belonged to the **culture of handwriting**. He employed a scribe, who wrote and made copies of his texts. The quality of the scribe was measured by the precision of his copies. In the age of print, copyists were still able to make a living, and indeed they were still to be found during the twentieth century, even if their status in the age of mass printing became increasingly marginal. They were useful when multiple documents were required that were not suitable for printing, e. g. in legal firms or administrative offices, where they only became redundant with the invention of the photocopying machine.

The figure of the **copyist** also plays an interesting role in literary texts. Practitioners generally have a hard time of it in nineteenth-century literature. In Charles Dickens' novel *Bleak House*, one rather unpleasant copyist dies from a mysterious illness called "spontaneous combustion", which casts a gloomy shadow over the act of merely copying what someone else has written – a chore that became less and less important in the age of print. A particularly striking example is to be found in Herman Melville's novella *Bartleby the Scrivener*. The eponymous protagonist is a copyist working in the Dead-Letter-Office.[23] This is a department of the

20 Chaucer (1969a), 118. Cf. Minnis (1984).
21 Chaucer (1969b), A 3176 f.
22 Shakespeare (1997a), III, 2, 34 f.
23 Melville (1987).

post office where letters are collected that have failed to reach their addressees. Bartleby's involvement with these 'dead letters' leads to him gradually adopting an attitude of refusal ("I prefer not to") that severs all his social ties, and eventually he dies utterly alone. In such narratives of copyists, literature reflects its own mediality.[24]

According to Francis Bacon, the three most important factors that ushered in the modern age were **gunpowder**, the **compass** and the **printing press**. These, he said, "have altered the whole face and state of things right across the globe."[25] He was right, for it was these inventions that opened up what had been a narrow vision of the world, and they all contributed in their different ways to geographical and political expansion. Without the compass, there could have been no transatlantic crossings, without gunpowder no conquests, and without the printing press, no mass multiplication of bibles and no extended missionary activity. The printing press was a technological revolution which completely changed the structure of the way information was recorded and distributed. Elizabeth Eisenstein, who wrote a history of this whole process, discovered that in the first fifty years of printing, some eight million books were published – more than all the books copied by all the scribes in Europe since the days of Constantine (4th century AD).[26]

2.3.2 Weak authorship

In times when tradition is dominant, authorship can only be weak; power then lies not with the **authors** who produce texts, but with the **authorities** whose texts have been handed down through the generations, followed, copied, compiled and annotated. The authorities are exclusively dead authors, and for a living individual to present himself as an author would be absurdly hubristic. The weak author can only be an intellectual shadow of the authorities; he presents himself as a reader. Whatever he writes, he has already read somewhere else. The weak author draws attention to the texts he is referring to, whereas the strong author conceals them. The American literary critic Harold Bloom has aptly described this as the 'anxiety of influence'.[27]

The weak author survived the introduction of the printing press, but did not perceive this new medium as a turning-point, and did not see the book market as an opportunity. In terms of publication practices (but of course not with respect to his literary genius), Shakespeare is a shining example of this: he himself never sent any of his works to the printer's, and the first collected edition of his plays was compiled by his company seven years after his death. By contrast, his con-

24 Mainberger (1995).
25 Bacon (2004), Aphorism 129, 195.
26 Eisenstein (1997), cf. Giesecke (1991).
27 Bloom (1973).

temporary Ben Jonson published an 'authorized' edition of his works during his lifetime.

Weak authorship is strikingly illustrated by a text published in the same year as the First Folio (1623). On the cover of this book is the title, the place of printing, and two names – those of the printer and the publisher. What you will not find there is the name of the author (John Earle). One can only assume that initially, the interest of technicians and entrepreneurs in the new medium took precedence over authorship. Indeed an author would only publicize himself if he needed to sell his work. For higher class personages this was considered objectionable. One such author must have been the man who wrote *Micro-Cosmographie*, published in 1628, as we can see from the foreword by the publisher Edward Blount:

> TO THE READER
>
> I have (for once) adventured to play the midwife's part, helping to bring forth these infants into the world, which the father would have smothered; who having left them lapt up in loose sheets, as soon as his fancy was delivered of them, written especially for his private recreation, to pass away the time in the country, and by the forcible request of friends drawn from him: yet, passing severally from hand to hand, in written copies, grew at length to be a pretty number in a little volume: and among so many sundry dispersed transcripts, some very imperfect and surreptitious had liked to have passed the press, if the author had not used speedy means of prevention; when, perceiving the hazard he ran to be wronged, was unwillingly willing to let them pass as now they appear to the world. If any faults have escaped the press (as few books can be printed without), impose them not on the author, I intreat thee; but rather impute them to mine and the printer's oversight, who seriously promise, on the re-impression hereof, by greater care and diligence for this our former default, to make thee ample satisfaction. In the mean while, I remain Thine, Ed. Blount.[28]

From this text, all the features of our second category of 'weak' authorship clearly emerge. The author has no thought of giving his intellectual product the chance of wider distribution and longer survival through the print medium. If he does get into print, he does so "unwillingly willing", and only in order to protect himself against pirates on the open market. Indifference towards his own intellectual products leads to others having to look after his 'orphaned children'. Alongside these current metaphors of literary production and birth go those of tutelage and upbringing.[29] Thus literary production could be split into two roles – those of the father and the tutor. In the aristocratic milieu, where the small middle-class family was not yet the norm, the two roles did not necessarily coincide, and the role of the warden – with responsibility for nurturing the child – was no less impor-

28 Earle (1811), xix f.

29 The topic of the text as a deformed suckling, changeling, foundling, foster child or orphan is dealt with by Richard Helgerson (1976), who speaks of a "paradigm of prodigality", and assigns these images to the motif of the Prodigal Son.

tant than that of the father. It is interesting to note that an older etymological meaning of the Latin word *auctor* re-emerges in this context, because part of its original legal definition was 'guardian of a ward'.

Thus the weak author is like a father who delegates the care of his child to a guardian. Whenever the progenitor neglects his product, inevitably the text will be full of inversions, omissions and especially unmarked additions to the original. Texts by weak authors are not stable but dynamic, and may be rewritten and altered at will.[30] Even though with our example later editions did identify John Earle as the author, it is no longer possible to tell which parts of the book actually came from his pen.

2.3.3 Strong authorship

The indeterminate assignment of texts and names ended with the standardized form of **strong authorship**. A legal precondition for this was the **Copyright Act**, passed in England in 1709, granting authors the right of text ownership. In addition to this legal and economic right, there were certain social conditions, of which we shall deal with just two: independence from patronage, and canonization.

Under the system of patronage, the writer was given social protection and economic support by someone in a higher position – generally a nobleman or prince – and in return he was duty bound to enhance the patron's reputation and make him be remembered for ever. Through this contractual arrangement, the patron was a participant in the work, for which he provided the materials and which was written for his glorification. The path from dependent to independent authorship was that of the patron to the book market. Samuel Johnson, respectfully dubbed "our doctor" and regarded as "the first professional man of letters" in England, was a prime example of someone who followed this path. When he was looking for a patron to finance his *Dictionary of the English Language*, he hoped to gain the support of a certain Lord Chesterfield, but without success. Eventually, the printing of the dictionary was financed by subscriptions.[31] After its publication, Lord Chesterfield wrote two glowing reviews. Johnson replied to these on 7 February 1755 with a famous letter that has gone down as a landmark in the history of authorship. He wrote:

> Seven years, My Lord have now passed since I waited in your outward Rooms or was repulsed from your Door, during which time I have been pushing my work through difficulties of which it is useless to complain, and have brought it at last to the verge of Publication without one Act of assistance, one word of encouragement, or one smile of favour. Such treatment I did not expect, for I never had a Patron before [...].

30 For further details, cf. Assmann, A. (1991b).
31 Regarding parallel developments in Germany, cf. Bosse (1981) and Rieger (1995).

> Is not a Patron, My Lord, one who looks with unconcern on a Man struggling for Life in the waters and when he has reached ground encumbers him with help.[32]

The circumvention of patronage through direct contact with printer and bookseller brought about the **professionalization** of authorship, thus opening up new commercial possibilities, especially for female authors.[33] However, along with professionalization, the expansion of education and literacy brought about a new distinction between strong and weak authorship. In the eighteenth and nineteenth centuries, this consisted (not exclusively but nevertheless significantly) in the border between the sexes. In other words, women generally were categorized as weak authors, and men (or some of them) as strong. One may well ask at this juncture what makes an author strong if it is not the great work or the independent act of printing.

This brings us to our second condition: the cultural practice of **canonization**. The canonization of literary texts follows the same principle as that of sacred texts: nothing must be added, nothing must be taken away, and nothing must be changed. The wording of such texts is fixed for ever, and all that is required is continuous interpretation and reinterpretation. The canonization of Shakespeare as a literary classic began in the eighteenth century with philologically researched editions of his works, separating authentic from non-authentic texts, and adding glossaries, i. e. explanations of obscure passages that give rise to secondary processes of interpretation. Literary classics are texts which are not only especially authorized and stable, but are also constantly reread and reinterpreted. Whose texts justified such attention? Why did this attention, schooled as it was on sacred and classical texts, suddenly spread to new works in everyday language and written by contemporary authors? The literary canonization of the classics was historically connected to the emergence of **national cultures**. The nations of Europe entered into cultural competition with one another by reinventing their historical origins and by producing national classics which became symbols of their national identity.

Shakespeare played a special role in this process, because not only was he hailed by the British as a classic, but towards the end of the eighteenth century the Germans too coopted him as their own 'national classic'. One reason was the German **concept of the genius** – a discourse in which Goethe took a very active role during his *Sturm und Drang* [Storm and Stress] period. Shakespeare was regarded as the archetypal, 'unruly' natural genius. Following their role model, young writers in Germany were able to free themselves from the chains of a rule-governed poetics. The idea of the genius, which in the mid eighteenth century pervaded the Protestant cultures of England and Germany, led to a celebration of individ-

32 Johnson (1992), 95 f; cf. Laurenson/Swingewood (1972).
33 In 1851, 69 % of men and 55 % of women in England were able to read and write, cf. Baumann (1986).

uality. It also led to the 'sanctification' or canonization of particular authors. This is an obviously sacral element of our modern secular culture. The embodiment of the strong author is the canonized one who qualifies being called a genius. The term 'genius' always implies **originality**, an innovative power that gives rise to a genuine and unmistakable individuality in the literary product. The genius's creative autonomy, no longer as a conveyor of traditions but as an innovator and liberator (Wordsworth in his *Prelude* calls on his imagination to inspire him, unlike Milton, who invokes the Muse) was directly linked to the legal protection of his intellectual property.[34]

This concept of the genius automatically meant the exclusion of female writers. For Kant, who in the late eighteenth century laid the basis for a philosophy of aesthetics, a 'female genius' would have been a contradiction in terms, or as Alastair Minnis puts it: 'an Impossible She'. Between 1750 and 1850 the image of the strong author was that of a **superman**. The germs of the idea are already to be found in Samuel Johnson, and subsequently in the Romantic poets such as Wordsworth and Shelley. With them the talk is of the poet as a prophet and lawgiver for the human race; these were offices and roles which would have been inconceivable for women at that time. Canonization not only entails editing and commenting on the work, but there is also a cultic dimension which manifests itself in the rhetoric of praise. In the case of Shakespeare, this extends from the young Goethe's enthusiastic endorsement to Harold Bloom's latest book on *Hamlet*.[35] A typical example of this genre of writing came from the pen of Thomas Carlyle in the first half of the nineteenth century: "For myself, I feel that there is actually a kind of sacredness in the fact of such a man being sent into this Earth. Is he not an eye to us all; a blessed heaven-sent Bringer of Light?"[36]

While the strong author writes if not directly for all time then at least for posterity, the weak author's impact is confined to the short-term economic cycles of the popular press. A large circulation means nothing or means everything: quantity and quality have nothing to do with each other. Rudolf Schenda points out that of the biggest selling German novel of the nineteenth century there remains only one incomplete copy.[37] Hawthorne, whose sales were never very high and

34 In his epic *Prelude. The Growth of a Poet's Mind*, Wordsworth (1970) writes that poets, like prophets, are endowed with a special gift "to perceive / Something unseen before." Of his poetic works that emerged from his own creative sources, he hoped "that work of mine, / Proceeding from the depth of untaught things, / Enduring and creative, might become/A power like one of Nature's." (Book XI, 1805, 306–312), cf. Woodmansee (1983).

35 Bloom (2003). In this book Bloom once more takes up his own original concept of 'bardolatry' (Bloom (1999), 271), which constitutes a quasi-religious worship of Shakespeare.

36 Carlyle (1926), 343. Cf. Assmann, A. (1995).

37 Schenda (1976).

who envied his contemporary females for their much wider circulation, spoke disparagingly of a **'mob of scribbling women'**. Clearly there is a hierarchy between writing and scribbling. However, what counts as one or the other is not decided by the printing press but by the social framework within which the writing and reading take place. What disappears in the ephemeral context of the present, no matter how high the sales or how widespread the acclaim, will still be 'scribble'; but what is selected by the present and the future for constant rereading and reinterpretation – and hence finally makes its way into the reading lists of schools and universities – most emphatically becomes 'writing', and therefore worthy of voluminous editions and critical studies, not to mention an indefinite place on the shelves of libraries.

An illuminating example of a 'mob of scribbling women' is Susan Warner, who wrote a novel called *The Wide, Wide World*, under the pseudonym of Elizabeth Wetherell. She was in financial trouble at the time, and wrote it in order to earn some money. It's a sentimental novel about the religious upbringing of a young girl who, by constantly reading the Bible, manages to remain physically and spiritually pure despite the repeated blows of fate and severe tests of her moral fibre. When the book was published in the United States in 1850, it was the biggest seller of its day: in the first two years alone there were fourteen reprints. It was also a success in England, remained in print until the turn of the century, but then was rapidly forgotten until Jane Tompkins rediscovered it and in 1987 republished it with an epilogue in the Feminist Press. Tompkins followed this up with a politico-cultural project whose aim was not only to recall the forgotten author to people's minds and memories, but also to include her in the literary canon. Her slogan for this was **'The other American Renaissance'**, in which female authors were to be included alongside the male classics named by F. O. Matthiessen, such as Hawthorne, Melville and Whitman. In this case it was not so much the text that was to be canonized – a text that was basically a sermon in the genre of female domestic fiction – but rather the feminist reading of the text, which Tompkins regarded as an important chapter of feminine history and the struggle for women's autonomy.[38]

The one-sided concept of genius excluded women from the literary canon.[39] Oscar Wilde summed up this manly gender-discourse as follows: "No woman is a genius. Women are a decorative sex. They never have anything to say, but they say it charmingly. Women represent the triumph of matter over mind, just as men represent the triumph of mind over morals."[40] However, the discourse on the possibility of strong women authors changed to the degree in which women

38 Cf. Rosenthal (2004).
39 We will return to the politico-cultural implications of literary canonization in the final chapter.
40 Wilde (2003), 64.

themselves began to take part in it. In her famous essay *A Room of One's Own*, Virginia Woolf posed the question of what actually keeps women from achieving the goal of strong authorship. She answered that it certainly was not a lack of talent or genius, but of an economic infrastructure and of an intellectual tradition.[41] A visit to the illustrious corridors of Oxbridge and then to an unprepossessing ladies' college made her acutely aware of the unbridgeable gap and inequality of opportunity between the sexes. Centuries of material and intellectual privilege gave male scientists, scholars and writers a solid foundation. None of this – whether financial, intellectual or even culinary – was to be found in the ladies' college. All the preconditions would first have to be created if women were to enjoy the same centuries-old access to success and immortality. Nevertheless, Virginia Woolf's essay was a start, and it laid a foundation stone on which a new, gender-conscious tradition of literature could be built.

2.3.4 The death of the author and the triumph of writing

The personality cult of the genius and the glorification of the strong author had a decisive effect on middle-class writing and reading habits until well into the twentieth century. In the revolutionary year of 1968, it was dealt a mortal blow by a short manifesto that fell on it with all the incisiveness of a guillotine. The author was Roland Barthes, and the title was **La Mort de l'Auteur** – the death of the author. Of course he did not mean the real live author, over whose life and death even Roland Barthes had no jurisdiction, but the author as a literary myth and as a construction created by middle-class reading habits. By desacralizing and so eliminating the great author figure, Barthes wanted to wipe out the reader's vanishing point or *telos*, and so remove the source of any stabilized meaning. Previously, people had believed that the more dominant the author, the more determinate and closed was the text, whereas now the attitude was: the further away the author, the more flexible and open the text. Once the author was 'dead', the text lost its origin, and neutral writing became separate from the biographical voice. Having lost its right to make any pronouncements, the author's voice also lost its authority over the text. Thanks to this strategy, the text took on a totally new structure of meaning, which demanded a totally different manner of reading: Instead of the author, now the network of signs was the final point of reference. The once strong author now became weak – so weak that he disappeared and became a **pure medium**. But a medium for what? No longer for the Muse, or for tradition, or for the authorities. Now it was for language, codes, and writing. With his help (for the author was still male), the language spoke for itself, and writing wrote for itself. The death of the author signalled the triumph of writing.

41 Woolf (2008a). See also the final chapter of this book.

It is important to point out that this form of writing has nothing to do with what we were discussing earlier. It is no longer writing as intermediate storage or as a medium to record speech. Nor is it subsequent annotation of past discussions or lives (which was what the author stood for originally), or a view expressed by someone outside the text. For this new form, we might use the French term **écriture**: the act of writing itself, or the **'inscription'**, as Barthes calls it. The emphasis he lays on the role of the writer in his manifesto shows how the long history of writing has come to an end which is astonishingly similar to its beginning:

> Having buried the Author, the modern scriptor can thus no longer believe, as according to the pathetic view of his predecessors, that this hand is too slow for his thought or passion [...] For him, on the contrary, the hand, cut off from any voice, borne by a pure gesture of inscription (and not of expression), traces a field without origin – or which, at least, has no other origin than language itself, language which ceaselessly calls into question all origins.[42]

The death of the author is the triumph of writing – this equation, established by Barthes in the 1970s, opened up not only new ways of reading, through the paradigm of **intertextuality**, but also **postmodern** and **deconstructive** modes of writing. At the same time, other doors began to open that led away from western traditions of strong authorship, and instead gave access to traditions that had been systematically repressed and extinguished by mainstream western culture. We shall end this section by briefly citing three examples in which **female voices** emphasize their belonging to weak authorship. The African-American author Alice Walker introduces her novel *The Color Purple* with a dedication 'To the Spirit'. She reminds us that the word 'spirit' – which has since been replaced by 'medium' – still carries connotations associated with the occult meaning of 'medium':

> To the Spirit:
> Without whose assistance
> Neither this book
> Nor I
> Would have been
> Written.[43]

Leslie Marmon Silko, a modern American author of Native American origin, introduces her novel *Ceremony* with a ritual saying, and places herself within a mythical genealogy. By interweaving traditional sayings, prayers and songs into her text, she makes it clear that as a writing author she is still bound by the oral narrative traditions of the Native Americans, whose origins go back to the mythical matriarch called the 'Spider Woman'. Stories provide links between people

42 Barthes (1990), 146.
43 Walker (1982), Dedication.

and generations because they can go on being spun through time. Silko embeds her literary text in the oral tradition of story-telling.

This consistent interweaving of written texts with elements of an oral culture is also a striking feature in the work of the African-American Nobel Prize winner Toni Morrison. In her novels, she finds many different ways of questioning the Puritan American tradition of individuality and autonomy, highlighting instead the importance of the community, without which her characters fall apart. What is crucial for them is not so much attempts at revolt or emancipation as the ways of connecting with their ancestors and the cultural memory that they embody.[44] Morrison sees herself as the heir and visionary medium of the suffering and traumata, but also of the creative resources of her ethnic community.

As a final example I would like to refer to the cross-over of oral and written traditions presented by the Indian-American author Sherman Alexie in the following self-portrait:

> 'Sherman', asks the critic, 'how does your work apply to the oral tradition?
> 'Well', I say, as I hold my latest book close to me, 'it doesn't apply at all because I type this. And I'm really, really quiet when I'm typing it.'[45]

2.4 Text and image

Ever since Antiquity an important role has been played by the relationship between the different art forms. In Roman rhetoric one art was held up as a model for others. *Ut pictura poesis* is a much quoted saying by Horace. He argued that poetry must present its content just as visually as painting.[46] Thus painting became the model for rhetoric. As the individual arts became more self-aware, for the first time the Renaissance focused on their particular strengths and limitations, which were critically set off against one another. And so a new discourse developed, called **'paragon'**, whose subject was the competition between the arts for individual qualities and for precedence. In the course of this competitive debate, poets and painters set out the specific advantages of their own art.

The competition between the arts spawned a **theoretical art discourse** which carried through into their practice. This marked the beginning of a new interest in the separation and purity of the arts, which reached its peak in the eighteenth century. In the Middle Ages there had still been a close association between writing and image – in initial letters, writing became a picture, and handwritten texts were framed with decorations and images[47] – but now the emphasis was on their separation, and on adherence to the rules that were intrinsic to each art. With

44 Morrison (1998).
45 Alexie (2000), 6.
46 Schweizer (1972).
47 Curschmann (1999).

this differentiation of the arts, there developed an increased professionalism and self-reflection. The most famous text arising from this discourse was written two hundred years after the *paragon*, and is still regarded today as a milestone in the history of aesthetics: Gotthold Ephraim Lessing's *Laocoön*.[48] Laocoön is the name of the central figure in a group of Greek statues representing a father and his two sons, who are suffering a terrible fate: a giant snake has attacked them, and is in the act of crushing all three men in its coils. What interests Lessing in this sculpture is an artistic problem: what can this image convey that cannot be communicated by a narrative? And what are we told by the narrative that has to remain outside the image? In other words, what are the specific advantages and limitations of the two different arts as forms of representation?

Lessing's answer is as simple as it is illuminating: painting and sculpture are **spatial arts**, while poetry and music are **temporal arts**. What can be depicted in space is simultaneous and synchronous; what can be represented by language and gesture develops discursively in a sequence. Unlike literary narrative, the visual arts cannot portray a process or development, but according to Lessing they must select one 'fertile moment' in which past and future are compressed into a single dynamic form. His argument continues that what applies to the production of the arts also applies to their reception. An image is a single unit whose power and pathos are packed into an instant, whereas a narrative fashions its impact over time, and proceeds through different turning-points.

This simple contrast between the timelessness of visual art and the time-dependence of linguistic art is not totally convincing in terms of their reception. Although images show everything at once and leave nothing in reserve, they are by no means perceived instantaneously in their totality. One needs long and patient study of a painting, and generally one's understanding of it will be guided by words. It is a common experience that a description will reveal details we had not observed for ourselves, and so the true composition of the picture is built up gradually, like a photograph in the course of its development. The literary critic Philip Fisher has described this process as the 'choreography of the gaze', which is no less time-dependent than the process of reading.[49]

The questions asked by artists and theorists such as Da Vinci and Alberti during the Renaissance and Lessing during the Enlightenment have lost none of their relevance today, even though the conditions that govern the media have changed. We will now take a look at the relationship between text and image with its modern and postmodern references, which will again entail consideration of sign systems (codes), formats of presentation (arts and genres), forms of representation (material media) and modes of communication (social contexts and institutions).

48 Lessing (1984).
49 Fisher (1997).

2.4.1 The 'iconic turn' around 2000

After the 'linguistic turn' at the beginning of the twentieth century, the end of the century saw another switch, this time away from language and towards the image. After more than 170 years of photography, 100 years of cinema, 50 years of television and 25 years of video, there can be no doubt that technological imagery has been making an ever deeper impression on our culture. A prophet of this turn is the Chicago literary critic W. J. T. Mitchell, who proclaimed an **'iconic turn'**, thereby pinpointing a change of structure in the composition of our culture.[50] According to this concept – if we may speak in terms of neurology – culture has shifted its emphasis from the left, language-processing half of the brain to the right, image-processing half. We are told that this change will also mark the end of the print age (the 'Gutenberg galaxy'), and with it the dominant medium of books will be replaced by that of images.

It cannot be denied that there is a great deal to be said for this thesis. Our everyday experiences are now shaped by images in a manner that was unimaginable in former times, when their production and distribution was difficult and expensive. However, if we take a closer look at the image culture of today, it will immediately become obvious that images are very seldom completely divorced from language. Generally they do not compete with language but appear in tandem with it. Wherever we find them, they are within a linguistic context – as commentaries or captions, sound tracks, balloons, interpretations. Images in art, film or advertising are always supplemented by language or reinterpreted in linguistic terms. Of course there are rigid borders and fundamental differences between pictorial signs and phonetic or written signs, but it is these same irreducible differences that create the need for bridging, for translation, thus leading to a productive interaction between the two sign systems.

The rhetoric behind the 'iconic turn' should not, therefore, be misconstrued as a radical turning point. The history of technological evolution is not one of competitive survival and extinction, and does not mean that every new invention automatically means the irreversible loss of whatever preceded it. What we have here is not **replacement** but **addition**, although it must be stressed that each new medium alters our relationship to older media, in the manner described by T. S. Eliot talking about the literary tradition (I have substituted my 'medium' for his 'work'): "The existing order is complete before the new medium arrives; for order to persist after the supervention of novelty, the whole existing order must be, if ever so slightly, altered; and so the relations, properties, values of each medium towards the other media are readjusted."[51]

50 Mitchell (1994; 2005).
51 Eliot, T. S. (1969), 50.

2.4.2 Images in the text

The heightened awareness caused by the 'iconic turn' has led not only art and media but also literary studies to reconsider their relationship to the image.[52] One of the central concepts of literary history, the imagination, already incorporates the term 'image', albeit in a pre-reflexive form. It needed a new approach to bring this aspect of literature to the fore as a subject of study in itself. **Intermediality**, which brought about a new awareness of the different forms and modes of representation, focused attention on the many types of image that had already been incorporated into the literary text. Within the sign system of writing, under the homogeneous cover of the letters, all kinds of images are concealed that form an essential element of the text. These include:

- **linguistic images** in the narrower sense of the word, i. e. metaphors and similes
- **verbally induced images**, which may be mimetically visual – serving to conjure up a scene and give vividness to linguistic expression – or alternatively non-mimetic but visionary in so far as they spring from abstract thought or free fantasy
- specific **material images**, existing outside of the text, that are referred to and represented by verbal description (*ekphrasis*[53])
- **embodied gestures and constellations** creating memorable images which arrest the flow of the narrative from the melodramatic scene up to the *tableau vivant*

Since the days of classical rhetoric, texts have always incorporated images, as we have already seen from the Horace quote (*ut pictura poesis*). In the history of art and media, this norm has constantly led to new exchanges in the relationship between the sister arts of painting and literature.[54] A famous example is to be found in Chapter 17 of *Adam Bede*, in which George Eliot informs her readers that her realistic writing has been schooled by the Dutch genre paintings of the seventeenth century. Her model is the pinpoint accuracy with which these depict even the tiniest, most monotonous details of simple, everyday life. She justifies her interest in the simple life by the fact that the vast majority of people have no say in the major actions that go to make up history, but move along quite differ-

52 Examples of this extended kind of art history are Hans Belting's 'Bildanthropologie' and Gottfried Böhm's 'Bildwissenschaft'. For what follows, cf. Rippl (2005).

53 *'Ekphrasis'* is a genre of description that has a long tradition. It is an attempt to give a detailed description of a picture with the aid of language. Its key term is *'enargeia'*. This means a vividness that will make the description so lifelike that the reader will feel he can actually see the thing being described. Thus *ekphrasis* translates sensory into mental visualization. Buch (1972).

54 Hagstrum (1958); Humm (2003).

ent paths that are dictated by everyday human needs. What she also admires about the Dutch paintings is the complete absence of picturesque compositions and sentimental clichés. Her realism is concerned precisely with the social stratum of ordinary people: "Therefore let Art always remind us of them; therefore let us always have men ready to give the loving pains of a life to the faithful representing of commonplace things."[55]

George Eliot was writing at a time when **photography** was in its infancy. The development of this new mass medium had an important impact on the history of the realistic novel. Paul Valéry stated that the norms of photography set new standards of accuracy, and therefore led to an increase in the descriptive passages of realistic novels. Photography became the embodiment of and the symbol for realistic art.[56] Its triumphal progress also contributed, however, to the fact that authors such as Virginia Woolf and D. H. Lawrence eventually abandoned the principle of **realism** in order to explore new and complementary styles of writing. They gave up the struggle to match what could be achieved more simply and more realistically in another medium. Henry James was another author who, in his narrative *The Real Thing* (1893), applied a critical gaze to photography as the norm for literature (along the lines of *ut photographia poesis*). Here a painter is commissioned to portray a couple who have already been photographed over and over again and are all too aware of their own 'photogenicity'. What may be an advantage for one medium can be a hindrance for another. The painter confesses:

> I could see she had been photographed often, but somehow the very habit that made her good for that purpose unfitted her for mine. [...] Do what I would with it my drawing looked like a photograph or a copy of a photograph.[57]

The following extract is from a conversation between the painter and his models on the relationship between reality and representation:

> "Do you think she looks like a Russian Princess?" Major Monarch asked, with lurking alarm.
> "When I *make* her, yes."
> "Oh, if you have to make her –!" he reasoned acutely.
> "That's the most you can ask. There are so many that are not makeable."
> "Well now, *here's* a lady" – and with a persuasive smile he passed his arm into his wife's – "who's already made!"[58]

The problem with the model as a 'real thing' is that art, whose very function is to make (the meaning of the Greek *poiesis* is 'making'), has nothing left to do. If there is no need for or possibility of transformation or translation, there is no

55 Eliot, G. (1996), 178.
56 Greiner/Kemmler (1979); Albers (2001).
57 James (1946), 195.
58 James (1946), 192.

need for art. This applies to artists and writers, but also to viewers and readers. They too will only get their money's worth if they can bring their **imagination** into play, and 'make' something out of the painting or text. In a situation in which the individual arts were competing with one another, James's interest lay in redefining their functions and reinstating the boundaries between them. Through the example of different models he showed that what was good for photography was bad for painting. The primary task of art and literature was not to copy or reproduce reality but, in his own words: "A studio was a place to learn to see."[59]

Around 1900, the new medium was **film**, which posed a challenge to literature similar to that already posed by photography. Leon Edel suggests that the invention of the novel was nothing other than an anticipation of the film camera. "Novelists have sought almost from the first to become a camera. And not a static instrument but one possessing the movement through space and time which the motion-picture camera has achieved in our century."[60] When this medium became a reality, it brought with it a new range of metaphors (point of view, the eye of the camera, tracking-shot, zoom), and led both authors and critics to a new self-reflexive awareness of this visual medium. Henry James was one of those who took particular care to make their texts as visual as possible.[61] He described himself as a "painter of life", and iconicity underlay all his literary writings. He was convinced that literature was the subtlest and most comprehensive form of the visual:

> The novelist can only fall back [...] on his recognition that man's constant demand for what he has to offer is simply man's general appetite for a picture. The novel is of all pictures the most comprehensive and the most elastic. It will stretch anywhere – it will take in absolutely anything.[62]

2.4.3 New Media

During the 1950s, **television** started to move into people's living rooms. In England, this development can be dated back to 2 June 1953, the day on which the coronation of Queen Elizabeth II was broadcast live. In Chapter 27 of her novel *Virgin in the Garden*, A. S. Byatt reconstructs this historic occasion, and asks herself the pointed question whether this was an event of national history or of media history:

> In those days, neither the public nor the private mores that went with the intrusive camera-eye and the obtrusive screen were established. The official BBC report on the coverage of the Coronation enquired of itself. 'Might there not be something un-

59 James (1946), 206.
60 Edel (1974), 177.
61 Bogardus (1984).
62 James (1986), 246.

> seemly in the chance that a viewer would watch this solemn and significant service with a cup of tea at his elbow? – there were real doubts […]'. Most of the Press was democratically statistically ecstatic. 'The Coronation brings the tiny screen into its own, turns it into a window on Westminster for 125,000,000 people … All these millions from Hamburg to Hollywood will see her coach jingle through rejoicing London *this very day* … 800 microphones are ready for 140 broadcasters to tell the world Elizabeth is crowned. But today is television's day. For it is television, reaching out to the Queen's subjects, which will give a new truth to the Recognition of the Monarch on her Coronation Day.'[63]

What interests Byatt in this new medium is the collapse of the boundary between the public and the private spheres. Television opened a window onto the world, bringing the coronation into the humblest home at the very moment of its happening, and the viewer did not even have to get up from his armchair. The social form of communication that was associated with the intimacy of this new mass medium was also a kind of anomaly to those living in the early 1950s. How could the historic splendour and ritual dignity of such an event be associated with 'home sweet home'?

The introduction of television as a new technological form of communication brought with it **new formats of presentation** – the news, live sport, quiz programmes, chat shows.[64] The new medium also had an impact on the primary level of signs. That is the thesis of Stuart Hall, who in a famous essay entitled **"Encoding/Decoding"** analysed the acoustic and visual form of TV discourse.[65] This study was part of a field which he dubbed 'audience research', in which questions like the following might be asked: How does the audience receive the televisional message? According to what rules is it compiled? What forms of direct and indirect influence are exercised? Hall's first argument is that the processes of encoding a message are never symmetrical with those of decoding it, and that communication never takes place as a circulation of information within a closed circuit. With the new medial situation in mind, he comes up with the following model of communication:

63 Byatt (1978), 238 f.
64 Morley (1992).
65 Hall (1980).

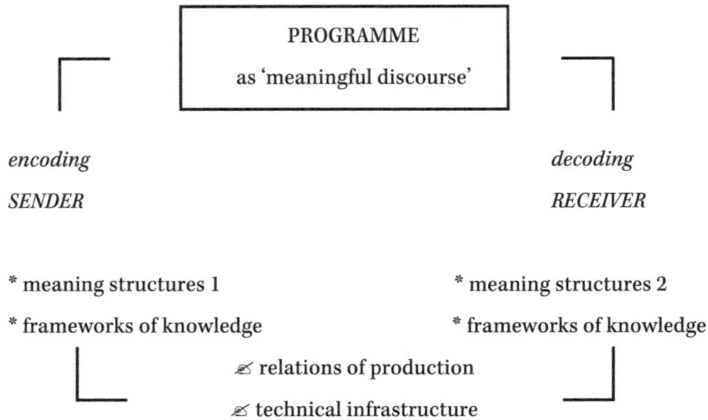

His most important findings in relation to the structure of medial mass communication are:

1. mass media communication is very different from the individualized form of reading
2. reality on TV can only be communicated if it is moulded into the form of particular codes (e. g. a story, a speech, a sequence of images, a structured programme)
3. the social structure, power and ideology of the dominant culture will always be inscribed into these codes
4. the ideological content will be conveyed not through denotation (clear signifiers) but mainly subliminally through connotation (additional associations, world view), which will be standardized within the cultural framework. Although there are explicit **'dominant codes'** that form the ideological dimension of communication, there are also what he calls **'negotiated codes'**, and these are so deeply internalized that their content and values are taken for granted.

While Lessing's concern was that the arts should each be as pure as possible, today we are faced with artworks in which the borders between the arts have been deliberately transcended. The new interest in border-crossing, subsumed under the heading of **'intermediality'**, brings into sharper focus the more or less hidden presence of images in texts and texts in images. This development is not independent of the new history of technical media, which has led to a progressive interweaving of media and presentation formats. Each new medium absorbs and frames an older one. Thus the computer has now become the hypermedium, in which all forms of presentation and formats of cultural history have been brought together: image, writing, photography, film, voice and sound.

Summary

The media are far more than just the basis for worldwide communications. They also mediate between humans and the world, as well as between humans and the mind or imagination. Because of their constructive character, the media are instruments that not only produce the world but also shape it.

In a narrow sense the media are bearers of sign systems because in addition to the components described by Saussure, signs must have a material exterior in order to become perceivable in the first place.

The term 'medium' itself can be divided up into different aspects, including sign systems, forms of presentation, sign bearers and means of storage, as well as modes of social communication. Specific works of art are thus produced through combinations of these different elements.

An important distinction in relation to the preservation and communication of cultural knowledge is that between oral and written. Storage techniques in orally based societies depend on the repetition of the relevant content, and hence on the use of particular mnemotechnic as well as regular performances. Writing, on the other hand, enables knowledge to be recorded independently of the memory. The multimedia composition of an oral performance is thus reduced to a non-sensual written code, and the wording of the information which is to be communicated is fixed in a permanent form. The knowledge that is stored in writing will survive independently of regular performances, and furthermore its extent is no longer limited to the memory capacity of a single human being. As it is bound to a particular and permanent form of words, a text provides repeated and repeatable information which in an infinitely expandable communications situation can bridge all spatial and temporal gaps.

Inseparably linked to the theme of the media is the figure of the author. While weak authors are intellectually confined to the shadows of socially recognized authorities, are frequently not even known by name, and in some cases have no interest in the fate of their own writings, strong authorship is marked by the author's claim to possession of his own work. He appears in public in his own right, and, since the Enlightenment, he has been 'constructed' in the form of a creative (male) genius who produces something completely original. The cult of the genius came to an abrupt end in the middle of the twentieth century. This was not only because Roland Barthes proclaimed the 'death of the author' and the 'triumph of writing', and replaced the author with the medium of *écriture.* The cult was also shaken by feminism and the inclusion of postcolonial literature in the western literary canon.

Towards the end of the 20th century, the literary critic W. J. T. Mitchell – following on from the 'linguistic turn' around 1900 – proclaimed the arrival of an 'iconic turn'. He pointed out that in our culture there had been a change from the main medium of the book to that of the picture. In fact, however, we very rarely encounter pictures in isolation – they are generally accompanied by the spoken or written word, so that it would be more appropriate to talk of a productive interaction between the two sign systems. In general nowadays the new media show a marked tendency towards such 'intermediality'.

Select bibliography

Briggs, Asa/Burke, Peter (2009) *A Social History of the Media. From Gutenberg to the Internet.* Cambridge: Polity Press.

Hodkinson, Paul (2011) *Media, Culture and Society. An Introduction.* London: Sage.

Jäger, Ludwig, ed. (2010) *Media, Culture, and Mediality. New Insights Into the Current State of Research.* Bielefeld: transcript.

Lull, James (2000) *Media, Communication, Culture. A Global Approach.* Cambridge: Polity Press.

Uricchio, William/Kinnebrock, Susanne, eds. (2006) *Media Cultures.* Heidelberg: Winter.

3. THE BODY

3.1 Body discourse

In Hofmannsthal's Lord Chandos letter, quoted earlier, there is a sentence that reads as follows: "I felt an inexplicable uneasiness in even pronouncing the words 'spirit', 'soul' or 'body'" (121). Obviously the writer of the letter had a problem with general concepts. Mind, soul and body are extremely abstract terms, which create difficulties for someone who has developed a compulsive need to focus on concrete details. Our situation is slightly different from that of Lord Chandos: we may share his resistance to 'mind' and 'soul', but 'body' is very much part of our vocabulary, and despite its abstractness we have invested it with a new aura. Since the 1980s, the word has enjoyed an almost inflationary boom; it is often used as if it were some magic formula, conjuring up more than it actually denotes. Attention is focused on the body as something universal and yet at the same time specific – i.e. as the forgotten or suppressed element or 'otherness' of discourse. The term 'body' plays a role in a variety of contexts, of which the following are just a selection:

- **Body and media:**
  The body is what remains beyond the text, i. e. is not convertible into alphabetical, numerical or digital signs. In this sense the body (Greek: *soma*) is the **opposite of the sign** (Greek: *sema*). The in itself meaningless structural writing of the digital code relates to image and sound as well as writing, but it cuts itself off completely from any interaction with the body. For this, it is necessary to create a virtual substitute (*avatar*). Among the bodily features that cannot be transformed into signs or numerical operations are feelings such as pleasure and pain, states such as illness or old age, the finiteness of the lifespan between birth and death, concrete positioning in space, time, family, generation and culture.
- **Body and gender**
  Another context in which the body becomes a theme is gender discourse. Initially, the questions asked by such discourse concerned differences: that between the sexes, and that between **'sex'** and **'gender'**. In the framework of constructivist and deconstructivist theories, these two differences again came under scrutiny with the recognition that the gendered body is culturally constructed by language and performativity.[1] This argument is meant to finally overcome the old gap between nature and culture. As a strategy of thought

1 Butler (1990).

and discourse, it may be illuminating, but the result is a paradox: the body, which traditionally has been defined as that which cannot be grasped by signs, appears to be a pure product of those signs – simply an effect produced by discourse. Lord Chandos would certainly not have been able to understand this theoretical twist; he linked his withdrawal from language with an emphatic return to objects and to a 'fluid thinking of the body'.

- **Body and 'agency'**
  In another context, the body gains in importance; this is when it is engaged in political resistance to colonial and imperial rule, including the effects of globalization. In opposition to all forms of cultural unification, indigenous traditions, concrete viewpoints and physical ways of life are invoked. With the *Location of Culture* (the title of a book by Homi Bhabha), attention is drawn to physical, spatiotemporal realities that cannot be circumvented. These different, concrete positions have to be regained in order to muster powers of resistance and to restore rights to those who have been deprived. Agency, in the sense of the **ability to act**, is the form in which nowadays the debate on 'the subject' (after its apparent demise) has been resumed in cultural studies (see Chapter 7). While the concept of the subject had previously been related to perception and consciousness, its new form is that of the body and its **voice**, by which is meant not only what is produced by the larynx, but also – if we may adapt an idea of Max Weber's – having a voice, in the sense of being given a hearing in matters of public discourse.

In this context, the Marxist literary theorist Terry Eagleton has suggested that "the concept of culture is no longer to be thought of in connection with the mind, but with the body."[2] In opposition to the view of culture as something that gets rid of all opposing realities through social constructs and discourses, Eagleton pleads for a political anthropology which will proceed from human physicality as a basis for all culture. In the fundamental conditions and needs that emanate from the body he sees the foundation for human solidarity, which might be practicable despite cultural differences and peculiarities.

To sum up, ever since the 1980s the body has figured prominently in discussions on what constitutes culture. In these discussions, different concepts of the body have marked the quest for something that takes us to the very frontiers of our various discourses. The starting-point of this chapter is the body as the **basis of knowledge** and the senses as our fundamental organs of perception. As the French phenomenologist Maurice Merleau-Ponty has pointed out, every form of knowledge is always embodied. Philosophy cannot therefore proceed from abstract maxims, but must begin with the information our senses give us about the world, and with the manner in which as embodied subjects we process this.

2 Große Kracht (2001), 263. Cf. Eagleton (2000).

3.1.1 The hierarchy of the senses

"The eye of man hath not heard, the ear of man / hath not seen, man's hand is not able to taste, / his tongue to conceive, nor his heart to report, what / my dream was."[3] Only one man is capable of such garbled perception, and that is Bottom on his awakening in Shakespeare's *A Midsummer Night's Dream*. His five senses have been left in such confusion that clearly it will take much time and effort to get them sorted out again. All this is because what he has experienced is far too miraculous for the master of the five senses, common sense, to impose any normal order on them. Throughout the history of western culture, these **five senses** have been arranged in different **hierarchical orders**. Roland Barthes comments on these shifts:

> At the beginning of the modern era, in Ignatius's century, one fact seems to begin to modify the exercise of the imagination: a reordering of the hierarchy of the five senses. In the Middle Ages, historians tell us, the most refined sense, the perceptive sense *par excellence*, the one that established the richest contact with the world, was hearing: sight came in only third place, after touch. Then we have a reversal: the eye becomes the prime organ of perception (Baroque, art of the thing seen, attests to this). This change is of great religious importance. The primacy of hearing, still very prevalent in the sixteenth century, was theologically guaranteed: the Church bases its authority on the word, faith is hearing: *auditum verbi Dei, id est fidem*; the ear, the ear alone, Luther said, is the Christian organ. Thus a risk of contradiction arises between the new perception, led by sight, and the ancient faith based on hearing.[4]

Barthes goes on to explain some of the reasons for the traditional downgrading of **sight**: image and vision are difficult to pin down; they are ambivalent, linked to the subconscious and are thus closer to the senses; images come low down on the scale of knowledge. To these reservations concerning imagination, image and eye, he adds a dogmatic argument: in the religious practice of meditation, imaginative vision is at the very bottom of the list of methods to be used; the Church regards mystic short cuts and techniques of direct communication as highly suspect. Similarly, the historian Lucien Febvre describes the transition from the Middle Ages to the Modern Age as an **'age of the ear'** giving way to an **'age of the eye'**. Regardless of one's attitude towards such generalized labelling of periods,[5] they do sharpen one's awareness of certain changes in cultural contexts. A truth established through the ear is obviously different from one affirmed by the eye. As opposed to St Paul, who insisted that faith be based on the spoken word,

3 Shakespeare (1997c), IV, 1, 204–207. On the hierarchy of senses, cf. Wulf (2004), 110–114.

4 Barthes (1989), 65.

5 One should also mention studies by Marshall McLuhan and a critique of these by Eisenstein, in which she writes of a change from a 'hearing public' to a 'reading public', (1997), 129.

there is the ever more modern figure of Doubting Thomas, who demanded a visual basis for his faith. As we all know, a need for visual empiricism has emerged from the Natural sciences, which prioritize the observable, focus the gaze, and use optical instruments to train and enhance the power of the eyes.

The empirical value of sight is also invoked by Shakespeare's Othello when he insists that Iago should provide visible evidence of his suspicions:

> OTHELLO [taking IAGO by the throat]:
> Villain, be sure thou prove my love a whore,
> Be sure of it. Give me the ocular proof,
> [...]
> Make me to see't[6]

The fact that in Renaissance artistic circles **the eye** went to the top of the sensory league table was the result of a fundamental cultural re-evaluation of sight. The Christian tradition recommended that the eyes be kept shut rather than open. St Augustine was highly suspicious of sight, and castigated it as being the gateway to sin.[7] He talked of 'ocular lust' (*concupiscentia oculorum*). Far from being reliable witnesses to truth, the eyes were for him a dangerously weak point through which humans were irresistibly drawn to the deceptive appearance of the world of the senses. Illusions and phantasms, Augustine argued, found their way into the human heart through the eyes, and stimulated sinful physical passions. Under the Puritans, this mistrust of the surface of things intensified to one where all beautiful appearances are seductive and therefore the most dangerous form of earthly deception.

The problem of beautiful appearance is taken up by Shakespeare in *The Merchant of Venice*, with the motif of the casket test. The three caskets are supposed to help select the right husband from among the wooers of Portia. The choice is between gold, silver and lead, and only one of the caskets contains her portrait, so everything depends on the suitor being able to distinguish between appearance and reality. This is a vivid illustration of the deep mistrust of surfaces that hide inner qualities, the message being that the eye is always susceptible to being misled, as it is unable to distinguish between **surface** and **depth.** One might say that the casket scenes are an eye test, though very different from those we take at the optician's. The test here is not of how sharp one's vision may be, but of how incorruptible it is.

Bassanio passes the test, because he has cottoned on at the right moment to the right lesson. With a fine piece of rhetoric, which is not so easy to take from such an opportunistic wastrel, he castigates the false lure of appearances:

---

6 Shakespeare (1997i), III, 3, 364–369.
7 St Augustine (2008).

> So may the outward shows be least themselves;
> The world is still deceiv'd with ornament. [...]
> Thus ornament is but the guiled shore
> To a most dangerous sea; the beauteous scarf
> Veiling an Indian beauty; in a word,
> The seeming truth which cunning times put on
> To entrap the wisest[8]

While Bassanio is meditating on the caskets, a song is sung in the background, and if he were to listen carefully to it, it would set him on the right track:

> Tell me where is fancy bred,
> Or in the heart or in the head?
> How begot, how nourished?
> Reply, reply.
> It's engend'red in the eyes,
> With gazing fed, and fancy dies
> In the cradle where it lies. (III, 2, 67-69)

In Christian Puritan anthropology, the imagination and the eyes were closely linked to lust and temptation. Bassanio passes the casket test thanks to his resistance to ocular lust and the lure of appearances. A hundred years later, at the beginning of the eighteenth century, these problems had largely disappeared: the Puritans' deep mistrust of the senses and of outer shows had given way to an **aesthetic appreciation of beauty**. With emphasis shifting from the religious to the aesthetic context, 'ocular lust' lost its negative connotations and became a force for productivity and sublimation. A manifesto for this new evaluation of sight is to be found in an issue of *The Spectator*, a weekly journal that was edited by Joseph Addison and Richard Steele early in the eighteenth century. The relevant text begins: "Our Sight is the most perfect and delightful of all our Senses."[9] This was the view of many Renaissance artists, but here the appreciation of sight is supported by a new argument. The eye is man's most perfect sense because it frees his physical range from restrictions and, so to speak, lays the whole world at his feet as far as the horizon. As a refined but more diffuse variation on the sense of touch, sight spreads its ethereal grasp unhindered over everything, and at the same time can absorb it all. Addison describes the new phenomenon of an aesthetically appreciative gaze, which he says has the following important qualities:

- **sensuousness** (*aesthesis*): everything that stimulates the imagination must first come to us (as Aristotle already knew) through the senses
- **internalization:** external perception by the senses is translated into an internal image

8 Shakespeare (1997j), III, 2, 97-101.
9 Addison (1965), 535.

- **intuition:** one only has to open one's eyes, and the whole image is present; judgement of the visual perception is equally spontaneous and unified
- **the 'inner eye':** transformation of the real into the imaginary: the eyes encompass the world and transform it into a *mental* possession
- **sublimation:** the aesthetic view transforms base sensual stimuli into something more elevated
- **leisure:** the aesthetic gaze opens up a sphere of leisure outside that of work; in this sphere, our mental powers are refreshed and stimulated

Aesthetics, according to Addison, form an intermediate realm between the senses and reason. The new view that leads to this area, freed from all needs and purposes, is particularly relevant to the prosperous middle classes, which are establishing their own culture of leisure (previously the privilege of the upper classes). The eyes now become more than just an organ of empirical perception; they are also an organ of **imagination**, and hence an organ for internal vision – in short, for a new kind of perception which since the eighteenth century we have called 'aesthetic'.

The theory of aesthetic perception, initiated by authors such as Addison, reached a peak at the end of the eighteenth century in the writings of Immanuel Kant, whose influence extended far beyond the German poets of his day.[10] Without the driving force created by **German Idealism**, as embodied by Kant, it is impossible to conceive of the English Romantics in the form of Wordsworth and Coleridge. Kant became the hero of the poets, because he highlighted 'productive imagination' as an indispensable ingredient of human perception. This constructive power is not, however, confined to poets and artists, but is an irreducible element of our humanity. Kant's philosophical insight into the constructive character of perception (and that is what is meant by 'Idealism' here) goes together with a positive evaluation of the imagination.[11] Thus two very different traditions emerged from the promotion of the eye to the top of the sensory hierarchy: **aesthetics** and **science**. When Wordsworth called the eye 'the most despotic of our senses', he was distancing himself not least from the empirical tradition of sight and its new standards of precision.[12] Just as two complementary modes of per-

10 Kant (2007).

11 There is a famous verse of Goethe's poem "Zahme Xenien" that describes the constructiveness of the eye as a metaphysical combination of divine creativity and human perception: "Wär nicht das Auge sonnenhaft, / die Sonne könnte es nicht erblicken, / lag nicht in uns des Gottes eigene Kraft, / wie könnt uns Göttliches entzücken?" Goethe (1988), 645.

12 "the bodily eye, in every stage of life / The most despotic of our senses"; and shortly afterwards: "such thraldom of that sense / Seems hard to shun." Wordsworth (1970), XII, 128 f; 150 f.

ception were based on the aesthetic and the empirical view, 'reality' in the nineteenth century could no longer be conceived of as an indisputable unit but was split up into a world of the natural sciences and (as they were to be known in the future) the arts or humanities. The arts, which claimed their own particular role in experiencing the world, as opposed to that of the concrete sciences, laid emphasis on the inner eye, the constructive gaze and the productive powers of imagination. The new evaluation of sight at the beginning of the eighteenth century marked a historical process which the sociologist Max Weber described as 'differentiation between the spheres of cultural values'. From now on, the arts and sciences would go their separate ways.

3.2 Body, sexuality and gender

3.2.1 Body, soul, mind

"A man's body and his mind, with the utmost reverence to both I speak, are exactly like a jerkin, and a jerkin's lining; – rumple the one – you rumple the other", wrote Laurence Sterne in his novel *Tristram Shandy*.[13] With this insight he was opposing the idea that humans could be neatly divided into two contrasting, unconnected components. Descartes' division between **mind** and **body** was basically only a rational confirmation of a long western tradition that began with Plato and was further developed by St Paul, St Augustine and Christianity at large. We can call this form of anthropology **'dualism'**: it splits man into two unequal elements that pull him in opposite directions. On the one side is the body, with all its needs, desires and fragility, while on the other are the mind, soul, reason and all the other forces that transcend the body and triumph over its weaknesses.

The deconstruction of this old European opposition is a central theme in the work of Oscar Wilde, who opposed the ascetic Victorian view of the body with a philosophy of sensual refinement and physical spiritualization:

> Soul and body, body and soul – how mysterious they were! There was animalism in the soul, and the body had its moments of spirituality. The senses could refine, and the intellect could degrade. Who could say where the fleshly impulse ceased, or the physical impulse began? How shallow were the arbitrary definitions of ordinary psychologists! [...] Was the soul a shadow seated in the house of sin? Or was the body really in the soul, as Giordano Bruno thought? The separation of spirit from matter was a mystery, and the union of spirit with matter was a mystery also.[14]

Like the mind, the **soul** counts as the 'other' of the body, but its meaning tends to be religious. It is part of the cosmos, creating a link between man and God,

13 Sterne (2004), 126.
14 Wilde (2003), 77.

and being immortal, it is part of the divine. This religious concept of the soul was fundamentally changed when at the beginning of the nineteenth century it became the subject of what Philipp Moritz called an empirical *Erfahrungsseelenkunde* [study of the experience of the soul]; this was later developed into what we now call psychology and psychoanalysis. The word *psyche* (Greek for soul) went together with a new scientific discourse concerning the soul, which was now completely divorced from its metaphysical context.

Connected with dualistic anthropology was a way of seeing and evaluating that had placed the material and immaterial components of man in an unequal hierarchy, which in western history (with interruptions in the Middle Ages and the Renaissance) had meant that the **body** was viewed as **inferior**, even satanic, and was therefore disregarded. Sterne had already written against this approach. He is considered a **sentimentalist** writer, who in the age of Enlightenment had rediscovered the importance of physically induced emotions. Seen from this perspective, grief, melancholy, sympathy and laughter are basic human impulses, and so constitute elementary expressions of human nature. The sentimentalist confesses to his emotions, and through them recognizes his commonality not only with people from other cultures, but also with every other creature.

Such convictions left their mark on literary texts. The focus on bodily processes in Sterne's work already takes up just as much space as it was later to do in Joyce's *Ulysses* (1922), which breaks away from the prudish norms of contemporary middle-class society. Sterne's *Tristram Shandy* begins with the unfortunate circumstances of the protagonist's conception, and more than a third of the book is taken up with the events that lead to his birth. Not only preparations for this, but also the labour pains of writing permeate the text, which self-consciously reflects on its own materiality, revealing the book to be a product of the mind and at the same time displaying its own 'text corpus'. With breaks in the linear sequence, reflections on narrative time and narrated time, an endpaper[15] bound directly between the printed pages, and two chapters on the meaning and function of chapter divisions (III, 9 and 10), the text is not only self-reflexive (thinking about itself) but also self-referential (referring to itself). Modern anthropology began with the insight that body and mind (or soul) were not two halves of human nature but formed an overall unit, and man could only be seen as a psychophysical being. Against this background we can say that Sterne's novel, obsessed as it is with the human body, is a manifesto for this new way of thinking.[16]

15 This is a marbled page that normally separates the outer cover from the printed pages.

16 Lippe (1987); Pfotenhauer (1987); Shilling (1993); Stafford (1991); Waldenfels (2000); Wulf (1997).

3.2.2 Bodily taboos and excesses

Let us now return to the literary preoccupation with bodily processes. A landmark in the history of taboo subjects is Joyce's *Ulysses*, which begins with the reader accompanying the protagonist Leopold Bloom on his morning visit to the lavatory. Generally, a literary description of such everyday routine matters would be subject to self-censorship, as conditioned by cultural taboos. Among the factors that Norbert Elias considers to constitute the process of civilization and bodily self-discipline are certain **rules of language** that proscribe the explicit mention of various body parts and functions. With the rise of the **middle classes** came a radical recoding of the body, which brought about a revolution in matters concerning propriety, taste and sensitivity. One example of this is the **representation of death**. Instead of the skeleton, which had been the universal symbol of death in the Middle Ages, cemeteries were now filled with abstract motifs such as columns, cherubs, or the genius with a lowered torch. In the eighteenth century the ageing, not to mention rotten body was strictly taboo as a subject of representation. All the radical realism that one finds in such abundance in medieval representations gave way to an idealized body based on classical Greek art. Not only the signs of death and disease were suppressed, but also physical signs of vitality, such as excessive eating and drinking, the digestive processes and sexuality.

The historian of this pre-middle-class discourse of the body is the Russian Hellenist Michail Bakhtin, who reconstructed the suppressed traditions of humour as a popular **'laughter culture'**, and followed their hidden tracks through literary history. In the *Canterbury Tales*, for instance, the medieval poet Geoffrey Chaucer reproduced the ribald jokes and stories (*fabliaux*) handed down through the oral tradition. Perhaps the most impressive literary opponent of the bodily canon of literary art and respectable talk in the Modern Age is Shakespeare's Sir John Falstaff[17], a liberating parody of the heroic knight figure. Falstaff's grotesque, fat, gluttonous, drinking, whoring **open** body is in every respect the opposite of the idealized, classical **closed** body. His exuberance, his language – exclusively in prose – and all his actions strikingly violate just about every aristocratic and bourgeois norm of rank and decency, which the audiences at the time did not in any way regard as a provocation but, on the contrary, greeted with uninhibited laughter. He goes to battle not with a pistol but with a bottle of sack: "Hal; 'Tis hot, 'tis hot. There's that will sack a city."[18] His philosophy is simply life, especially when faced with death and the sight of dead men on the battlefield: "I like not such grinning honour as Sir Walter hath. Give me life."[19] Falstaff is the personification of an indomitable will to live, and he cannot be led from his chosen path

17 Cf. Bakhtin (1968).
18 Shakespeare (1997b), V, 3, 53.
19 Shakespeare (1997b), V, 3, 56–58.

by fine-sounding words or exalted values. As Harold Bloom points out, "he subverts everything [...] that would constrain him: time, the state, virtue, the chivalric concept of 'honour', and all ideas of order whatsoever."[20] Bloom places him alongside Chaucer's Wife of Bath, Cervantes' Sancho Panza, and Rabelais' Panurge. He considers him to be the greatest of all carnivalesque characters, and offers him to the reader or spectator as a psychological personality test:

> Falstaff, to most scholars, is the emblem of self-indulgence, but to most playgoers and readers Sir John is the representative of imaginative freedom, of a liberty set against time, death, and the state, which is a condition that we crave for ourselves. Add a fourth freedom to timelessness, the blessing of more life, and the evasion of the state, and call it freedom from censoriousness, from the superego, from guilt. [...] You define who you are by your reaction to Falstaff [...]. Those who do not care for Falstaff are in love with time, death, the state, and the censor.[21]

Bakhtin's impressive studies of the European laughter culture, and its close connections with the emergence of the dynamic, amorphous genre of the novel, opened up a wide new field of research, and found many disciples. One can include in this list Terry Eagleton's **political anthropology**, which takes our basic physical condition to be a foundation for human solidarity and an all-inclusive culture. Nevertheless, Bakhtin's theses remain a matter of controversy: does this laughter culture really stem from popular tradition or is it, rather, derived from the aristocracy? Should it be seen as a subversive tradition that survived the repressions of western culture? Or are the carnivalesque rituals which temporarily overturn established codes and hierarchies and periodically relieve pent-up social tensions in fact a means of stabilizing existing systems? Can we still maintain this opposition of power and subversion in our own, present-day culture? The following observation by Ruth Mayer can be applied to both Bakhtin and Foucault:

> We need to reconsider the whole image of a controlling centre and subversive margins. Pop has long since lost the status of something marginal and oppositional. The carnivalesque subversion of the 1970s may have had an equally provocative and liberating effect. In the late 1990s, however, in a world in which polysemy has become a central code of the media and subcultural styles are celebrated by TV stations and glossy magazines, it is no longer easy to understand why or exactly how these representational strategies are supposed to convey resistance. The question arises whether in a postmodern media society the ironic, parodic and carnivalesque might not take on the function that in former times was fulfilled by supervision and censorship.[22]

---

20 Bloom (1999), 311.

21 Bloom (1999), 288. Although Bloom emphasizes the subversive aspect here, he sees Falstaff less as a figure of disorder or disruption than one of exuberance and virtuoso playfulness (299).

22 Mayer (1999), 241 f, refers to the theorists Gilles Deleuze and Félix Guattari, whose paradigm of the 'rhizome' (which means something like an inextricable tangle of roots) offers an alternative to hierarchical models of society.

3.2.3 Sexuality as a literary subject

There is probably no more popular or indispensable subject in literature than love. The erotic attraction between characters gives order, dynamism and magnetism to the fictitious worlds performed on the stage and narrated on the page. Who desires whom, who offends whom, who gets whom – these are the questions that continue to grab the sympathy and curiosity of audiences and readers with undiminished powers of fascination.[23] Literature's almost obsessive preoccupation with **love** is countered, however – up to the twentieth century – by the absence of **sexuality**. While every vivid detail of love as passion or destiny is explored, the physical dimension is excluded. For centuries, literary love consisted of tender emotions and violent passions, but never of physical excitement, let alone action. The ban on the sexualized body in literary love discourse was one of the longest and most firmly established conventions of western, Christian culture. The sexual act never took place on stage. Romeo and Juliet discuss the lark and the nightingale after their night of love, while the stresses and strains of day-to-day business in Cyprus leave Othello and Desdemona with scarcely a moment to enjoy themselves backstage. Whatever sex may have taken place has been pushed into the wings – into the gaps which spectator or reader must fill in for themselves. The word obscene can be associated with 'off scene'.[24] Anything that runs contrary to social decorum (the Latin *decorus* means 'seemly') is banned from the stage. Of course this self-censorship was not always adhered to, and indeed from the eighteenth century onwards there was actually a growing market for pornographic literature and performances.

The power of moral repression during **Victorianism** can be gauged from Robert Louis Stevenson's novel *Dr Jekyll and Mr Hyde.* Here the dual moral code of the Scottish Calvinist milieu from which Stevenson came leads to a personality split and a *Doppelgaenger*-narrative. What Dr Jekyll is unable to act out in the daylight of social conventions is loaded onto his alter ego, who lives as he pleases with no regard for norms or even the law. Sexuality does not in fact play any part in Stevenson's novel, or even in "Henry Jekyll's Full Statement of the Case"; in this case, the author Stevenson himself is a 'Mr Hyde'. He attributes the shameful, degrading dark side of the character to a 'certain impatient gaiety of disposition', thereby paying his dues to the prudish code of the Victorians. In 1886, when the novel was published, other authors had already freed themselves from these bourgeois repressions and explored new subjects relating to the body. The poet Dante Gabriel Rossetti wrote this sonnet on the moments following sex:

---

23 "Love is the result of particular cultural conditions; it depends on the myths and rhetorical forms of a society, and is socially controlled." Wulf (2004), 122. See also Wulf (1985).

24 According to its etymology, the word stems from the Latin *caenum*, meaning dirt or filth.

Nuptial Sleep

At length their long kiss severed, with sweet smart:
And as the last slow sudden drops are shed
From sparkling eaves when all the storm has fled,
So singly flagged the pulses of each heart.
Their bosoms sundered, with the opening start
Of married flowers to either side outspread
From the knit stem; yet still their mouths, burnt red,
Fawned on each other when they lay apart.
Sleep sank them lower than the tide of dreams,
And their dreams watched them sink, and slid away.
Slowly their souls swam up again, through gleams
Of watered light and dull drowned waifs of day;
Till from some wonder of new woods and streams
He woke, and wondered more: for there she lay.[25]

This situation is very different from that of Romeo and Juliet or even Adam and Eve, to whom it may perhaps allude to indirectly because, as the title indicates, it is about sexuality *in* and not – as is usually the case in literature – *before* or *outside* marriage. What is new in this variation of the (Petrarchan) love sonnet is the fact that it is not addressed so much to the loved one as to love itself as a creative energy. The word 'sleep' in the title is ambiguous: it refers both to intercourse and to the sleep that follows it. The point of the poem is that the two forms of sleep merge into one another. In the gradual separation of the two bodies after their embrace, the sexual act of intercourse is already implied, their exhaustion incorporates the physical effort, and the coitus is inherent in the post-coital sleep.

The period around 1900 was characterized by a tension between continuing social taboos on the one hand and a movement towards sexual freedom on the other, and this affected not only authors' freedom of expression but also people's way of life. **Homosexuality** as well as **lesbian love** played a major part in this conflict, to which Victorian society had reacted by criminalizing it and destroying the reputation of those concerned. Oscar Wilde's 'love that dare not speak its name' for the young Lord Alfred Douglas landed him in jail in 1894.[26] E. M. Forster, who was also homosexual, kept within the confines of obligatory heterosexuality in the plots of the novels and stories that were published in his lifetime. Those in which he made no concessions to the public or his readers were not published until after his death.[27] Similar restrictions applied to women writers.

25 Rossetti (1970), 193. The poem was originally conceived as part of the sonnet cycle *House of Life*. When a critic took exception to its 'fleshliness', Rossetti withdrew it from the cycle.

26 This is the last line of the poem *Two Loves* by Lord Alfred Douglas, published in the journal *Chameleon* (London 1894).

27 They included the novel *Maurice*, in which the theme of homosexuality is explicit.

Virginia Woolf had a relationship with Vita Sackville-West; Gertrude Stein lived with her friend Alice B. Toklas; the poet H. D. (Hilda Doolittle), who was engaged to Ezra Pound and married to Richard Aldington, lived most of her life with a female friend. These explosive changes in people's attitudes in the early twentieth century led to a radical **sexual revolution**, and it was not only artists who took part in it. Here one must mention the work of Sigmund Freud and Havelock Ellis,[28] both of whom wrote about the structure of human instincts, thereby making important contributions to the process of enlightenment and helping to break through the crust of bourgeois double standards.

There was, however, a literature of sexual freedom even in the nineteenth century. The American poet Walt Whitman saw himself quite openly as a poet of the body, and never tired of expressing this in his poems. *I Sing the Body Electric* is the title of a sequence of nine poems in which he praises the body and sexuality in his hymnal verses. The last of these consists of a long list of body parts from top to bottom, including the following:

> Broad breast-front, curling hair of the breast, breast-bone, breast-side,
> Ribs, belly, backbone, joints of the backbone,
> Hips, hip-sockets, hip-strength, inward and outward round, man-balls, man-root,
> Strong set of thighs, well carrying the trunk above,
> Leg-fibres, knee, knee-pan, upper-leg, under-leg [...][29]

In another poem he compares the masculine potency of his semen to the power of his poetic creativity, which will shape the future. In the following act of procreation, he even imagines himself as Father of the Nation:

> It is I, you women, I make my way,
> I am stern, acrid, large, indissuadable, but I love you,
> I do not hurt you any more than is necessary for you,
> I pour the stuff to start sons and daughters fit for these States,
> I press with slow rude muscle,
> I brace myself effectually, I listen to no entreaties,
> I dare not withdraw till I deposit what has so long accumulated within me.[30]

For all the concreteness of his imagery and the precision with which he names things, what Whitman is trying to capture with language is general and sometimes even abstract. The terms body and soul are inextricably linked, and whenever he talks of the body, he also has the soul in mind: "I am the poet of the Body and I am the poet of the Soul." Even when he speaks of the male body, he also speaks of the female, and when he speaks of the white body, he also speaks of the black. His poems are highly **explicit** – he writes directly in violation of the taboo and the current disparagement of the body – and also **inclusive**, in so far

28 Ellis (1918).
29 Whitman (1958), 104.
30 Whitman (1958), 106.

as they collect all the variations together and try to encompass them linguistically in one sweeping democratic gesture.[31]

Whitman's political enthusiasm led unquestionably to an inflation of language. This was the view of another author who at the turn of the century committed himself to the cause of sexual freedom. D. H. Lawrence's *Lady Chatterley's Lover* was first published in 1928, but was immediately banned, and was not allowed to be published in England until 1960. He wrote it as a riposte to the double standards of a repressive society which savoured pornography but would not openly recognize the importance of sexuality. "It's the one insane taboo left: sex as a natural and vital thing."[32] D. H. Lawrence had little respect for the lofty tone of Walt Whitman's poetry, and wrote the following on Whitman's 'Sexual Activity as a National Productive Force':

> I AM HE THAT ACHES WITH AMOROUS LOVE.
> What do you make of that? I AM HE THAT ACHES. First generalization. First uncomfortable universalisation. WITH AMOROUS LOVE! Oh, God! Better a bellyache. A bellyache is at least specific. But the ACHE OF AMOROUS LOVE! Think of having all that under your skin. All that!
>
> I AM HE THAT ACHES WITH AMOROUS LOVE.
> Walter, leave off. You are not HE. You are just a limited Walter. And your ache doesn't include all Amorous Love, by any means. If you ache you only ache with a small bit of amorous love, and there's so much more stays outside the cover of your ache, that you might be a bit milder about it.[33]

The examples we have looked at offer different **male views** on the theme of sexuality. A new chapter in the literary history of this subject was opened with the inclusion of female perspectives, which not only concentrated on the specifically feminine view of sexuality,[34] but also analysed the sexual phantasms to be found in male literature.[35] At this point, however, the body as an interface between nature and culture began to lose its focus, and the borders between sexuality and gender became blurred. Between the 1970s and the 1990s feminist theory moved

31 In her essay 'Secret Sewers of Vice'. Disgust, Bodies, and the Law" (1999), Martha Nussbaum writes: "Disgust at the body and its products has collaborated with the maintenance of injurious social hierarchies. The health of democracy therefore depends on criticizing and undoing that social formation." She describes these verses as "an elaborate undoing of disgust" (118).

32 Lawrence (1994), 277. How much the standards of decency change in matters concerning the body is evident from the foreword that Richard Hoggart wrote for the second edition of the novel in 1961. He begins with the words: "*Lady Chatterley's Lover* is not a dirty book. It is clean and serious and beautiful." Ibid. V.

33 Lawrence (2003), 392 f.

34 Among the major female writers who have written about lesbian love are the American poet Adrienne Rich and the Scottish novelist Jeanette Winterson.

35 Hill Rigney (1978); Bronfen (1994).

from physical sexuality to a more systematic focus on the body as a social and political gender construct.

3.2.4 Gender

To the Ancient Greeks and Christians, the body was the **prison of the soul**. In death, this prison was broken open, and the soul – the nobler part of man – was able to escape and return to its original state of immortality. Nietzsche, the specialist in radical rethinking, turned this concept on its head by arguing that the soul was the prison of the body. In this sense, the soul is the network of cultural norms and social constraints (Freud would call it the super-ego) which exercise power over the body, discipline it, and inhibit its development. Gender studies have taken up this theme and looked into the cultural programming that is responsible for the laying down and the evaluating of the respective roles of the sexes. In gender studies, male and female are not natural givens but cultural patterns imposed by the power of the state and internalized through socialization until they are rooted in the unconscious. Precisely because they are unconscious, they become effectively the foundation for self-images, identities and attitudes towards life. In establishing **norms for the sexes**, it is not only such institutions as the family or the school that play a major role, but so too does literature, which is just as likely to perpetuate normative models as it is to undermine them (cf. Chapter 7). It was only through the new perspective of gender studies, which demanded a rereading of canonical and non-canonical literature, that it became clear how little was due to nature and how much was the result of culture. The history of relations between the sexes has been extremely changeable, and is an area where virtually nothing is fixed and virtually everything is controversial. The core issue of gender studies is man's patriarchal power over the female body – a power that is present in social hierarchies and oppressive family structures, both of which are deeply anchored in the foundations of culture. By developing a discourse about these embodied power relations, gender studies at the same time create political strategies to weaken and transform the norms. This sets off a process of self-reflection and social change from which new possibilities of emancipation and self-determination may emerge.

3.3 Concepts of man – historical anthropology

The concept of the body includes that of man in general. The different anthropological disciplines offer various views: from the standpoint of evolutionary theory, the focus is on the history of the human species going back over millions of years; ethnologists are concerned with the living conditions and the customs and traditions of non-writing and non-European societies; historians may tackle general living conditions and symbol systems throughout European history. A less concrete and much more speculative approach is that of philosophical anthropology, which traditionally defines humankind as being distinct from the animal kingdom (cf. Chapter 1). One of these 'human images' stems from the German philosopher Helmut Plessner (1892-1985), who defined man by way of man's **'ec-centric positioning'**. He meant that unlike beasts, man is not fitted out for any one specific environment in which he can act instinctively, but must constantly assert himself outside any such fixed centre, and this gives him the ability to detach himself, to resist settlement, to move around and to reflect. Plessner also stresses that we have a twofold relationship with our bodies: he distinguishes between **'having a body'** and **'being a body'**. We have a body when we confront, and master, train, or model it (e. g. through cosmetics or at a fitness centre). We are a body because as animated organisms we cannot exist without it. Will and mind are unthinkable without our physical infrastructure, with its unfathomable moods and sensitivities.[36] Man is therefore always and simultaneously inward and outward, both possessing his body and being a part of it.

3.3.1 The materiality of the body

The body forms a paradigmatic point of intersection between nature and culture. As soon as we go to the doctor, the body becomes the subject of measurements and diagnoses that promise an objective assessment of its condition. It is equally the subject of cultural practices, discourses and institutions set up to define and direct it, interpret and evaluate it, shape and reshape it. What is regarded as the 'nature' of the body has changed dramatically since early modern times.[37] During the Renaissance, for instance, there was a totally different concept of its materiality. At that time, they still believed in the doctrine of the so-called **'humour pathology'** handed down by Aristotle and Galen, according to which man was composed of four fluids: blood, phlegm, yellow bile and black bile. Ideally, these fluids should be in perfect harmony, but if the balance is disturbed and one of the fluids dominates, the gateway is open to all kinds of illnesses. The temperaments of different characters are also explained by a surfeit of one or other of the fluids: a merry, sanguine person would have too much blood; a phlegmatic character, with too much of the white fluid, would suffer from a lack of drive; the choleric, with an excess of yellow bile, would be short-tempered; and the melancholic, with too much black bile, would be a victim of depression. Undoubtedly the most interesting symptom within this system was that of the **melancholic**, whom Aristotle described as being not only pathologically sad but also prone to have visions and to be endowed with particular forms of creativity. Around this type there developed a special 'body history' of the aesthetics of genius. Robert Burton, a contemporary of Shakespeare, wrote a voluminous *Anatomy of Melan-*

36 Plessner (1928). The human image that Plessner develops in his philosophical anthropology is in many respects that of the modern European in the twentieth century.
37 Van Dülmen (1995).

choly.[38] The most famous melancholic in the history of literature is Hamlet, who enters the stage dressed in black, and adopts the then familiar, paradigmatic pose, with hat drawn down low over his brow, arms folded across his chest, signalling the introversion common to the mourner, the lover, and the poet.

A **cultural history of the body** must focus not only on the history of medical knowledge but also on cultural attitudes towards sexuality, death and grief,[39] passions[40] and pain,[41] the importance of food and drink,[42] and an assessment of different phases in life, such as childhood,[43] youth and old age – to mention just a few of the relevant topics.

3.3.2 Artificial and symbolic bodies

The word 'body' is used not only for individual organisms but also for **collectives** and for other **non-sensory concepts,** which are endowed with a symbolic body in order to give them substance. One example of this is Thomas Hobbes' view of the State in his book *Leviathan* (1651). The cover does not show a mythical sea monster but a giant man towering over a landscape of mountains and villages. This man, visible down to his waist, bears the insignia of kingship, with crown, sword and sceptre. If one inspects this figure more closely, one will see that his body consists of countless tiny human bodies lined up and turned towards him. Hobbes refers to this image in his introduction, and explains that this is an artificial man who is composed, like the engine of a machine, out of individual parts: "For by Art is created that great LEVIATHAN called COMMON-WEALTH, or STATE (in latine CIVITAS) which is but an Artificiall Man; though of greater stature and strength than the Naturall, for whose protection and defence it was intended."[44] Hobbes continues his description by assigning a **political function** to each part of the body. Here, the human body is not meant just as a concrete representation of something abstract, or as a mnemonic for the organization of the State; the emphasis on the body's artificiality puts man in the position of the divine Creator and shows that he has as free a hand in the realm of man-made affairs as God has in the realm of Nature.

38 Burton (1972).
39 Ariès (1980); Ecker (1999); Horn (1998).
40 Fisher (2002).
41 Scarry (1985). The basic thesis of the book is succinctly summed up by a sentence in Jean Paul Sartre's *L'être et le néant*: "My body is everywhere: the bomb that destroys my house also destroys my body, because the house was already an indication of my body." See also Assmann, A. (1989).
42 Neumann (2000); Wierlacher et al. (1993).
43 Ariès (1975).
44 Hobbes (1997), 9.

Hobbes' megabody of individual bodies is a hypostasis or allegory for the State. Prior to this, there was another symbolic body which did not represent the State but the kingdom. In the late Middle Ages, the king was regarded as having **two bodies**: the mortal one of man and the immortal one of his office.[45] The first put him on a par with everyone else, while the second made him a giant among men. This was because his office had been given to him by God and was therefore everlasting. The doctrine of the king's two bodies ensured the continuity of the office beyond the mortality of its holder, thereby excluding the effects of time and contingency. The death of the king, which implies an immediate threat of chaos and revolution and the demise of the existing world order, is overcome by the device of the second, immortal body of the king. Shakespeare alludes to these two royal bodies in *Richard II*[46]. In this play a legitimate but incompetent king is replaced by a competent but illegitimate rival, Henry Bolingbroke, and then finally killed. With his excessive theatricality, Richard constantly oscillates between his two bodies: at one moment he is the anointed official body whose numinous power cannot be denied, and the next he is the bare human body, stripped of his royal attributes, exposed and defenceless. Richard's theatrical inner conflict consists precisely in the conflict between these two bodies of the king.

We shall now leap from the Middle Ages and early modern times to the present: in this age of **biotechnical programming**, human nature is no longer unfathomable. Thanks to new scientific findings and technology, man is now capable of intervening in his own evolution and even changing his own genetic constitution as well as that of his descendants. The concept of being and having a body has taken on a new meaning: man, who is a body, modifies the body he has. 180 years before this self-transformation entered the realms of the possible, Mary Shelley anticipated the problem in a gothic novel that is as relevant now as it was then. In *Frankenstein*, the main character is a **modern Prometheus** – a scientist who manipulates the building blocks of life and so usurps the divine power of giving life and the female power of giving birth. However, man is not definitively formed at the moment of his entry into the world, but continues to develop through upbringing and experience, and so the product of this experiment, when abandoned by everyone and left to fend for itself, develops into a monster.[47] Shelley presents us with a researcher who loses control of his project and degenerates from self-confident action to helpless despair.

With cloning we have long since transcended the borders between what was once clearly distinguishable as 'natural' and 'artificial'. Nowadays research laboratories are full of cloned creatures that have been created artificially but never-

45 Kantorowicz (1957). Cf. Ernst/Vismann (1998).
46 Shakespeare (1997d).
47 Shelley (1965). See also Chapter 7.

theless reproduce naturally. The related ethical problems are similar when it comes to the human organism, in which more and more functions are being taken over by digital chips. Here we already have the outline of a **'post-human body'** – a concept discussed in an important essay by Donna Haraway, "A Cyborg Manifesto", in which she takes up the questions raised by Mary Shelley and relates them very pertinently to the present, using the imagery of a **cyborg** body.[48] The background to this fictive technology is the phantasm of immortality through a technically enhanced body. With the decline of the Christian vision of salvation, people nevertheless cling to hopes of salvation by means of medicine and technology. In general the new cultural technology of electronic writing has created new anthropological conditions. The tendency towards a separation of body and writing, which was already the basis of alphabetical writing, has been strengthened still further by this new technology. The material, three-dimensional body of the user remains outside when he goes into chat rooms and cyber worlds, and in its place a so-called avatar – a virtual substitute body – enters the digital world. From an anthropological standpoint this leads to a new division, which is no longer between mind and body but between an organic and a digital body.

3.3.3 Body techniques, body histories, modes of conduct

The cultural elements of the human image do not consist solely of symbolic actions representing a person's identity, status or culture, but also of unobtrusive everyday practices that reflect things we take for granted. One important dimension of historical anthropology is therefore the cultural use and characterization of the body. The French ethnologist Marcel Mauss coined the expression **'body techniques'** for this new area of research. He explains what led to it:

> I made, and went on making for several years, the fundamental mistake of thinking that there is technique only when there is an instrument. [...] The body is man's first and most natural instrument. Or more accurately, not to speak of instruments, man's first and most natural technical object, and at the same time technical means, is his body.[49]

Mauss illustrates his argument with reference to his situation as an academic teacher. In every seemingly trivial action, these body techniques come into use:

> Here let us look for a moment at ourselves. Everything in us all is under command. I am a lecturer for you; you can tell it from my sitting posture and my voice, and you are listening to me seated in silence. We have a set of permissible or impermissible, natural or unnatural attitudes. Thus we should attribute different values to the act of staring fixedly: a symbol of politeness in the army, and of rudeness in everyday life. (105)

48 Haraway (1998). Cf. Schwab (1994).
49 Mauss (1979), 104.

One historian of body techniques, whom we mentioned in the Introduction, was Norbert Elias, who studied the dynamics of the **'civilization process'** and its social conditions. By 'civilization process' Elias meant "the structural change of humans towards greater determinacy and differentiation in their control of affects and hence also of their experiences – for instance, in the form of advancing the threshold of shame and embarrassment – and of their conduct – e. g. when eating, in the form of differentiating between items of cutlery."[50] In his richly researched study, he traces the long and difficult process of bodily and affective control which society has imposed on its members since the early modern age. The aim of this restraint is the internalization of the norms that will lead to a smoothly economical self-control. Elias regards this action of knocking off rough edges as a civilizing process. His most important source is a genre of literature which had previously attracted little attention among historians – namely **conduct books**, which give detailed insights into rules of behaviour in public and private spheres. From these we learn about such different activities as how to eat correctly with knife and fork, how to deal with members of the opposite sex, and how to control one's physical and emotional instincts.

A concept concerning the cultural conditioning of the body came from the French sociologist Pierre Bourdieu. He talked of the **'habitus'**, by which he meant a collection of cultural characteristics that had become ingrained through learning, repetition and internalization, and had penetrated so deeply that they took effect without any prompting from the conscious mind. His historical example is the 'normative authority' of the medieval school, where attitudes and modes of conduct were incorporated in such a manner that they became second nature. 'Habitus' is the name given to this 'incorporated' collection of cultural schemata which become all the more effective and established in proportion to the degree in which they become unconscious. Bourdieu[51] regards the function of the school as being explicitly "to transform the collective heritage into both an individual and a collective unconsciousness" (139). Linking up with Chomsky's generative grammar, he defines 'habitus' as a "system of internalized patterns which allow for the production of all the typical thoughts, perceptions and actions of a culture – and for no others." (143) This habituated knowledge is different from a code or repertoire of rules and solutions, because of its 'incarnate' nature, which places it beyond the reach of consciousness.

Another French historian of body techniques was Michel Foucault, whose life's work was the study of different social institutions in which the body is defined, disciplined, modelled etc. according to specific norms. The institutions Foucault focused on included psychiatry, hospitals and medication, marriage and sexual-

50 Elias (1977), 13.
51 Bourdieu (1974).

ity, prison and penal practices. He saw society and its institutions as the extended arm of a disciplined power that manifested and affirmed itself through its influence on the body.[52] He switched the historical perspective from the national and international deeds of great men to ordinary people's everyday subtle, though sometimes painful mastery of their bodies. This together with a new sensitivity to the whole subject led to the discovery and heightened evaluation of sources on whose basis one can reconstruct a **'history of the body'**, with particular attention to the female.[53] The Italian philosopher Giorgio Agamben further developed Foucault's thesis, introducing the concept of 'naked life' into the discussion, defining it as what is left when all legal and social connections are subtracted. The gruesome emphasis on this minimal stage of existence, Agamben argues, was not only the work of the Nazis, who annihilated the Jews and other minorities with their policy of 'destruction through work', but is also to be seen nowadays in an age of forced migration and deportation – the reverse side of a politically destabilized form of existence.[54] In his later works, Foucault turned to yet another aspect of the body. He fastened onto the motto *cura sui*, which in Latin texts refers to physical self-healing, and which one can perhaps equate with the idea of **'body consciousness'**.[55] In this case, the power over the body does not come from outside, with the imposition of rigid codes and patterns, but from a power within, from an autonomy of the body with its own culture of internal life and feelings.

3.3.4 Body writing

The cultural conditioning of the body is not confined to the history of self-discipline and outside influences. It is also a sign-bearer which can be read as well as drawn, written on and painted. There are two different fields to be explored here: the **readability** of the body, and tattooing.

The readability of the body is part of the discourse of **'physiognomics'**, a study that extends from Antiquity right through to the present day. This subject reached its peak in the eighteenth century (and had already lost its status as an academic field in the nineteenth century), when the philosopher Johann Kaspar Lavater (1741–1801) embarked on the ambitious project of deciphering the human character by way of its external features. The dream of 'physiognomics' was to read the hidden, inner being through involuntary physical signs, and thus bring it out into the open. These signs might be physiological, e.g. the shape of the nose, or uncontrollable forms of expression, such as raising the eyebrows or blushing. Hamlet's resistance to such transparency and readability has already

52 Foucault (1967; 1990; 1994).
53 Duden (1998).
54 Agamben (2002).
55 Foucault (1985).

been noted (see Chapter 1). For him, the outer manifestations of mourning are not unmistakable, metonymic signs emanating from his body that reveal something hidden, but instead they are conditioned and controlled.

This is in contrast to the spontaneous, involuntary reactions he invokes in Claudius by means of the play within the play. Here Hamlet himself becomes the physiognomist, hoping to gain insight into the interior of a fellow human by deciphering the outer signs.

Goethe was critical of the 'science of physiognomy', and he played a not insignificant role in its loss of scientific status. He never got tired of deconstructing the opposition between pure interior and pure exterior, and he replaced it with an open process of interaction. This study, he wrote,

> [...] makes conclusions from the outside to the inside. But what is the outside of man? Certainly not his naked figure, involuntary gestures that denote his inner powers and their interplay! Status, customs, possessions, clothes – everything modifies and covers him. To penetrate through all these veils into his innermost self, and to find in all these alien circumstances fixed points that might give clear indications of his essential being, seems difficult in the extreme, indeed impossible. But take comfort! What surrounds man does not only affect him, but he in turn affects it, and as he modifies himself, so he modifies all around him. [...] Nature fashions man, he refashions himself, and the refashioning is once again natural.[56]

While the physiognomist reads the body like a piece of writing, the cultural practice of **tattooing** makes the body itself into a writing surface on which it inscribes indelible signs. It is this indelibility that distinguishes tattoos from clothes. They are an exterior which at the same time is also an interior because they are engraved into the skin. In Melville's *Typee* (1846), the protagonist Tommo – who ends up on a Polynesian island – is conscious of this distinction. He thinks it would be a good idea to adapt himself to the ways of the islanders on whom his survival depends: "When at Rome do as the Romans do, I held to be so good a proverb, that being in Typee I made a point of doing as the Typees did."[57] He wears the same clothes as them, eats their food, and fits in as well as he can with their way of life. The proverb he quotes, however, shows clearly that his adaptation to their customs is only a façade, a necessary adjustment that can be reversed, and not something that affects his innermost being. His decision becomes a problem when the tribesmen want to tattoo him so that he can become a full member of their island society. His native servant Kory-Kory is a living example of the art of the tattooist, who was no doubt convinced that he could make vast improvements on the work of Nature by painting the whole body. In the description of this Polynesian, ironically the indigenous oral culture of the

56 Goethe (1981), 11.
57 Melville (1968), 209.

South Seas encounters the American culture of print, archives, sciences and museums:

> The entire body of my savage valet, covered all over with representations of birds and fishes, and a variety of the most unaccountable-looking creatures, suggested to me the idea of a pictorial museum of natural history, or an illustrated copy of 'Goldsmith's Animated Nature'.[58]

As soon as Tommo sees this artistic masterpiece coming towards him, his ironic reflections on tattooing give way to sheer horror at the **cultural otherness**, because he sees this step as a profound threat to his identity. Particularly the tattooing of the face will mean overstepping a boundary which will forever bar him from a return to the civilized world. Across the bodily frontier of the skin, tattooing shifts the exterior to the interior. Seen from this standpoint, the exotic cultural representations become stigmata: "I should be disfigured in such a manner as never more to have the face to return to my countrymen, even should an opportunity offer itself."[59]

Melville, who had himself been a seaman and had lived among the South Sea islanders as a beachcomber,[60] returned to the theme of tattooing in his later novel *Moby Dick* (1851). Through the example of the native Queequeg, whose body is also covered with tattoos, he reflects not on inclusion and exclusion and the boundaries of community, but more generally on the borders of cultural meaning. Here, significantly, the talk is of 'hieroglyphs' that have been engraved on him by a medicine man:

> [He] had written out on his body a complete theory of the heavens and the earth, and a mystical treatise on the art of attaining truth; so that Queequeg in his own proper person was a riddle to unfold; a wondrous volume; but whose mysteries not even himself could read, though his own live heart beat against them; and these mysteries were therefore destined in the end to moulder away with the living parchment whereon they were inscribed, and so be unsolved to the last.[61]

These are signs from an alien culture which might possibly contain the key to this culture. The sailor is described as an embodied book which, however, he cannot read because he is incorporated in it himself.[62] Melville's narrator makes

---

58 Melville (1968), 83.

59 Melville (1968), 219. On the ambivalence of decorations (ornaments) and stigmata, cf. Caplan (2000) and Frank (2011).

60 This makes him a kind of 'go-between' for white and Indian cultures. He too jumped ship and was stranded on an exotic island, where for a while he voluntarily conformed to the lifestyle of the natives. Cf. Frank (2006).

61 Melville (1998), 480 f.

62 The word 'volume' is derived from the Latin *volumen*, and denotes the papyrus scroll, whereas parchment was processed in the form of the codex (see the paragraph on the forms of the book in Chapter 2).

it clear that this incarnation of the traditions of a tribal oral culture differs in two respects from the traditions of a written one. Firstly because it is inscribed on the body, it cannot be the subject of reflection and interpretation, as a written text can be, but must remain an insoluble mystery that resists understanding and explanation. Secondly because it is inscribed on the body, it cannot survive the man himself; it will vanish along with his life, leaving no trace behind such as might be preserved in an archive and become available to study for posterity.

3.3.5 Incarnate and excarnate culture

The opposition between body and mind is closely connected with the history of media which we dealt with in the preceding chapter. Developments and improvements in technological systems of recording have resulted in a radical breakaway from the human body. In this context, the alphabet already constituted an irreversible abstraction by separating human language from the live voice. Through writing, we might say that speech was 'excarnated', i. e. detached from all physical substrata. **Incarnation** is a theological term and stands for the Word being made flesh, as we learn at the beginning of the St John gospel. Something immaterial like the Greek *logos*, and something written like the Hebraic *Torah*, can according to St John, take on a flesh and blood human form. The incarnate Christ is the embodiment of the holy Word. In terms of media technology, however, every act of writing entails the exact opposite: concrete experience, embodied speech, and the sensory voice are all transformed into black letters on a white background. A culture that depends above all on this achievement and extends it for its own purposes is radically different from a culture that depends on orality and bodily staging (see Chapter 1). These are the two cultures that I call **'excarnate'** and **'incarnate'**.[63] An excarnate culture creates libraries and archives, storage and scholarship. An incarnate culture forms itself through interpersonal contacts, physical staging, festivals and rituals – in brief, by giving cultural meanings a sensory present through performance in space and time.

The distinction between excarnate and incarnate cultures should not be understood as an opposition in which both poles mutually exclude each other. There are incarnate cultures that flourish without alphabetical writing, but there are no excarnate cultures that can do without the principle of embodiment, presence and live participation. Nevertheless, it is useful to make this distinction in order to be able to describe the different orientations and emphases that exist within the cultures.[64] My pairing of excarnate and incarnate has a sort of parallel in the distinction introduced by the culture historian Carl E. Schorske. With regard to

63 Cf. Assmann, A. (1993b).

64 We can link this typological approach made by the historian of Europe, Carl E. Schorske, to the study of 'cultural patterns' developed by Ruth Benedict and Margaret Mead in ethnology.

the history of Austria he speaks of a **'culture of grace'** and a **'culture of the word'**.[65] 'Grace' can relate to either God's kindness to man or to elegance, and both meanings apply to the culture of the Catholic Counter-Reformation, with its baroque splendour, its courtly and ecclesiastical performances, its love of images, outer beauty, aesthetics and sensual pleasure. The culture of the word, on the other hand, points to the Protestant tradition of iconoclasm, abstraction, rationality, enlightenment and asceticism. Schorske's concepts denote the different developments within western, Christian culture, though he sees these not as unique historical manifestations but as structures that recur throughout history under changing circumstances. The typological differences do not by any means lead to a basic polarization, but preserve themselves as sensitive instruments with which to describe a complex, sometimes tense relationship and interaction.

Just as western Protestant and Catholic cultures both polarize and intersect, on a more general level it can be said that an excarnate culture cannot survive without elements of an incarnate culture, and vice versa. In the USA, for instance, where the culture has emerged from a very clear writing-orientated Puritan movement, there exists not only the countermovement of fundamental scepticism towards writing (as with the mystic philosopher Ralph Waldo Emerson,[66] who held the authority of the critical individual to be above all the wisdom of books) but also a strong tradition of rhetorical self-staging.[67]

In this context, a much more tangible distinction is that between **white** and **black culture**, both of which come together in the USA. It begins with the very concrete experience of body. How does one live, asks Toni Morrison in *The Bluest Eye*, as a young girl in a black community when the normative white ideal of beauty is blue eyes? What does such an ingrained but alien image do for the self-respect of black women? The difference is not, however, confined to racial features, but also applies to **body consciousness** and the different emphasis on the body within black and white culture. In African-American literature, which since the Harlem renaissance in the 1920s had fought primarily for social and later cultural emancipation, white culture was perceived principally as written and excarnate. It was based on encoded traditions and institutions like libraries, schools and universities, museums and concert halls, to which it was difficult if not impossible for blacks to gain access. Black culture, which because of its history of deprivation and social oppression had long been regarded as inferior, had to be rediscovered and reinvented. It is an incarnate culture derived from the 'spirit' of the body, with all its live traditions of dance, music (jazz), orality, and a vast store

65 Schorske (1999).
66 Emerson (1971).
67 One only has to think of the many American films that end up in a courtroom, where the outcome of the plot is decided by convincing rhetoric.

of songs and folktales.[68] The literary theorist Henry Louis Gates pinpointed the differences between the two cultures and made the body-related sign practices of African-American culture the subject of an illuminating book.[69] His interest lies not just in the (incarnate) culture of the body and of orality itself, but especially in the stagings of this incarnate culture in the written (excarnate) medium of writing.

3.4 Body stagings

With the era of the book coming to an end, which in the 1970s the media theorist Marshall McLuhan called 'the end of the Gutenberg Galaxy', the hitherto dominant perspective of an excarnate culture was on the wane, leaving an open view of developments and phenomena associated with an incarnate culture which for a long time had been out of sight or devalued. This change, which has also been described as the **'return of the body'**, has manifested itself in many aspects of cultural life. They include the direction of cultural studies, which have detached themselves from their adherence to texts as the privileged subject and now seek other approaches to culture. One such possibility lies in the study of cultural history as a "history of body stagings":

> From the standpoint of research policy, there has in recent times been a shift of cultural paradigm from the text model to the performance model. Compared to making culture readable as a text, processes of exchange, the nature of action, cultural practices, rituals, ceremonies, games, festivals – in current terms, stagings of culture and experiential values of culture – deserve more attention than the mere representations, images and self-portraits that can be derived from texts. What needs to be studied are texts as cultural patterns, which within precisely definable limitations of time and space produce a communicative, culturally describable event.[70]

This is the path taken especially by **New Historicism**, which we have already glanced at in the Introduction. New Historians have not rejected the text as an historical source – of course it remains the most important means of access to forms of expression prevalent in the past – but they eliminate the hierarchical distinction between canonized texts and those, which they read in order to gain insights into social practices within the framework of a cultural history of the body. The journal of this branch of cultural studies is called *Representations*. This indeed is the keyword for the whole approach: the word can refer to the **presentation**, with emphasis on the specific sign systems and media involved, and it can

68 Ellison (1994); Morrison (1993); cf. Bröck (1988).
69 Gates (1988).
70 Scherpe (1999), 29. Scherpe is associated with the Research Group 447, 'Cultures of the Performative', Berlin/Potsdam, and with the postgraduate course on 'Body Stagings' at the Institut für Theaterwissenschaft at the Free University, Berlin.

refer to the **staging**, with special emphasis on the embodied performances and their effects on the audience. The conditions, premises and procedures of these public (self-) representations have been analysed in detail by Stephen Greenblatt, co-founder of the journal and leading light of New Historicism, in his book *Renaissance Self-Fashioning*. The subject of this book is the symbolic use of the body as a medium of publicly displaying power, status and identity in the culture of Renaissance courts.

'Representation' is a key term not only for Renaissance courts but also for the present-day (incarnate) culture of the media. In contrast to the (excarnate) book culture, a decisive role is played here by categories such as representation, theatricality, staging and performance. Together with these categories the physical body, which in the era of book culture had been immobilized and marginalized, reappears in concrete situations as a bearer of emotion, action and meaning.

Summary

Since the 1980s, the word 'body' has taken on an increasingly important role in a variety of fields (e.g. the media, gender, and 'agency'). Down through the centuries, the hierarchy of the five senses has undergone many religious and cultural re-evaluations. For instance, during the Renaissance it was sight that predominated, whereas earlier it had been condemned as the gateway to sin. From this new status of the eye there emerged two very different modern traditions: aesthetics and the Natural sciences.

Unlike animals, humans are not bound to one particular environment. This 'eccentric' position is conducive to reflection. In addition to this affirmative, humanistic approach of philosophical anthropology, cultural uses and decorations of the human body ('body techniques') constitute important features of historical anthropology.

This latter position is concerned with the relationship between body and mind, or body and soul. The modern-age anthropology of the Enlightenment, which set body and soul against one another, has a long history in Christianity, but was constantly being undermined by the concept of a unified whole.

Elias sees the process of civilization as being progressive self-control over body and affects. Bourdieu uses the term 'habitus' to cover a wide range of cultural characteristics whose effectiveness is proportionate to the degree in which they are detached from consciousness.

A taboo on the sexualized body was a component initially of Christian and later of bourgeois culture and literature. The period around 1900 was marked by tensions between these sexual taboos and movements in favour of sexual freedom. In this context, Nietzsche described the soul as a web of cultural norms and social constraints that controlled the body. Gender studies focus on these cultural programmes which may be internalized to the point of unconsciousness. Central to these studies is the masculine power of the patriarch over the female body. Foucault's new perspective on body control laid the foundations for a history of the body.

In cultural history, 'body writing' relates both to the tradition of physiognomy, which sought to make people 'readable' by way of involuntary physical signs, and to the ethnographical practice of tattooing, which uses the skin as a writing surface for cultural signs.

There is a basic distinction between incarnate and excarnate cultures. Incarnate cultures turn the body into a kind of theatre by emphasizing its appearance through performative acts; excarnate cultures dispense with the body and focus on non-sensual phenomena such as texts, which provide a kind of stepping-stone to transcendental values. In this context, Catholicism places a different emphasis on the body from that of Protestantism.

Select bibliography

Armstrong, Philip (2008) *What Animals Mean in the Fiction of Modernity.* London (et al.): Routledge.

Carlson, Marvin (2003) *Performance. A Critical Introduction.* London (et al.): Routledge.

Douglas, Mary (2007) *Natural Symbols. Explorations in Cosmology.* London (et al.): Routledge.

Kosut, Mary/Moore, Lisa J. (2010) *The Body Reader. Essential Social and Cultural Readings.* New York: New York UP.

Spry, Tami (2011) *Body, Paper, Stage. Writing and Performing Autoethnography.* Walnut Creek, CA: Left Coast Press.

4. TIME

4.1 Cultural bases for the experience of time

Generally time isn't as clear-cut to us as the date on the calendar or the hands on the clock, but it passes in many almost imperceptible ways through our actions, experiences, observations and memories. From a cultural perspective, **space** and **time** are neither purely physical phenomena nor a priori categories of human perception, but **cultural constructs** themselves. These coordinates, within which all our human activities take place, are not stable or independent of our influence, but are means of orientation and interpretation that constantly change throughout history. In the next two chapters we shall consider various examples of how we look at these cultural frameworks and how literary texts in different periods have helped to shape them. How did and how do people think of time? How is it compressed, extended, and made accessible to experience?

4.1.1 The ambivalence of time

Perhaps the least sensuous description of time in the whole of literature comes from Virginia Woolf:

> It was November. After November, comes December. Then January, February, March, and April. After April comes May. June, July, August follows. Next is September. Then October, and so, behold, here we are back at November again, with a whole year accomplished.[1]

Shakespeare's *Winter's Tale*[2] offers a bit more to the senses. The action does not take place within the contracted space and time, typical of classical drama. Presenting itself as a narrative, the play gives itself the freedom to unfold between two geographical locations (Sicily and Bohemia). It begins in the ninth month of Queen Hermione's pregnancy, her daughter Perdita is born in Act II, and by Act IV she is already a young woman of marriageable age. At the beginning of this act, Shakespeare introduces a winged figure to announce the fact that sixteen years have passed. This personification of Time is holding an hourglass that he tips over in a single movement, after presenting himself to the audience as follows:

> I that please some, try all, both joy and terror
> Of good and bad, that make and unfold error,
> Now take upon me, in the name of Time,
> To use my wings. (IV, Chorus, 1–4)

---

1 Woolf (2008b), 254.
2 Shakespeare (1997h).

With this embodiment, Shakespeare has followed the Renaissance theme of Truth as the daughter of Time (*veritas filia temporis*). There are three figures in the constellation: Father Time with long beard and wings, his daughter – a naked female figure freed by her father from a cave to which she had fled from her adversary, and Error, who is portrayed as an ugly female. Time rules over good and evil, punishes Leontes with years of suffering for his blind jealousy and defamation of character (with fatal consequences for Mamillius), but does not allow Error to triumph and finally brings truth to light.

The modern counterpart to the allegorical personification of time is the **clock**, which does not represent time but measures it by dividing the hour into 60 units of equal length. Bacon, who regarded the compass, gunpowder and the printing press as the three great agents of modernization, might well have added a fourth in the shape of the mechanical clock, which was invented simultaneously at various places in Europe during the fourteenth century and has since then provided an indispensable foundation for our time-governed modern age.[3] In Shakespeare's Sonnet 77, the clock together with two other objects brings out the ambivalence of time with both its destructive and its productive effects:

> Thy glass will show thee how thy beauties wear,
> Thy dial how thy precious minutes waste;
> The vacant leaves thy mind's imprint will bear,
> And of this book this learning mayst thou taste.
> The wrinkles which thy glass will truly show
> Of mouthed graves will give thee memory;
> Thou by thy dial's steady stealth mayst know
> Time's thievish progress to eternity.
> Look! What thy memory cannot contain,
> Commit to these waste blanks, and thou shalt find
> Those children nursed, deliver'd from thy brain,
> To take a new acquaintance of thy mind.
> These offices, so oft as thou wilt look,
> Shall profit thee and much enrich thy book.[4]

The poem names three everyday objects through which we experience time in different ways: mirror, clock and book. The mirror and clock are media which bring home to us the negative character of time: it steals our youth and beauty, and drives us towards disintegration and death. This image corresponds to the old one of **Time as Kronos**, who eats his children and is represented in baroque symbols as *tempus edax*. However, this sonnet also brings to the fore the positive side of time. It is an agent not only of theft and destruction but also of creative forces that allow the person to develop and grow. This is where the third object comes into play: the **book**, which in this case is to be imagined as having blank

3 Dohrn van Rossum (1992).
4 Shakespeare (1997f).

pages and is to be thought of as a concrete gift from a friend, with the sonnet simply providing instructions on how to use it. With the aid of this book, so the argument goes, the negative effects of time can be cancelled out and turned into something positive and productive. As soon as things are written down, the empty pages will at first passively accept the overflow from memory in the form of thoughts and poems; however, through the act of rereading, not only is nothing lost but this encounter with the written word will enable something new to emerge and grow. The creative force of time is here described in terms of biological reproduction: "thou shalt find / Those children nursed, deliver'd from thy brain."[5]

4.1.2 Lifetime

The moment we view time not as a physical constant but as a basic framework for our human life and experience, we cannot help but be struck by its different qualities. The prime example is life itself, which we commemorate with each birthday and which all generations of writers have contemplated in their own way. This time is, above all, limited and indeed far too short, as Andrew Marvell bemoans in his poem *To His Coy Mistress* (1681):

> Had we but world enough, and time,
> This coyness, lady, were no crime.
> We would sit down, and think which way
> To walk, and pass our long love's day;
> Thou by the Indian Ganges' side
> Shouldst rubies find; I by the tide
> Of Humber would complain. I would
> Love you ten years before the Flood;
> And you should, if you please, refuse
> Till the conversion of the Jews.[6]

Such a slow, long-drawn-out passage of time can only exist in this witty, unreal subjunctive form; the reality of human life is that it races by: "But at my back I always hear / Time's winged chariot hurrying near." Here too the wings of time symbolize the speed with which it overtakes us, no matter how hard we try to outrun it. In matters of love, the shortness of time makes shyness and aloofness impracticable and indeed, according to the frustrated wooer, criminal ("This coyness lady were no crime"). The motto has to be *carpe diem*, and the poet does not hesitate to play his final trump card:

> The grave's a fine and private place,
> But none I think do there embrace.

5 See metaphors of weak authorship in Chapter 2.
6 Marvell (1999).

Our limited **lifespan** is not just an excuse for getting a move on when it comes to enjoying ourselves; it also fixes a frame within which we must achieve whatever goals and tasks we have set ourselves. Marvell's contemporary John Milton wrote some autobiographical sonnets in which he asks how he can possibly fulfil all his poetic ambitions within the short time available, especially when burdened with such hindrances as his blindness:

How soon hath Time, the subtle thief of youth,
Stolen on his wing my three-and-twentieth year!
My hasting days fly on with full career,
But my late spring no bud or blossom shew'th.
Perhaps my semblance might deceive the truth
That I to manhood am arrived so near;
And inward ripeness doth much less appear,
That some more timely-happy spirits indu'th.
Yet, be it less or more, or soon or slow,
It shall be still in strictest measure even
To that same lot, however mean or high,
Toward which Time leads me, and the will of Heaven.
All is, if I have grace to use it so,
As ever in my great Task-Master's eye.[7]
(1631)

In the first quatrain time once more is personified as a winged creature, with the emblematic wings corresponding to Peirce's iconic symbol for the unstoppable movement ("My hasting days fly"). The speaker's late spring, however, has not yet produced any flowers, and he feels as immature as he looks. In the following six lines, there is a change of perspective from a comparatively active to a somewhat passive view of the situation: in the face of various contrasting possibilities, he adopts a more acquiescent attitude, no longer seeing time as a thief but as a guide working according to God's will. The final couplet underlines but also transcends this feeling of acceptance, in so far as the poet now looks towards eternity and the granting of **God's grace** ("if I have grace to use it so"). For Puritans in the seventeenth century, God's grace stood for the motivation behind their deeds and works, but it also held them in check. No matter how important their own actions and ambitions were within their programme of self-determination, the decisive factor was always God's grace, because that and that alone would settle the question of whether a life had been fulfilled or not. The fact that the concern which underlies this whole poem has not disappeared even at the end and has not given way to a true, God-given peace of mind is clear from the manner in which the poet addresses his God in the very last line: "my great Task-Master". The speaker remains very much like a schoolboy who has not yet done his homework and fears the wrath of the teacher.

7 Milton (1968), 29.

When I consider how my light is spent,
  Ere half my days in this dark world and wide,
  And that one talent which is death to hide,
  Lodged with me useless, though my soul more bent
To serve therewith my Maker, and present
  My true account, lest he returning chide,
  'Doth God exact day-labour, light denied?'
  I fondly ask: but Patience to prevent
That murmur, soon replies, 'God doth not need
  Either man's work or his own gifts. Who best
  Bear his mild yoke, they serve him best: his state
Is kingly: thousands at his bidding speed.
  And post o'er land and ocean without rest;
  They also serve who only stand and wait.[8]
(1652)

Milton's famous sonnet on his blindness, written twenty years after the first one, varies both the theme and the basic pattern of the metaphors. The circumstances are now much more dramatic, and his preoccupation with the problem of time and the limits of human will and ability runs much deeper. The poem is in the form of a psychomachia – a conflict between soul and body – in which the two vie with each other for dominance. Now, instead of the schoolboy metaphor, we have the image of the talent, taken from the New Testament, according to which those who use the money given to them and succeed in increasing it will be rewarded, in contrast to those who bury it and then return it without profit. This interpretation of the parable expresses the new self-confidence of the middle classes, who have changed the world through their capitalist activities and have thrust open the gates to the modern age. The link between the Protestant ethic and the spirit of capitalism, as explained by the sociologist Max Weber, was obviously the new economic attitude towards the value and scarcity of time, which had to be saved and exploited to the full by every possible means. The dialogue in Milton's poem formulates this new philosophy but at the same time counterbalances it with the voice of pious self-restriction.

The Puritans – and we may for the first time partially include women – experienced time principally in economic terms of duties and responsibilities, accounts and accountability both to themselves and to their Creator. They developed the **diary** as an important cultural medium of self-examination and self-guidance through time. One example of this is Daniel Defoe's Robinson Crusoe, who shipwrecked on a desert island in the Caribbean and soon comes to realize how important this inner dialogue by means of paper, ink and calendar is for the self-preservation of a civilized man in conditions of 'barbarism'. In his isolation, it is essential for his identity that he should regain control over time. The diary and

8 Milton (1968), 80.

the **calendar** are both indispensable as instruments of order and guidance. Every day he carves a notch on a tree trunk, extending each seventh cut. His management of time enables him not only to maintain his cultural identity as a Christian by honouring the Sabbath, but also to celebrate non-religious occasions such as the day when he was saved and also his arrival on the island. Like ecclesiastical and national **holidays**, these have the function of giving him regular reminders of identity-forming events, and they place his life within the framework of an individual history of salvation. The fact that he names his native companion Friday not only tells us that the man came to him on that particular day, but also shows the colonial superiority of the white man's calendar.

4.1.3 'Cold' and 'hot' cultures

The thesis that time is a cultural construct includes the fundamental observation that every culture produces specific frames for time to evolve (Jan Assmann)[9]. Whether time passes and the world changes more slowly or more quickly is a question of cultural context. There are some cultures that stabilize their identity through rituals and traditions, whereas others – like our own western culture – have at some time in their history switched more or less universally to constant innovation and change. In this connection, the ethnologist Claude Lévi-Strauss speaks of 'cold' and 'hot' cultures.[10] **'Cold cultures'** are those which, out of wisdom rather than lack of ability, block off any tendency towards so-called progress or change by organizing themselves around repetition, recognition and consistency, guided by the cyclical processes of Nature. **'Hot cultures'**, on the other hand, embrace invention and alteration as a governing principle of their development, and for them time is simply a neutral measurement. In western Europe, cultures changed from cold to warm to hot during the period between the Middle Ages and early modern times, when stabilizing influences such as religion and tradition increasingly gave way to the dynamic movements of science, technology and economics, so that they were sucked into a general process of change which was subsumed under the metaphysical concept of 'progress'.

This polarization between 'cold' and 'hot' can be a useful aid to description provided we avoid value judgements applying the Hegelian norm of evolution, which would downgrade cold cultures as deficient and would maintain that eventually they must turn into hot. The concept in fact works the other way, as it enables us to discern certain grey areas in which we can identify cold elements in hot cultures and vice versa. Cold elements in hot cultures arise out of self-imposed obligations in the form of sacrosanct values that are not open to alteration. They may be ethical or social, like human dignity or the equality of the sexes, but they can also be aesthetic, as manifested in an artistic canon of works that are per-

9 Assmann, J. (1996), 31.
10 Lévi-Strauss (1966).

manently exposed to reception and interpretation. Hot elements in cold cultures are now taken for granted in our age of globalization: in a village in Upper Egypt you will find an internet café, although everyday life continues to be shaped by archaic conditions that include women and girls having to get water from a central well and carry it home on their heads. Such phenomena of global but partial technological expansion were described by the art historian Wilhelm Pinder as long ago as the end of the nineteenth century as the 'simultaneity of the non-simultaneous'.[11]

4.1.4 Relations between generations

If innovation is to become a basic principle of cultural change, it requires specific driving forces. One such was the mass exploitation of the writing medium through the invention of the **printing press**. Without this, innovative advances through science and technology would have been as impossible then as scientific and technological differentiation and specialization would be today without the computer. Another driving force of change on a social level is the **sequence of generations**. In cold cultures, the younger generation is generally obliged to accept the norms and values of the older generation, thereby adapting to the existing society. In this respect, each new generation brings a piece of Nature or 'barbarism' into the culture, and the aim of upbringing and socialization consists in 'civilizing' the barbarian in accordance with the cultural code that is in operation. In hot cultures, however, the natural gap between generations leads to the younger constantly finding fault with the older, thereby paving the way for innovation and hence for an acceleration in the process of cultural change. In hot cultures, youth is a positive asset that stands for creative energy, potential for innovation and openness to the future. As Ralph Waldo Emerson wrote:

> Nature abhors the old, and old age seems the only disease: [...] We call it by many names, - fever, intemperance, insanity, stupidity, and crime: they are all forms of old age: they are rest, conservatism, appropriation, inertia, not newness, not the way onward.[12]

In hot cultures, youth not only can but in fact must question all the old and hallowed traditions. The first literary generation to claim this right was the German *Sturm und Drang* (Storm and Stress), which rebelled against the schoolmasterly poetics of the eighteenth century, gave literary expression to unbridled passions, and established the concept of the genius as a new artistic norm. What the ***Sturm und Drang*** movement introduced so dramatically, with the new generation throwing down the gauntlet to the society it had been born into, set an historical precedent for every subsequent generation. This was also aided by biological factors: general improvements in living conditions and hygiene prolonged

11 Pinder (1926).
12 Emerson (1979), 188 f.

and indeed doubled life expectancy during the nineteenth century. This in turn meant that the generations did not succeed one another but lived side by side in a 'simultaneity of the non-simultaneous', which resulted in social clashes and cultural tensions that also contributed to the acceleration of cultural change. Each new generation, which recognizes, defines and identifies itself by way of shared historical experiences, values and aims, contains the potential for a new and dynamic onward movement in the evolution of its culture.

4.1.5 The acceleration of time

Since the last quarter of the eighteenth century – dubbed the **'saddle period'** by the historian Reinhart Koselleck – western cultures have been going through an ever hotter phase at an ever increasing speed of evolution. The French Revolution, a new wave of secularism, the Industrial Revolution, the founding of new universities and the democratization of culture through the spread of writing and of literacy have each contributed to the feeling of an all-encompassing acceleration of time through an acceleration of change.[13]

We shall now focus on a particularly concrete aspect of this process of acceleration: the change in transport technology and its effect on literature. We shall not confine ourselves to the effects of the fundamental changes in living conditions and modes of perception, for which literature offers us a rich archive, but will also consider changes in the different forms of writing itself.

Cultural history is one of changing time rhythms. One important intervention in the way we experience time came about through the **Industrial Revolution**, which brought the **steam engine** and the **railways**. The first English railway was constructed in 1825 between Stockton and Darlington (five years before the Liverpool – Manchester line). In America, Henry David Thoreau, who had retreated to the remote forests of New England in the mid-nineteenth century, was able to maintain contact with the outside world by means of this new form of transport. He saw very clearly how it introduced a new concept of time and accelerated the pulse of life, speech and thought:

> The startings and arrivals of the cars are now the epochs in the village day. They go and come with such regularity and precision, and their whistle can be heard so far, that the farmers set their clocks by them, and thus one well-constructed institution regulates a whole country. Have not men improved in punctuality since the railroad was invented? Do they not talk and think faster in the depot than they did in the stage-office?[14]

13 This acceleration has continued: the amount of literature published since the Second World War exceeds the sum total of all the works printed before then. See Cavalli (1991), 208.

14 Thoreau (1995), 114.

From now on, time was directed less by the natural rhythms of day and night or the seasons, and more and more by the exact time on the clock – e. g. in the form of timetables – which synchronized social time with ever greater precision. Thoreau observed all these changes, and as a modern American did not have the slightest objection. On the other hand, he was far from glorifying the progress of technology as progress in civilization, as was common in the second half of the nineteenth century. The historian Frederick Jackson Turner, for instance, hailed the advance of the railways into the wilderness and the whole expansion of the network as a harbinger of progress. The wilderness, he wrote, "has been interpenetrated by lines of civilization growing ever more numerous. It is like the steady growth of a complex nervous system for the originally simple, inert continent."[15]

Heinrich Heine, who was present at the opening of the lines between Paris, Orleans and Rouen in 1843, talked of a new paragraph in world history which would change our modes of perception and our ideas and would shake the elementary concepts of space and time. Just as we react today to globalization, with vast communications and transport networks that have so dramatically shrunk the world, Heine too reacted to the **new era of speed** which had shortened distances and produced a different feeling for space: "It feels to me as if the mountains and forests of all countries were advancing towards Paris. I can already smell the scent of German lime trees; the North Sea is surging outside my door."[16] While admirers of technology and progress saw all this as man's increasing mastery of space and time, critics viewed it as the "destruction of space and time"[17]. As one looked out of what the poet Joseph von Eichendorff called the 'flying salon', the shapes and contours of the landscapes disappeared in the headlong rush.

In the introduction to her novel *Felix Holt*, George Eliot remarks with a slight note of nostalgia that the technological progress of the railways has been accompanied by an impoverishment of sensual experience and thus of narrative potential:

> O youngsters! The elderly man has his enviable memories, and not the least of them is the memory of a long journey in mid-spring or autumn on the outside of a stagecoach. Posterity may be shot, like a bullet through a tube, by atmospheric pressure from Winchester to Newcastle: that is a fine result to have among our hopes; but the slow old-fashioned way of getting from one end of the country to the other is the better thing to have in the memory. The tube-journey can never lend much to picture and narrative; it is as barren as an exclamatory O! Whereas the happy outside passenger seated on the box from the dawn to the gloaming

15 Turner (1963), 37 (see Chapter 5).
16 Heine (1981), 449.
17 Schivelbusch (1977) describes contemporary reactions to this turning-point in cultural history, 35 f.

> gathered enough stories of English life, enough of English labours in town and country, enough aspects of earth and sky, to make episodes for a modern Odyssey.[18]

150 years later, Eliot's future fantasies have not yet come true: despite the development of transrapid systems, our everyday experience of overland travel is still a long way off being shot through a tube. However, air travel has certainly brought this nineteenth century Utopia to life, making travel – apart from the spectacular views – into a non-sensory experience which we compensate for by watching films on board. Like the loss of sensory perception, the decline in the social art of narration is connected with this acceleration, because observing and talking need and use time, of which in our modern society there is less and less at our disposal.

Narrative, which appears to be at risk under these conditions, is itself a basic cultural mode of time construction. Stories organize events in such a way that they are endowed with connections and meanings. Narrative form, time structure and meaning are all interwoven. The processing of biographical and historical experiences "is an indispensable medium for the cultural orientation of actions and the formation of a convincing personal and social identity"[19]. The past as such does not exist; it can only be made present by selecting, shaping and interpreting, which generally means moulding it in order to lend support to an argument or an attitude. As we shall see in more detail in the final two chapters, this use of the past is indispensable for self-understanding and for future orientation. In order to make the past present, one needs impressive images and vivid narratives. Within a narrative framework made up of particular **narrative schemata** (the historian Hayden White uses the term 'emplotment', and Stuart Hall 'encoding'[20]), events that are important for the message are selected and organized to point the way towards a particular goal or meaning.

Virginia Woolf made the relationship between **changing eras**, changing lifestyles and experiences the subject of her novel *Orlando*. Here time plays a vital role on different levels. One of these is historical time, which changes from period to period, each of them with its own characteristics. This historical uniqueness is what she calls 'the spirit of the age'. The representation of each ***Zeitgeist*** is an ambitious, historico-cultural project, because Woolf reconstructs the physiognomy of the individual periods not just from their political and intellectual features but also from mentalities, objects, fashions, social and life styles, as well as the values and world views inherent in all of these. Orlando, the eponymous protagonist, is a remarkable person – partly because after the first half of the book he is transformed into a woman, partly because he lives from the sixteenth

18 Eliot, G. (1998), 5.
19 Rüsen (1990), 12.
20 White (1973).

through to the twentieth century, and over the four hundred years of his life gets to know a wide variety of *Zeitgeister*.[21]

Whereas on earlier adventures Orlando travels by ship, coach or on horseback, in the last chapter the protagonist takes the railway during the Victorian era and later goes by car during the 1920s. When she wants to take the coach, she is informed that she must catch the 11.45 train to London. She sits down in a compartment "without giving a thought to 'that stupendous invention, which had (the historians say) completely changed the face of Europe in the past twenty years' (as, indeed, happens much more frequently than historians suppose)." (260) When the Victorian episode comes to an end, ten strokes of the clock bring her straight back into her writing present: "It was the eleventh of October. It was 1928. It was the present moment." (285) This moment, when **discourse time** and **story time** coincide, marks a fragile dividing line between literature and life.

Back in the present, Orlando sits in a car and drives off. She has to make her way through heavy traffic, and takes in a variety of individual images:

> [S]he noticed sponges, bird-cages, boxes of green American cloth. But she did not allow these sights to sink into her mind even the fraction of an inch as she crossed the narrow plank of the present, lest she should fall into the raging torrent beneath. (285)

The objects that fleetingly enter her field of perception have no connection with one another – they might just be goods displayed in shop windows. As she drives along the street, Orlando instinctively adopts the perceptive mode of the new age; she only observes the surface of things and does not allow them to 'sink into her mind'. As Woolf wrote in another tale, "the eye is not a miner"[22]. This ties in with a phenomenon which psychologists and sociologists at that time described as an **'overflow of stimuli'** and linked to a new nervous disease called neurasthenia. Everything forces itself *onto* Orlando, but at the same time nothing goes *into* her. As the car moves along, a fragmented world races past:

> Here was a market. Here a funeral. Here a procession with banners upon which was written 'Ra – Un', but what else? [...] Amor Vin – that was over a porch. A woman looked out of a bedroom window, profoundly contemplative, and very still. Applejohn and Applebed, Undert –. (292 f)

To this sequence of isolated and fragmented images the narrator appends a remarkable reflection that summarizes the very essence of the modern experience of time:

---

21 "The transaction between a writer and the spirit of the age is one of infinite delicacy, and upon a nice arrangement between the two the whole fortune of his work depends. Orlando had so ordered it that she was in an extremely happy position; she need neither fight her age, nor submit to it; she was of it, yet remained herself." Woolf (2008b), 254.

22 Woolf (1994), 156. See the following chapter on 'Space'.

> Nothing could be seen whole or read from start to finish. What was seen begun – like two friends starting to meet each other across the street – was never seen ended. After twenty minutes the body and mind were like scraps of torn paper tumbling from a sack, and, indeed, the process of motoring fast out of London so much resembles the chopping up small of identity which precedes unconsciousness and perhaps death itself that it is an open question in what sense Orlando can be said to have existed at the present moment. (293)

4.2 Literary stagings of the present

An age-old subject of poetry is the savouring, intensifying and **immortalizing of the moment**. *Ars longa, vita brevis*: what is fleeting in life can be prolonged and given a lasting presence through art. Immortalizing the moment is also the poetic programme of the Victorian writer Dante Gabriel Rossetti, as he says explicitly in the poem that begins his cycle *House of Life*: "A sonnet is a moment's monument"[23].

In Virginia Woolf's *Orlando*, on the other hand, the unmediated and pure present comes as a shock to the protagonist: "For what more terrifying revelation can there be than that it is the present moment? That we survive the shock at all is only possible because the past shelters us on one side and the future on another." (285) This experience gives a new slant to an old problem that has long troubled philosophers: does the present exist at all? Does it not break up infinitesimally into smaller and smaller segments which ultimately are no longer accessible to perception or experience? St Augustine grappled with this problem in the eleventh book of his *Confessions*, and he came up with a solution.[24] Dividing time up into the three dimensions of past, present and future (as laid down by the rules of Latin grammar) seemed to him too simplistic, because we have no direct sensory access to either the past or the future. **Perception of time** can only take place exclusively in the present, and so only the present actually exists; there is therefore a present-relating-to-the-past (memory or historical reconstruction, which is always reproduced in the present), and there is a present-in-relation-to-the-future (the particular expectations that we have of the future in our present). Still, suppose it turns out that we have no guaranteed way of experiencing the present either? Neurologists and perception psychologists assure us today that the brain is not a passive container of minimalist sensory perceptions swirling around chaotically in our heads, but that our faculties of perception are a platform on which whatever is perceived is already set out in a form that is accessible to consciousness. However, this automatic process itself needs time, approximately three seconds, which is why they speak of a **three-second window** in

23 Rossetti (1873), 176. The first part of the cycle in particular contains several poems that deal with the fleeting nature of life and time.

24 St Augustine (2008).

which a sensory image is generated.[25] Whether this image is retained, focused on and taken up by the conscious mind, subsequently to be worked on and committed to memory, or immediately discarded is not decided by the infrastructure of the brain but by the individual interests of what are called our 'mental maps'.

4.2.1 Fragmentation of perception

Many artists in the early twentieth century took the new fragmentation of experience to be the hallmark of their era. In this they were following in the footsteps of the French poet of city life, Charles Baudelaire, who in the nineteenth century had already realized that acceleration and the concomitant fragmentation of perception lay at the heart of modern experience: "La modernité, c'est le transitoire, le fugitif, le contingent."[26] As for the city, it "changes more swiftly than the human heart."[27] This insight had direct consequences for a new **modern aesthetics**. The long and leisurely epic narrative was no longer suited to these conditions, and so writers experimented with short and ever shorter forms. The **short story** developed during the nineteenth century as a genuinely modern genre, while **imagism** – an early twentieth-century movement involving British and American poets – used extremely condensed images. Instead of protracted development, the narrative – as in Joyce's collection of short stories, *Dubliners* – consisted of an impressive sequence of concise but unconnected episodes. When the novel itself expanded and regained its epic format, nevertheless its time span was radically restricted: the plot of *Ulysses* covers sixteen hours of a single day and the following night – 'Bloomsday', 16 June 1904.

With Virginia Woolf, the fragmentation of perception led to the literary 'stream of consciousness' technique, in which disconnected images and associations merge with one another inside the head of the protagonist, and the process of writing runs parallel to the flow of thoughts. This leads to the character herself dissolving into a variety of self-portraits, and we shall return to this theme in the chapter on identity. At the opposite end of the scale to the active staging of the self is the passive overflow of stimuli, through which human consciousness is transformed into a mere reflector – a piece of apparatus akin to a camera. Unconsciousness and proximity to death, but also a mystical form of self-transcendence are linked to this extension of consciousness. After such states of self-dissolving, it requires an act of immense effort and discipline to bring perception back under conscious control. Whoever achieves it will emerge with a sharper awareness for social conventions and for how identities are constructed.

25 Pöppel (1988).
26 Baudelaire (1995).
27 Cf. Cavalli (1991), 202.

4.2.2 Apotheoses of the moment

Experience of temporal acceleration and worldly fragmentation intensify our perception of each individual moment. Disconnected from its contexts, it is fragmented into **isolated experiences**. Generally, it is trivial matters that have a lasting effect and can assume an almost unfathomable significance. As an example, we will look at a poem by Ezra Pound which was written under remarkable circumstances. The idea first came to him when he left the Paris metro at La Concorde one day in 1913. Suddenly, amid the everyday mass of people and traffic, he found himself noticing individual faces whose beauty he wanted to capture in a poem. The initial result was a 30-line poem which six months later he reduced by half, and then after another year condensed into a two-liner:

> IN A STATION OF THE METRO
> The apparition of these faces in the crowd;
> Petals on a wet, black bough.[28]

The scene is a non-sensual place of dark shafts and tunnels, pulsating with speed and general bustle. In such a place, perceived images are reduced to fleeting, unconnected apparitions. The characteristic city experience of movement, fragmentation and transitoriness is compressed into the first line of the poem, but we do not learn what sort of faces these are, and before the eyes can take them in, they have gone. "Apparition" is usually used to describe ghosts, and this enhances the fleeting, insubstantial quality of the faces, as well as providing a link with the Underworld, in the form of the dark shafts of the metro. But it is the image in the second line that creates the extraordinary tension within this poem: an image from Nature, which Pound himself described as 'superimposed' on the first image, producing a kind of filmic dissolve which for a second opens up a surprising similarity between two contrasting worlds. Surprise and **suddenness** are the key emotions of this 'imagist' poem, whose effect is achieved through the technique of a swift cut and an abrupt montage of images. It is the same technique that was developed simultaneously in the new medium of **film**. The new mode of visual perception was thus both imitated and corrected in modern poetry, which aspired to wrenching our dull vision out of its lethargy and in the midst of the urban overflow of stimuli giving it a new sharpness of focus. Imagist poetry aspired to an art form composed of verbal images that hone the senses and enhance perception.

At the core of the imagist movement was the thesis formulated by T. E. Hulme that it is not words and sounds that are the decisive material of poetry, but the image. The imagists reinforced the visual quality of their work at the expense of aural qualities such as rhyme, assonance and rhythm.[29] When it comes to describing the

28 Pound (1968), 113.
29 Hulme (1962).

relevant image, however, it is easier to say what it is not than what it is. It is not a metaphor, it has no illustrative character, nor is it the bearer of a subjective, emotional value. The route from the metaphor to the image, and from subjectivity to objectivity, leads through **alienation**, i. e. through a violation of linguistic conventions and stereotypical perceptions. The quest is for the sensuous power of the concrete, which must be stripped of all ingrained connotations and traces of expressiveness. What is important here is the absolute **purity of the image**, its 'pure visibility' (Lambert Wiesing), and its complete emancipation from the tyranny of language. This struggle for purity links the American imagist poets to other modern artists who also sought for pure forms of painting, sculpture and music. For them a pure image was a form of energy. The tension aroused in the reader was not meant to be resolved through shock or catharsis, but had to be maintained through the configuration of contrasting images. Only then could the work attain the quality of objectivity – it ceased to mean something and instead began to be. Ezra Pound, who in 1912 coined the name 'imagist' with reference to his friend the philosopher and art historian T. E. Hulme, repeatedly described his new poems in terms of hardness and truth at the cost of expressiveness and emotion: "It will be as much like granite as it can be, its force will lie in its truth."[30]

For his two-liner, Pound borrowed not only from the new medium of film but also from Chinese writing, which does not provide arbitrary signs for sounds – as our letters do – but produces words as stylized images (ideograms), and from Japanese literature, through which he had got to know the *haiku*, a poem limited to seventeen syllables. The point of such poems is that they say more through **omission** than through what is said. Modern montage and ancient *haiku* come together in Pound's poetic practice, where the linear sequence is replaced by spatial **juxtaposition**. The enhanced richness of the images, however, is always at the expense of wider contexts. Perception is reduced to the shortest impulses, so that the imagist poem forces a kind of pointillism onto the reader. In this way, the 'image' isolates an 'instant of time' that has no before and no after; it shatters the monotonous chain of time with its linear flow, and extracts a moment in which time is frozen. In 1913, the same year in which he wrote the metro poem, Pound defined what he meant by 'image' in the journal *Poetry:*

> An 'image' is that which presents an intellectual and emotional complex in an instant of time. I use the term 'complex' rather in the technical sense employed by the newer psychologists, such as Hart, though we might not agree absolutely in our application. It is the presentation of such a 'complex' instantaneously which gives that sense of sudden liberation; that sense of freedom from time limits and space limits; that sense of sudden growth, which we experience in the presence of the greatest works of art.[31]

30 Pound (1963), 12. "The first use of the word 'Imagiste' was in my note to T. E. Hulme's five poems, printed at the end of my Ripostes in the autumn of 1912." (4)

31 Pound (1963), 4.

The key term 'complex' provides a technical and neurological association, because Pound's poetics not only strive to create new language patterns but also to extend the boundaries of perception. 'Complex' means the joining together of incommensurables (man and nature, intellect and emotion) and also the interlocking of opposing elements that release new tensions. The poetics of imagism present themselves in terms of psychic energy. But above all, this definition makes clear the close relationship between image and time. The image that breaks the continuum of time simultaneously allows us to break free from time and to transcend it – which is the goal and the test of great art.

4.2.3 Epiphanies

From Pound's intensified moment it is only a short step to the 'epiphanous' moment. The intensified moment celebrates a sensuous impression, whereas the epiphanous opens up a window to **transcendence**. It was James Joyce who described such quasi-religious moments as 'epiphanies'. The word goes back to the day of Epiphany, 6 January, when the Three Wise Men realized that an everyday, worldly event (the birth of a child in humble circumstances) was of metaphysical importance (the arrival of the Saviour). Such events are **epi-phanous**, i. e. literally after-revealing, but they are also and especially **dia-phanous**, i. e. through-revealing, in the sense that they denote an indeterminate, deeper meaning. In Joyce's epiphanies the religious dimension has disappeared, but what remains is the moment of reverence, which focuses attention on something unknown.

Joyce's interest in epiphanous moments was not solely due to his Catholic upbringing, and nor was he by any means the only writer to be attracted to them. Reality for many authors around 1900 was no longer as clear-cut as in the realistic literature of the nineteenth century, but on the contrary it was something arcane that would only reveal itself at unexpected moments. Against this background, literature became a privileged medium in the search for revelation. Herein lay the mysticism of the modern age, which now focused on moments that might uncover the hidden depths of reality and – as with the imagists – might give an instantaneous insight into the true essence of things. This 'essence' (as Heidegger called the hidden truth) is the otherness of time: to get to it, one must break the continuum. An authentic moment, free from the fabrications of narrative and imagination, cannot be sought or found, but can only be experienced suddenly and unexpectedly. The prime example is Proust's **'mémoire involontaire'**. It is always a trivial, sensuous perception which, he writes, releases "for a moment brief as a flash of lightning [...] a fragment of time in the pure state."[32]

With Proust this sensation can be set off by the sound of a spoon on the plate, the sight of a church tower, the taste of a madeleine dipped in tea, or the feel of

32 Proust (1996), 224.

two uneven cobblestones. At such unlikely moments, the involuntary memory jerks the subject out of time by suddenly merging two different instants – one past, one present – into an unpredictable synchrony.

The concealment of reality is also a starting point for James Joyce, and the concept of 'essence' plays an equally central role in his work. Just as Proust was convinced that "the work of art was the sole means of rediscovering Lost Time"[33], Joyce believed that it was the task of literature to uncover the hidden side of reality and to reveal the **essence of things** – which, if it could actually be revealed, would be encapsulated in subjective experiences and would not be communicable in itself. One can only approach it by exiting from the dimension of time. For Proust the exit was through the little gateway of the involuntary memory, whereas for Joyce it is the epiphanous moments that break the continuum of time and suddenly, unexpectedly bring reality into view. But as with Proust these moments are sensuous, trivial everyday experiences, and Joyce's aesthetic also depends on a mystic 'reverence for the insignificant' (Aby Warburg), which finds God in the detail and deciphers the profound in the superficial.[34]

Joyce gave the heading 'Epiphanies' to a series of short sketches he wrote between 1900 and 1903, which came to light between 1956 and 1965 and were identified by the publishers as building blocks for his early autobiographical novel *Stephen Hero*. They are little scenes, fragments of narrative, and records of conversations, all taken out of their context and thus appearing to be spontaneous transcriptions of reality. The form presents a kind of immediate "photographic realism" – as if reality has been directly inscribed into the silver bromide of the photographic plate, and this is precisely the way it should manifest itself in the epiphanous moment (see Chapter 2). Joyce used a concentrated form of most of these sketches in his other works. Their importance is made clear by a statement in *Stephen Hero* concerning the hidden character of reality. According to Joyce, what hides it is not habit or convention but above all our **cultural patterns of interpretation**:

> The ancient method investigated law with the lantern of justice, morality with the lantern of revelation, art with the lantern of tradition. But all these lanterns have magical properties: they transform and disfigure. The modern method examines its territory by the light of day.[35]

The modern method, which Joyce also calls **'vivisection'**, combines the ethos of art with that of science. Both have the task of representing the world through precise and incorruptible procedures as straightforwardly as possible, i. e. as independently as possible from human projections.

33 Proust (1996), 258.
34 Kany (1987).
35 Joyce (1969), 190.

Within this framework, Joyce secularized the religious concept of epiphany and conceived it as a counterpart to scientific experimentation. What is crucial here is the discontinuous, fragmentary nature of these epiphanies. By being lifted out of the flow of time, each trivial scene takes on the quality of a mysterious sign – a 'revelation', an 'illumination', a 'spiritual manifestation'. The 'hero' Stephen develops the artistic project connected to this procedure as follows:

> This triviality made him think of collecting many such moments together in a book of epiphanies. By an epiphany he meant a sudden spiritual manifestation, whether in the vulgarity of speech or gesture or in a memorable phase of the mind itself. He believed that it was for the man of letters to record these epiphanies with extreme care, seeing that they themselves are the most delicate and evanescent moments.[36]

Again just like Proust, Joyce combines transience and eternity in his paradoxical aesthetics. In this context, he does not talk of eternity but of 'stasis' – although this term does not have any of the negative connotations that we associate with it nowadays. The negative equivalent for him is 'paralysis'. By contrast, stasis has nothing to do with the inability to move, but relates to the productive moment of standstill which defies the flow of time and is transplanted into the structure of the artwork. On this aesthetic structure is founded the ***contretemps***, the chronotope of the work of art. For his aesthetic theory, the Irish Catholic Joyce borrows from the traditions of scholasticism: At the centre of his thinking is the connection between timelessness and essence. In *Stephen Hero* he systematically summarizes the three phases of aesthetic perception:

> First we recognize an object as *one*, i.e. as a unified thing, then we recognize its structure as a combination of parts, the *thing*, and finally, when the relation of the parts to one another is complete, when they have been organized to a particular point, we recognize that it is *the* thing and no other. Its soul, its white-ness, leaps at us through the veil of its appearance. We experience the soul even of the commonest thing, organized according to its structure, as a glow. Then the thing has achieved its epiphany.[37]

The three steps of aesthetic perception are divided into **'integritas'**, **'consonantia'** and **'claritas'**. In the third and final phase, when order and light merge together, the hidden essence of things appears – a moment variously described by Joyce as 'claritas', 'quidditas' and 'epiphany'. The essence is always taken out of the flow of time and suddenly revealed in involuntary moments, deepening perception and giving validity to the aesthetic shaping of reality.

36 Joyce (1969), 216.
37 Joyce (1969), 218. See also Joyce (1993).

4.3 The nightmare of history

In Chapter 2 of James Joyce's *Ulysses*, we watch the protagonist Stephen Daedalus giving a history lesson. He makes every effort to drum names and dates into his pupils' heads, but all in vain, partly because they have no interest in boring textbook knowledge, but also – and this is a far weightier reason – because their teacher himself has no regard for a history that comprises nothing but military victories and defeats. In the second half of the same chapter, the protagonist's role changes; the teacher no longer stands in front of the pupils but in front of his superior. After he has been given his pay, they have a conversation about history from a different perspective. In the course of this discussion, the Anglo-Irishman Mr. Deasy develops his conspiracy theory: the Jews are responsible for the downfall of the British Empire. Here Joyce notes how anti-Semitism has massively increased with the fall of the Empire. At this moment, Stephen is thinking of how the Jews throughout history have endured thousands of years of suffering, always for different reasons, and he reacts defensively. There follows a sentence which will be repeated several times in the course of the novel: "History, Stephen said, is a nightmare from which I am trying to awake."[38] The fanatical Mr. Deasy thinks the exact opposite, he wants to be a part of the historical process: "I am a struggler now at the end of my days. But I will fight for the right till the end." (40 f) Here Deasy is formulating an 'Armageddon mentality' that compels him to enter history, knowing that he is on the right side. To do this, he must name his arch enemies and know for sure that they are guilty, and as far as he is concerned they are the Jews (with women not far behind). For him, history is a religious revelation with an eschatological driving force: "The ways of the Creator are not our ways, Mr. Deasy said. All history moves towards one great goal, the manifestation of God." Stephen initially reacts to this statement in a completely incomprehensible manner. Instead of answering, he points towards the window; outside, one can see and hear the schoolchildren playing hockey during their PE period.

> – That is God.
> Hooray! Ay! Whrrwhee!
> – What? Mr. Deasy asked.
> – A shout in the street, Stephen answered, shrugging his shoulders. (40)

In contrast to Mr. Deasy's presumption that God will manifest himself in history (in a different context, Americans talk of **'manifest destiny'**), Stephen experiences an **unexpected 'epiphany'** of God in the trivial things of the everyday world. Mr. Deasy stresses that God will become accessible through the facts and figures of political power, while Stephen insists that such manifestations are inaccessible, and recognizes the signs of God independently of collective needs and individual aspirations.

38 Joyce (1997), 40.

4.3.1 Transcending time: T. S. Eliot's Four Quartets

The modern age has not only accelerated the experience of time and intensified its individual moments, but it has also continuously sought ways and means of reining it in or escaping from its tyranny. Joyce published *Ulysses* in 1922; his pessimistic view of history is undoubtedly connected with his experience of the First World War. At this time the promotion of national ideologies – as he diagnosed with great clarity – was already being reinforced by a new wave of anti-Semitism. After the Second World War even more people came to share Stephen's feeling that history was a nightmare from which they longed to awake. The postwar period, after 1945, was one of **deceleration**, of trying to get away from the ever increasing pace of time and to find some kind of metaphysical reassurance. This was the climate that gave birth to the later poetry of T. S. Eliot, who was awarded the Nobel Prize for Literature in 1948 and whose *Four Quartets* were the most important and most widely read poems of the 1950s.[39] By now, Eliot had left behind the experimental phase of his youth; he described himself as a "classicist in literature, royalist in politics, and Anglo-Catholic in religion." The cycle consists of four poems that are each named after places of particular biographical or historical significance. Out of these inconspicuous locations Eliot creates his own **'lieux de mémoire'** (Pierre Nora) of Anglo-American history. Each of the quartets reflects not only on the place but also and especially on the time, each establishing its own individual tone. The thread that runs through all of the poems is the transcending of time. The musical connotations of the word 'quartet' are already an indication of this theme: **music** is the model for such transcendence, as it opposes time's passing with memorable forms of melody, rhythm and modulation. Eliot's way of defeating time requires an artistic figuration, which also includes the structuring of his own identity. While 'memory' and 'desire' entangle us in past and future, thus holding us ever more tightly in time's net, the need is to create a deeper awareness of **simultaneity**. Hemmed in between past and future, consciousness shrinks: "Time past and time future / Allow but a little consciousness" (16) we learn in the first quartet, and "the world moves / In appetency, on its metalled ways / Of time past and time future." (18) This is another allusion to the tracks of the railway age, which have become the backbone of the modern era. The emphasis on temporality is not, however, just a consequence of technology but, above all, a physical condition of our bodies: "the enchainment of past and future / Woven in the weakness of the changing body." Eliot would like to free himself from this condition, just as he would from his memories. In his poem he tries out different ways of overcoming time – through mysticism, ritual and art.

In the context of mysticism, he combines Christian and eastern traditions, in order to rid himself of illusions and to empty out his conscious mind. Both traditions try to overcome time by overcoming the body through spirituality:

---

39 Eliot (1963).

The inner freedom from the practical desire,
The release from action and suffering, release from the inner
And outer compulsion, yet surrounded
By a grace of sense, a white light still and moving,
Erhebung without motion, concentration
Without elimination. (Burnt Norton 2, 16)

The third part of the first quartet sounds like instructions for a yoga exercise: "Emptying the sensual with deprivation / Cleansing affection from the temporal" (17). The high proportion of technical Latin expressions adds to the de-sensualization of language:

Descend lower, descend only
Into the world of perpetual solitude,
World not world, but that which is not world,
Internal darkness, deprivation
And destitution of all property,
Desiccation of the world of sense,
Evacuation of the world of fancy,
Inoperancy of the world of spirit. (Burnt Norton, 3, 18)

What consciousness needs to be emptied of (rather like Hamlet's tables, see Chapter 6) is chaotic sensory impressions, and fragments of images and memories, which were the material of imagist poetry and of the literary stream of consciousness. The ephemeral perceptional images with which Pound and Woolf created their poetics of the city are mere refuse according to the world-weary Eliot. One only needs to compare the tenderness of the faces in Pound's vision of the metro with these lines from the *Four Quartets*:

Only a flicker
Over the strained time-ridden faces
Distracted from distraction by distraction
Filled with fancies and empty of meaning
Tumid apathy with no concentration
Men and bits of paper, whirled by the cold wind
That blows before and after time,
Wind in and out of unwholesome lungs
Time before and time after. (Burnt Norton, 99–107)

Eliot diagnoses distraction and fragmentation as a disease of culture, the therapy for which is **concentration** and **collection**. For him, collection is possible among other things through the ritual of the Christian sacrament and through prayer: "and prayer is more. / Than an order of words, the conscious occupation / Of the praying mind, or the sound of the voice praying" (51). Concentration and collection, however, are also gifts of art and an effect obtained through the ordering of words. Eliot's verbal ordering and rearrangement of temporal concepts permeate all four quartets:

Time present and time past
Are both perhaps present in time future,
And time future contained in time past. (13)

Or say that the end precedes the beginning,
And the end and the beginning were always there
Before the beginning and after the end.
And all is always now. (19)

In my beginning is my end. (23)

In my end is my beginning. (32)

What we call the beginning is often the end
And to make an end is to make a beginning. (58)

One can well imagine that after the Second World War nightmare of history, such lines worked on the dazed reader like a kind of drug. The syntactic simplicity and litany of repeated, elementary words create an almost hypnotic charm that soothes the shattered soul to restfulness. Eliot's verses aim to **transcend time** and enable the reader to break away from linear history. His most important aesthetic stratagem to achieve this is order, together with ornament. Poetry, like music, is an art of time, and both pursue the same goal of using an artistic figuration to eliminate time.

Words move, music moves
Only in time; but that which is only living
Can only die. Words, after speech, reach
Into the silence. Only by the form, the pattern,
Can words or music reach
The stillness, as a Chinese jar still
Moves perpetually in its stillness. (19)

Eliot's term **'stillness'** is reminiscent of Joyce's 'stasis', which we noted had nothing to do with the inability to move. Words like 'form', 'pattern' and 'stillness' skirt round this figurative quality of time-transcendent classical art, which is not the opposite of movement but absorbs movement into itself and holds it still: "at the still point, there the dance is, / But neither arrest nor movement" (15); or: "The detail of the pattern is movement" (19).

Breaking away from linear time also means learning and accepting a new kind of humility, because one always has to start again from the beginning: "And so each venture / Is a new beginning, a raid on the inarticulate." (30 f) "There is only the fight to recover what has been lost / And found and lost again and again." Within this time frame there is no progress, no stability, no achievement – nothing but the repeated attempt. This has very little to do with playful experimentation, and everything to do with discipline and effort, as one can tell from the violent imagery in which this aesthetic theory is couched, for each beginning is 'a raid'.

4.3.2 In the time train

In the middle of the third quartet, Eliot describes a train journey which at the same time is man's **journey through time** from the past into the future. This image, however, undermines the obvious commonplaces of the general time model: the past is not closed off behind the passengers like the departure station, and the future does not lie ahead like their destination. The superficial idea that the dimension of time can be equally illustrated through the dimensions of space is denied by Eliot. His railway carriage stands for a place outside both time and space, in which fixed identities are dissolved and a perspective can be opened up to create a new balance between past and future. This is the moment of the pause which is to be wrested from the one-way flow of time – the moment in which past and future intersect in a new and surprising manner. More than a hundred years after its invention, railway travel has become part of everyday life. The train is no longer associated with the excitement of speed and technology, but its lulling movements and sounds have a calming effect. The compartment is a **non-place**, an intermediate space in time which loosens all the bonds of both space and time that bind us to the place of departure and the place of arrival, to the past and to the future. In this non-place and this **non-time**, the network of connections that holds our lives together is temporarily dissolved. This gives us the chance to create a new configuration of past and future in a moment of illumination or stasis. Ironically, the setting for Eliot's moment of stasis is the headlong-rushing 'flying salon' of a railway train.

> When the train starts, and the passengers are settled
> To fruit, periodicals and business letters
> (And those who saw them off have left the platform)
> Their faces relax from grief into relief,
> To the sleepy rhythm of a hundred hours.
> Fare forward, travellers! not escaping from the past
> Into different lives, or into any future;
> You are not the same people who left that station
> Or who will arrive at any terminus [...]
> You shall not think 'the past is finished'
> Or 'the future is before us'. [...]
> 'Fare forward, you who think that you are voyaging;
> You are not those who saw the harbour
> Receding, or those who will disembark.
> Here between the hither and the farther shore
> While time is withdrawn, consider the future
> And the past with an equal mind.' (Dry Salvages, 3, 41 f)

Summary

Time exercises its influence on human life in many subtle ways. Space and time, seen from the perspective of cultural studies, are cultural constructs that serve as dimensions of orientation and as bearers of meaning.

The (mechanical) clock which provides the basis for the time-governed modern age is the opposite of the allegorical embodiment of time; it is purely and simply a measuring instrument which divides time into exactly equal sections, thereby removing all the imagery associated with the topos of transience.

Seventeenth-century Puritans saw time as the basic religious framework that conditioned human life and experience. The modern focus on effective use of time goes back to these Puritans, who calculated the degree of God's grace in accordance with the degree of their material prosperity. The most important instruments that guided them – and also Robinson Crusoe – to a mastery of time were the diary and the calendar. While the diary is the medium in which the meaning of one's own life is deciphered from a transcendental perspective, the task of the calendar is to provide periodic reminders of personal, identity-shaping experiences and religious festivals.

Whether historical change should be seen as positive or negative depends on its cultural framework. Whereas so-called 'cold' cultures channel the flow of time into repetition and consistency, 'hot' cultures are based on innovation and change. Since the early modern age, western European nations have switched to technical progress and evolution, i. e. from cold to ever hotter cultures. In addition to the use of writing and new technology (e. g. the clock, the compass and gunpowder), a driving force for cultural change is the sequence of generations. When children break away from their parents, they also break with the continuity of tradition and open culture up to new ways of shaping the future. Both the French Revolution and the Industrial Revolution led to an all-encompassing acceleration of time through the ever increasing rate of change within the world of everyday life. In particular the railways, which provided a new experience of speed, also brought in a new attitude towards time and a new awareness of space.

In the modern age, the prevailing feeling of fragmentation that characterized people's experience of time also led to an aesthetic confrontation with the fragmentation of perception. A new 'aesthetics of the moment' became the central focus of artistic activity, to which a major contribution was photography and the then new medium of film. The 'image' compressed into a single sensual impression became a basic element in poetry, while 'epiphanous moments', in which everyday trivialities provide insights into transcendental experiences, play an important role in the novels of Proust and Joyce. After the Second World War, people had had enough of revolutions and historical change. There followed a period of restoration, in which poets like T. S. Eliot explored new modes of access to time. This entailed breaking away from linear history and attempting to forge new links between the dimensions of past, present and future.

Select bibliography

Bender, John/Wellbery, David, eds. (1991) *Chronotypes. The Construction of Time.* Stanford: Stanford UP.

Currie, Mark (2007) *About time. Narrative, Fiction and the Philosophy of Time.* Edinburgh: Edinburgh UP.

Kern, Stephen (2003) *The Culture of Time and Space. 1880–1918.* London: Harvard UP.

Ricoeur, Paul (1990) *Time and Narrative.* Vol. 1. Trans. K. MacLaughlin and D. Pellauer. Chicago: Chicago UP.

Schleifer, Ronald (2009) *Modernism and Time: The Logic of Abundance in Literature, Science, and Culture, 1880–1930.* Cambridge (et al.): Cambridge UP.

Whitrow, Gerald J. (1988) *Time in History. The Evolution of Our General Awareness of Time and Temporal Perspective.* Oxford (et al.): Oxford UP.

5. SPACE

Recent studies have repeatedly argued that too much attention has been paid to time, and not enough to space, and so while the modern age prioritized the former, the **postmodern** has opted for the latter. Now that the 'great tales' (Jean François Lyotard), with their long-term visions of history and the future, have lost their powers of conviction, time has been foregrounded as a dimension that needs to be reduced: by faster means of transport and by nanosecond communication.

The new interest in space has been sparked by a number of impulses, including economic location factors, the increasing touristic importance of cultural and historical sites (*lieux de mémoire*), and also awareness of ecological threats. Apart from geographical, we also have virtual space, in which more and more interactions, events and experiences are taking place.[1] While new worlds open up in virtual space, at the same time real-life milieux take on additional significance because of their specific sensual qualities. The same applies to the advance of globalization: in proportion to the expansion of consumer patterns across the globe, the unmistakable individuality of the local community gains in importance – as summed up by the term **'glocalization'**. In the light of these new developments, there is talk today of a **'spatial turn'** which, after the extensive period in which history and narrative held sway, some would say is long overdue.[2] However, it is seldom possible to draw such a clear-cut distinction between space and time as the two dimensions of human life; experience and action. The invention of new forms of transport such as the railways and the airplane has had just as powerful an effect on our experience of space as it has on that of time. In order to emphasize the interconnection of both dimensions, the Russian literary theorist Michael Bakhtin coined the term 'chronotope'[3].

One can say of both dimensions that the basic categories of perception are anthropological and have as their starting-point the spatial position of the human body. Examples of the embodied experience of time are our biological lifespan, with its key elements of birth and death, growing up and growing old, the sequence of generations, and – as far as the individual is concerned – the biological

---

1 See Nowotny (1996).

2 Weigel (2004). This essay is recommended as an introductory survey of the wide international spectrum of cultural space theories. As long ago as 1989, Edward W. Soja asked for a "spatialization of historical narratives" and a cultural-geographical study from a non-western perspective.

3 Bakhtin (1981).

clock with its alternation of sleeping and waking, range of perception and attention, and the need for repetition and renewal. With regard to space, basic factors are our orientation to the front (conditioned by the features of the face), our blindness and insecurity in relation to what is behind us, our reaching out to the left and right (spatial concepts that have also taken on political and normative connotations), standpoints that govern perspective, the distance of the horizon, the overall 'superior' view from above, and the respectful or even fearful view from below, the closed nature of surfaces, and plumbing the depths.

All of these play a role in, for instance, *anthropological* discourse on space. People always orientate themselves in space, and they develop not only their sensory faculties but also their imagination, memory, and social skills within basic spatial structures. From a *sociological* perspective, space is principally the setting for social interaction, which is produced basically by communication, everyday practices, and representations both of and in space. One might call it a three-dimensional stage for social life and activity.[4] In addition to these time- and space-bound interactions, which are mainly dependent on reciprocity, there is also *political* space, which relates mainly to national self-determination, and to conquest and government. In the political sphere, space is territory that has to be defended, discovered, crossed, colonized, measured, mapped, occupied etc. It is the central focus of colonial reshaping and the exercise of power. *Historically*, the topography of particular places must be studied, because these are the 'frozen' storehouses of compressed time, in which one can find signs and traces that must be verified and deciphered.[5] This approach inquires into the **readability** of landscapes, towns and villages where (as Walter Benjamin puts it) history has wandered onto the scene. There is a distinction between such historic sites and **non-places** like car parks and airports, which are strictly functional and are devoid of any individual historical features.[6]

Another cultural concept of space includes what is variously known as 'interstitial space', 'space-in-between' and 'contact zone', which plays a particularly important strategic role in postcolonial studies, undermining the colonizers' hegemonic organization of space from their minority perspective. In postcolonial times – in an age of both forced and voluntary migration – **interstitial space** as something that has not been and cannot be colonized has become a vital intellectual resource in discourses that reclassify colonialism into nationalism and transnationalism. This is where the traditional, polarizing categories of (colonial)

4 De Certeau (1984); Lefebvre (1991).
5 Bachelard (1994); Miller (1995); Schlögel (2003).
6 Augé (1995).

territorial states give way to new discursive definitions of space.[7] Cultural studies are also concerned with the imaginary **psycho-space** of nightmares and horror stories,[8] with imaginary ethno-spaces,[9] and with the new field of **virtual spaces** as created by cyber-space and the electronic media.[10] In the course of globalization, the static concept of space has increasingly lost ground to the view that space is dynamic: "[It] entails a deterritorialisation of culture and its subsequent reterritorialisation, and challenges culture's equation with location or place."[11]

The importance of geographical space and climate for human life and experience, thought and ideas, actions and creativity, was highlighted by Gertrude Stein. The American writer grew up in Vienna, had a Czech tutor and a Hungarian governess, and in later years moved to Paris, so that from very early on she had experienced the effects of moving between geographical and cultural spaces: "After all anybody is as their land and air is. Anybody is as the sky is low or high, the air heavy or clear and anybody is as there is wind or no wind there. It is that which makes them and the arts they make and the work they do and the way they eat."[12]

We will now discuss in more detail three different concepts and experiences of space: metropolitan London as a framework for individual experience and social action, colonial space with its categories of centre, periphery, frontier and threshold, and Native American cultural space outside the sphere of western imagination, though not without western interventions and influences.

5.1 London – the metropolitan labyrinth

The modern city, which we discussed in the last chapter as both a crystallization of and condition for a changed perception of time, is equally important for a new experience of space. This can be seen from three literary texts that have London as their setting for experience, action and perception. Our source for **experience of space** will be the English Romantic Thomas De Quincey (1785–1859), who be-

7 Clifford (1997); Pratt (1986); Bhabha (2008). Interstitial space also plays an important role as a thinking space in which all the things that take place undermine contrasts and hinder or prevent understanding: ambivalence, indeterminacy, openness, polysemy. According to Ruth Mayer, this space-in-between is a "place of subversion and the starting point for quests for alternative meanings and lifestyles, and has long since become a privileged place and a densely inhabited area." (1999), 239.
8 Vidler (1992).
9 Mayer (2002).
10 Of a very different nature are the 'intellectual spaces', in the sense of knowledge stores and thought spaces, including *topoi* (places) and commonplaces, which help us to think and to understand one another.
11 Grossberg (1996), 169.
12 Stein (1968), 419.

came famous throughout Europe as the "English Opium Eater". Our source for **action within space** will be an eighteenth-century satirical text by John Gay, and for **perception of space** we will turn to Virginia Woolf, a more modern experimentalist.

5.1.1 London as a space of experience – Thomas De Quincey

The metropolis of London plays a leading part in De Quincey's autobiography. In 1802, at the age of 17, he ran away from school, wandered round Wales, and ended up hiding himself in London. This period lasted from the winter of 1802 until spring 1804, and was anything but a glorious taste of freedom. A chronic shortage of cash left him half starved, and led to gastritis with complications that were to form the basis of his later addiction to opium.

In a short chapter of his *Confessions*, De Quincey talks about the "Pleasures of Opium" before then spending far more time describing the "Pains of Opium".[13] The pleasures relate to his experiences in London. During the first eight years of his addiction he deliberately indulged because he enjoyed the stimulation. He describes two pleasurable experiences which he regularly repeated and which he initiated every time with a warm drink of laudanum without sugar. On each of these occasions he had what we would now describe as a typical experience of 'flow'. One example he gives is a visit to the opera. He bought a seat in the gallery for five shillings and found himself intoxicated by the voice of a singer named Guiseppina Grassini, of whom it was rumoured that she was the mistress of both Napoleon and Wellington. The highlight for the opera fan was the moment when as Andromache she sang her heart out with grief at the grave of Hector.

Another metropolitan attraction that he discovered promised a similar opium-induced flow. One Saturday he mingled with the poorest of the poor, a group of labourers who were free for two evenings and one night from the daily grind and the grim realities of their weekdays. Latching on like a parasite, De Quincey joined in their brief euphoria at the removal of the yoke. Ironically he stresses the fact that he was quite different from the reformer, because he was empathizing with their joys and not with their miseries. Over the weekend he observed and accompanied these people, imagined being in their shoes, and shared their pleasure or dismay when they went to do their shopping in the market. He felt his way into their lives in much the same way as a sensitive reader identifies with characters in a novel. The opium helped him not only to blur the distinction between reality and fiction, but also to block out the depressive impressions and give precedence to those of enjoyment.

With the same high expectations as he had for the opera, De Quincey sought out the many markets scattered all over London. Under the influence of his drugs,

13 De Quincey (2008).

distances were no problem for him. He travelled far and wide within the city, and left himself totally at the mercy of chance and his own moods. What proved much more difficult, however, was the return journey. He tried to use navigational devices, directing himself by the northern star and hunting for a northwest passage, but only rarely did he manage to find his way straight home. Frequently he ended up in strange places he had never seen before. At such times, London turned into a **labyrinth** in which he could get hopelessly lost: "I came suddenly upon such knotty problems of alleys, such enigmatical entries, and such sphinx's riddles of streets without thoroughfares." (47)

The language here merges the city plan with the structures of reason. Under the influence of opium, the exterior and interior worlds come to resemble each other more and more, and the labyrinth of the city changes into the labyrinth of the human mind. At this point we might perhaps allow ourselves our own little diversion down a side alley. Like De Quincey, T. S. Eliot in an early poem also draws a parallel between the unnavigable streets of London and the unnavigable human mind:

> Let us go, through certain half-deserted streets, [...]
> Streets that follow like a tedious argument
> Of insidious intent
> To lead you to an overwhelming question ...
> Oh, do not ask, 'What is it?'
> Let us go and make our visit.[14]

De Quincey uses a second image to describe his wanderings – that of the explorer of new lands:

> I could almost have believed, at times, that I must be the first discoverer of some of those *terrae incognitae*, and doubted, whether they had yet been laid down in the modern charts of London. (47 f)

The expression **"modern charts"** suggests that the city is somehow rational, orderly, and under control. But running counter to modern systems of order is De Quincey's experience of the wilderness in the heart of the city, a *terra incognita* in the midst of civilization.[15] Through the parallel between the city and the human mind there emerges the impression that the nocturnal adventurer is wandering along paths of the unconscious, the dark regions of his unknown self. De Quincey did not go unpunished for these experiences. The images of his wanderings returned and haunted him in the shape of nightmares, and the pleasures of opium were later overshadowed by their torments:

14 Eliot (1967), 11.

15 The idea of a plan of London used as a topography of the human soul and all its dark districts was taken up again by R. L. Stevenson in his early novel *Dr Jekyll and Mr Hyde*, also by Peter Ackroyd (1993) in *Hawksmoor*.

> [T]he perplexities of my steps in London came back and haunted my sleep, with the feeling of perplexities moral or intellectual that brought confusion to the reason, or anguish and remorse to the conscience. (48)

There is a biographical episode underlying these references to **moral lapses** and guilt. During his time in London, De Quincey had an affair with a 15-year-old prostitute named Ann. However, his relationship with this young girl was by no means a source of shame (the Victorian era had not yet begun). On the contrary, he declared that it was quite natural for a philosopher like himself, a wanderer of the streets, to link up with female peripatetics who earned their living roaming the same streets.[16] It was to this prostitute – an orphan and also the victim of a dishonest relative who had robbed her of the few belongings she had – that De Quincey owed food and shelter during the months when he was most destitute; night after night he walked up and down Oxford Street with her. Indeed he actually owed her his life. Quite apart from his material problems, he suffered from fainting fits, and one day in his half-starved state he collapsed, whereupon she spent the little money she had on a glass of port and some herbs to bring him back to life. He remained for ever in her debt, but could never repay her because eventually he lost contact with her in the labyrinth of London's streets. This broken bond was to remain a spiritual wound for the rest of his life. He expresses this lasting feeling of gratitude and guilt in a long and convoluted sentence that begins with an emotional "Oh! youthful benefactress!" and ends with the wish that just as the curse of the father strikes the son, so exceptionally should the blessing of a grateful heart have the power to find the benefactress and reward her for her kindness:

> I wished that [...] the benediction of a heart oppressed with gratitude [...] might have power given to it from above to chace – to haunt – to way-lay – to overtake – to pursue thee into the central darkness of a London brothel, or (if it were possible) into the darkness of the grave – there to awaken thee with an authentic message of peace and forgiveness, and of final reconciliation! (22)

The syntax of this sentence, with its lists, parentheses, corrections and insertions expresses something of the **hopelessness** attached to De Quincey's quest. His gratitude cannot reach the addressee, for he does not even know where he should send it, to someone alive or dead, to a brothel or a grave. The desire for a reunion and for reconciliation is as profound as the pain of losing her. This pain consists above all in the fact that life, unlike novels, brings about separation and loss, and that in the labyrinth of the city there is no coherence, no logic, but only chance, meaninglessness, and the law of "perplexities".

How did this loss happen? When lack of money forced De Quincey to make a journey from London to Eton, he had to leave Ann for a week. From his point of view, the parting was full of hope, and from hers full of tears. They arranged to

16 De Quincey (2008).

meet on his return. The time was to be 6 pm after the fifth day of their separation and each subsequent day; the place, the end of Great Titchfield Street, so that they could avoid what he called "The great Mediterranean of Oxford Street" (27). One thing, however, he had overlooked: he never knew his companion's family name. On his return, he was unable to find her. She did not come to the agreed meeting-place, and although he searched for weeks and months, it was all in vain. Looking for a familiar face in the anonymous masses of the city **without a name and address** is as hopeless an enterprise as finding the proverbial needle in the haystack. He imagined that at some time he might have come close to her:

> If she lived, doubtless we must have been sometimes in search of each other, at the very same moment, through the mighty labyrinths of London; perhaps, even within a few feet of each other – a barrier no wider in a London street, often amounting in the end to a separation for eternity! (34)[17]

De Quincey begins the second half of his *Confessions* with an emotional farewell to London: "So then, Oxford-street, stony-hearted stepmother! thou that listenest to the sighs of orphans, and drinkest the tears of children, at length I was dismissed from thee." (34)

Like Yeats, who later in the midst of the hubbub of modern London had the epiphany of a very different pastoral life in the Arran Isles – "I will arise and go now, and go to Innisfree" runs the first line of his famous poem[18] – De Quincey envisioned **a pastoral life in the north**. The north-west passage which was his route home after his nightly wanderings was also the compass that directed his yearnings. From Oxford Street, in the heart of the stone desert, he used to raise his eyes along the rows of houses, gazing towards the north and promising himself in the tone of a psalmist: "that is the road to the north, and therefore to – [the blank was Grasmere, Wordsworth's home, A. A.] – And if I had the wings of a dove, *that* way I would fly for comfort." (35)

De Quincey ultimately married a farmer's daughter, and spent the rest of his life in close proximity to his friends Wordsworth and Coleridge. But the dark images of London and the unresolved events that had taken place never ceased to haunt him. Many years later, he travelled to London and on the way spent the night in a hotel, but even before he arrived, the city posed a terrible threat: "now rose London – sole, dark, infinite – brooding over the whole capacities of my heart."[19] In his dream, it took on the form of an "unfathomed abyss [...] into which I was now so wilfully precipitating myself." (346 f) London, the scene of his youthful escapades, aberrations and deprivations, stayed with him into old age. At the centre of his nightmares was the face of the lost prostitute Ann, always remind-

17 On the importance of the face in literature, cf. Von Matt (1983).
18 Yeats (1999a).
19 De Quincey (1897), 346.

ing him of the fleeting, fragmentary and ultimately futile character of his life, which may well have been the driving force that made him write his confessions.

5.1.2 The anonymous crowd in the city – John Gay, Edgar Allan Poe and Virginia Woolf

The romantic nature of De Quincey's London only becomes apparent when one compares his descriptions to earlier and later examples. A hundred years before, in 1716, the English poet John Gay, on whose work Bertolt Brecht modelled his *Dreigroschenoper*, wrote a poem about London. He called it "Trivia; or, The Art of Walking the Streets of London". Trivia is the name of the goddess who is invoked as a muse at the beginning of this comic epic. The 'banality' implied by the name 'Trivia' conveys Gay's unheroic concept of everyday life in eighteenth-century London. The invocation of the muse, obligatory in the epic genre, is clearly a counter to Milton's invocation of the heavenly muse Urania at the beginning of the seventh book of *Paradise Lost*, in which she is to lead the blind poet through hell and heaven along paths that no man has ever trodden before. Gay's invocation reads as follows:

> Thou, Trivia, Goddess, aid my song,
> Thro' spacious streets conduct thy bard along;
> By thee transported, I securely stray
> Where winding alleys lead a doubtful way.
> The silent court and op'ning square explore,
> And long perplexing lanes untrod before.[20]

The confusing topography of the metropolis is described in words that we will later find in De Quincey. Unknown areas are "explored", and the writer finds himself in "perplexing lanes". Milton is not the only model for this didactic work, Virgil's *Georgics* may also be seen as a forerunner, though here the art to be learned is not agriculture but wandering through the streets of the city. This art, described in three epic books, begins with instructions concerning the correct equipment (suitable shoes, coat and cane), and the right way to tackle the various problems that will arise. One learns, for instance, what to do when caught in a shower, what to watch out for during the day and during the night, which people to avoid, which people to be polite to, what vehicles and what tradesmen one will encounter and what cries will emanate from the latter, which areas of the city to go to and which areas to steer clear of. The charm of the poem undoubtedly lies in the fact that everyday, trivial events are observed, described and amusingly cloaked in terms of epic mythology. However, the poem also shows that the city as a **"social laboratory"** has produced a new social formation, that of the **anonymous crowd**, to whom it is addressed: "O ye associate walkers" (157, Book II, 501). The countless people who are constantly on the move in this nar-

20 Gay (1974), 135 (Book I, 5–10).

row space must learn amid the hustle and bustle how to walk past without bumping into one another, a manoeuvre in which good manners are as important as various techniques of self-defence.

London is also the setting for Edgar Allan Poe's short story *A Man of the Crowd*.[21] In this tale, city life is perceived from the perspective of an **observer** watching the stream of passers-by through the window of a coffee-house. There is no order in this flood of people; in the narrowest of confines there is a mixture of all classes and professions – the whole social spectrum, from beggar to millionaire, from upright citizen to low-class felon, all pass by his window. The story consists of two parts. In the first, the observer's standpoint is fixed. From there he tries to 'read' the anonymous crowd, which he does to a degree with the aid of a catalogue of types that he develops along lines of class and social hierarchy. They are of no interest to him as individuals, but only as examples of particular groups and professions. He describes the superior class of office workers (upper clerks) as follows:

> They were known by their coats and pantaloons of black or brown, made to sit comfortably, with white cravats and waistcoats, broad solid-looking shoes, and thick hose or gaiters. – They all had slightly bald heads, from which the right ears, long used to pen-holding, had an odd habit of standing off on end. I observed that they always removed or settled their hats with both hands, and wore watches, with short gold chains of a substantial and ancient pattern. (216)

In the second half of the story, the narrator leaves his fixed vantage point and himself becomes part of the anonymous seething mass. His motive has now changed: there is one particular face which has set him an intriguing puzzle that he seeks to solve. He follows a scruffy old man, who is apparently wandering aimlessly through the streets, and he hopes somehow to garner a few clues about this person's character and history. However, none of the speculations and projections that have aroused his curiosity are either confirmed or corrected. After spending the whole night following the stranger, he must finally concede in his exhaustion that he has not come up with any information, direct or indirect, from which he might reconstruct the story of a man or a crime. The city and its passers-by remain anonymous, opaque and unreadable.

Poe's narrator is one of a type that became very popular in the nineteenth and early twentieth centuries – the **flâneur**. The city produced him as its observer who merges into the stream of passers-by. He is an idler, directed by no pragmatic needs or purposes, and whose attention is therefore freely available to focus on the city itself and its different forms of life. The *flâneur* is the figure in whom the life of the city becomes **self-reflexive.** There are also female *flâneuses*, for example in Virginia Woolf's short story *Street Haunting: A London Adventure* (1927). In this prose the narrator attaches herself to the "vast republican army of

21 Poe (1984).

anonymous trampers" who walk the streets of London day and night.[22] She feels an irresistible urge to get out of her room for a while and to join them. While the room is a home whose enclosing walls, utensils and memories allow her to take on a particular identity, the anonymous flood of walkers will allow her to dissolve this fixed identity for a time: "As we step out of the house on a fine evening between four and six we shed the self our friends know us by." (481) Woolf compares the conventions of identity to an oyster shell that can be temporarily opened, allowing its occupant to be nothing but an observer: "The shell-like covering which our souls have excreted to house themselves, to make for themselves a shape distinct from others, is broken, and there is left of all these wrinkles and roughness a central oyster of perceptiveness, an enormous eye." (481)

For Virginia Woolf, narrator of the stream of consciousness, strolling through the streets of London is a pleasant form of existence. The street is an image of modern life amid the confusing welter of diffuse sensual impressions which the observer perceives as a continuous wave. Her passivity is not unlike that of the cinema-goer. At the same time as Walter Benjamin and Franz Hessel,[23] Woolf wrote a precise description of *flânerie*, which we have already referred to in the chapter on 'Time':

> [W]e are only gliding smoothly on the surface. The eye is not a miner, not a diver, not a seeker after buried treasure. It floats us smoothly down a stream, resting, pausing, the brain sleeps perhaps as it looks. (482)

There follows a series of **visual impressions**, arranged according to values of light and shade, forms and fields of colour. The aesthetic view, which is made possible by an ecstatic departure from the self, changes the city into an Impressionist painting. However, the eye is also inquisitive, and so it rests on the sights and curiosities of the city, the eccentricities and deformities, capturing them in little narrative vignettes. Among the army of pedestrians, the self can break free from the constraints of its reality and for a moment slip into a variety of contradictory forms. By temporarily sacrificing its own identity, it can try out other identities. Through observing what goes on in the city, one can enjoy experiences similar to those one has when reading a novel, although unlike Poe, Woolf is not concerned with analytical deciphering but with **empathetic immersion**:

> Into each of these lives one could penetrate a little way, far enough to give oneself the illusion that one is not tethered to a single mind but can put on briefly for a few minutes the bodies and minds of others. One could become a washerwoman, a publican, a street singer. And what greater delight and wonder can there be than to leave the straight lines of personality and deviate into those footpaths that lead

22 Woolf (1994), 480. See also Woolf (1993). The text "Oxford Street Tide" was published in 1931 in the magazine *Good Housekeeping*, and is one of five short prose pieces under the collective title "The London Scene".

23 Benjamin (2002); Hessel (1984).

> beneath brambles and thick tree trunks into the heart of the forest where live those wild beasts, our fellow men?[24]

Like De Quincey, the narrator feels her way into the strangers of the city, sharing their joys and sorrows, as if they were characters in a novel. Still none of this lasts more than a few moments, because experiences here are not only anonymous, they are also **fleeting**. The *flâneuse* cannot hold fast to anything – she must rein back her fantasy, which always strives to penetrate into the depths. These are rules of conduct very different from those of John Gay, who had discovered the city as a new social space, and formulated the rules of human interaction. In De Quincey's city, the collective social space was already taken up with the biography of an individual self, who filled the whole town and found it to be a mirror of his own mind and soul. Virginia Woolf radicalizes this **subjectivity** even further, but she also deliberately cuts the biographical threads of identity and concentrates on the self purely as an observer.

The differences between the city texts we have looked at can best be summarized as follows: John Gay describes the city as a new, anonymous social space in which one must learn to be considerate and to allow others to pass unhindered; De Quincey sees it as the setting for a deep and lasting autobiographical episode; for Poe and Woolf, it has lost its quality as a romantic space of experience, and has become in parts an opaque, modern space of perception.

5.2 Centre and periphery – Frederick Jackson Turner and Joseph Conrad

5.2.1 Colonization, conquest, colonialism

Centre and periphery are **relational concepts**. The one is inconceivable without the other. Each is defined by the polarity of the other, and changes its meaning according to shifts or changes in the other. The meaning of these two terms also changes according to whether we are speaking of colonization, conquest or colonialism.

In the context of **colonization**, periphery is something which initially lies out of range but through particular cultural techniques can be brought within the ruling grasp of the centre. Colonization entails uninhabited or uninhabitable regions being made habitable by draining swamps, irrigating deserts, or cultivating plains. One can talk of colonization wherever a territory is expanded with the **spade** (as opposed to the sword) – where the acquisition or reclamation of land is not accompanied by the expulsion of its original inhabitants. The shaping and preserving of peripheral areas as human living space requires constant work and attention.

24 Woolf (1994), 690 f.

The **sword** is by far the most common means of gaining and occupying peripheral space. **Conquest** is the violent subjection of the original inhabitants, to either being forced to leave their land, exterminated, or allowed to stay on but with no powers of their own. The history of Europe and North America is one of violent expansion by the strong at the expense of the weak. Imperialism can be defined as a mixture of colonization and conquest. A typical example was how, between the seventeenth century and the late nineteenth, settlers with spades and guns kept shifting the boundaries further and further west to extend the territory under American rule. Along this **'frontier',** wilderness is tamed by civilization, and the original contrast between centre and periphery is dissolved. Imperial territorial expansion through conquest is still going on even today, with the continuous absorption of marginal zones that are made part of a homogeneous whole. Once they have all been arranged to fit in with an overall political organization and bureaucracy, the initial distinction between centre and periphery loses its meaning.

On the other hand, the hierarchical structure of centre and periphery is absolutely essential and also permanent for **colonialism**, through which colonies are formed by a central motherland whose authority radiates into spatial distance, with one state owning and governing people of a different language and culture. The relation between master and servant takes on a special quality here: "a whole society is robbed of its own historical evolution, governed by strangers, and converted to serve the – mainly economic – needs and interests of its colonial masters."[25] The geographical distance between centre and periphery remains inherent to the structure, with the former evaluated as **culturally superior** to the latter. The centre legitimizes its power over the periphery not only through this cultural superiority but also through the 'backwardness' of the natives, which gives rise to a civilizing mission, or "missionary doctrines of ideological justification"[26].

The colonial relationship between centre and periphery arises from the combination of two interacting perspectives. It functions in much the same way as the master-servant relationship: without each of the opposite parties recognizing one another's position, one cannot talk meaningfully about either. Masters must be acknowledged by servants, centres by peripheries, and the seat of power by all those under its authority. Centres that have no chance of symbolic recognition, of normative influence, or of commanding obedience are hollow and unlikely to last long. This already tells us that there are several, sometimes very different factors that make centres into centres and peripheries into peripheries. The former have four basic, closely interwoven attributes: physical force, eco-

25 Osterhammel (2003), 19.

26 Osterhammel (2003), 21. According to Osterhammel, one of the characteristics of the colonial state is "that generally an unbridgeable cultural gap opened up between the rulers and the ruled." (64)

nomic superiority, normative power, and symbolic authority. If these four are separated, the result is a crisis of legitimation and a weakening of the relational structure.

Historical research shows that there have never been any centres that have been able to indefinitely maintain their position unopposed. An essential driving force of history consists in the very fact that centres are constantly being overthrown or displaced, so that they become peripheries and vice versa. One example is the geo-cultural centrality of Europe with its symbolic centre of a first and second Rome. The existence of the second, easterly Rome, named Byzantium and later Constantinople, already demonstrates that any centre with aspirations to permanence and power will always be challenged and restricted by opposing aspirations. The everlasting centre or hub of the world (*omphalos*) exists only as a mythical **phantasm**, and is inherent in all claims to permanent centrality. The two texts that we are now going to look at illustrate the theme of power and space, in the one case with respect to mythologizing, and in the other in the sense of demythologizing. Our first example is by F. J. Turner, inventor of the American myth of space, and our second is Joseph Conrad's critical analysis of the Empire.

5.2.2 Border and threshold – Frederick Jackson Turner's myth of the 'frontier'

The creator of the **American myth** of the frontier was the historian Frederick Jackson Turner. When he wrote his influential study, the phenomenon he was describing had just come to an end. In 1890 the United States Census Bureau issued an official announcement that since 1880 the US no longer had a frontier line that could be extended further west through colonization and settlement ("westward movement").[27] Turner regarded this piece of bureaucracy as a key date in US history. Looking back, he did not – as one might have expected an historian to do – see the now ended 300-year history of the American settlers as a 'pre-history' heralding a new phase, but instead transformed it into a national myth that would transcend time. By myth we mean here that what has finished in history is not left behind but is endowed with **identity-forming importance** for the future. How, then, did Turner transform a chapter of American history into myth?

The answer is that he made the frontier itself into an agent which in turn transformed the pioneers into paradigmatic Americans. The movable western frontier, fought for and wrested from the wilderness and from the Native Americans, was, he said, a 'crucible' in which the many heterogeneous immigrants became mem-

27 Turner (1963), 27.

bers of a single, united nation. At the western frontier, civilization conquered the wilderness and overcame the resistance of the Native Americans, thereby establishing the essence of American history and nationhood:

> Up to our own day American history has been in a large degree the history of colonization of the Great West. The existence of an area of free land, its continuous recession, and the advance of American settlement westward, explain American development. (27)

This 300-year expansion, and not the War of Independence or the Civil War, was the fulcrum of American history and for him defined the nature of the American nation. "The frontier is the line of most rapid and effective Americanization" (29), he writes, and goes on to trace all the stages of this **national metamorphosis**. Initially, the colonizer is a man in European clothes, armed with European instruments, weapons, vehicles and ideas. At the frontier of civilization, this European is transformed into a Native American, whose clothes, tools and survival skills he copies in order to adapt to the environment. After he has reshaped an area of the wilderness and made his mark on it, this former European is able to call it his own. At this point, though, the immigrant does not change back into his old European self, because what he has created is the new America, and so with this new America the colonizer mutates into the American. "Little by little he transforms the wilderness, but the outcome is not the old Europe [...]. The fact is that here is a new product that is American." (29) Turner wants to establish a national experience through which America can detach itself from its European roots and affirm its own separate identity. The territorial westward shift of the frontier was accompanied by a widening in the east of the cultural barrier between the USA and Europe. It was not only the acquisition of land but also the increasing distance from Europe that Turner regarded as "the really American part of our history". He adds: "Thus the advance of the frontier has meant a steady movement away from the influence of Europe, a steady growth of independence on American lines." (30). After the nation had fought for and won its independence, further forms of liberation had to follow. The westward expansion led to the **'essence of Americanism'**: "To the frontier the American intellect owes its striking characteristics." (57) By pinpointing this as the essence, he mythologizes unique, contingent historical experiences into permanent national qualities.

What is vital for Turner's concept of the frontier is that there is no fixed border but only a threshold which is there to be crossed, and it is this very **overstepping of borders** that Turner considers to be the essence of Americanism. The onward drive mobilizes specifically American reserves of energy. In the geopolitical sphere, colonial expansion may indeed have come up against a fixed frontier, but the essential impetus to move on can easily be transferred from space to time and the future: "He would be a rash prophet who should assert that the expansive character of American life has now entirely ceased. Movement has been its dominant fact, and [...] the American energy will continually demand a wider field for its exercise." (57) NASA's space programme in the 1950s and 1960s, the advance of science and technology, and also the spread of economic and political hegemony in a globalized world are all forms in which Turner's invention of a national character, so effectively adopted by the Americans themselves, has continued to manifest itself in the late twentieth and early twenty-first centuries.[28]

Part of this national character, as stylized by Turner, is a powerful orientation towards the future, accompanied by a denigration of the past: "Each frontier did indeed furnish a new field of opportunity, a gate of escape from the bondage of the past." (57) The European pre-history of the settlers is to be forgotten, but not the now ended colonization chapter of American history, written in the flesh and blood of the people, and which determined their national character, and gave them their sense of direction. Also to be forgotten are certain aspects of this history, which the American philosopher Ralph Waldo Emerson called "black events"[29] – the expulsion and slaughter of the Native Americans. Turner mentions them as being armed with modern weapons, which suggests a fair and even contest.[30] He describes the military project of expansion in terms of self-defence: "keeping alive the power of resistance to aggression" (38). There is no mention of confrontation, conquest, force – instead there is an image of **organic growth** which alone has enabled the land to come to life:

> Thus civilization in America has followed the arteries made by geology, pouring an ever richer tide through them, until at last the tender paths of aboriginal intercourse have been broadened and interwoven into the complex mazes of modern commercial lines; the wilderness has been interpenetrated by lines of civilization growing ever more numerous. It is like the steady growth of a complex nervous system for the originally simple, inert continent. (37)

The myth of the frontier, as Turner has constructed it, turns a heterogeneous collection of immigrants and of states into a **unit** which genuinely sees itself and feels itself to be a nation. "If one would understand why we are today one nation, rather than a collection of isolated states, he must study this economic and social consolidation of the country." (37) This is the self-portrait of America, of modernization, of white male dominance, and of the 'melting pot' that finally began to be questioned during the 1970s. Ultimately, it was something that grew from a nostalgic impulse. A new wave of immigration together with economic and social upheavals characterized the years between 1880 and 1920. As society then became increasingly heterogeneous and fragmented, it was no longer possible to maintain the concept of a monocultural American nation. To counter

28 In another essay, Turner himself broadens the scope: "In place of old frontiers of wilderness, there are new frontiers of unwon fields of science, fruitful for the needs of the race; there are frontiers of better social domains yet unexplored." Turner (1962), 300.

29 Emerson (1979).

30 Turner (1963).

such developments, there was a strong need for national and cultural unity. What was missing from reality had to be provided by myth.[31]

More than one hundred years later, Salman Rushdie refers directly to Turner's text in his essay "Step Across the Line". Rushdie, a habitual crosser of borders, discusses the general function and meaning of the border.[32] Based on anthropological statements he alludes to the fundamental meaning of border-crossing for human life and for narration: "In our deepest natures, we are frontier-crossing beings. We know this by the stories we tell ourselves." (350) He describes himself as a "migrant, the man without frontiers" (356), which for him is the archetype of our age. He argues that "the emergence, in the age of mass migration, mass displacement, globalized finances and industries, of this new, permeable post-frontier is the distinguishing feature of our times, and, to use Turner's phrase, explains our development as nothing else can." (365) Rushdie is convinced of this 'post-frontier' credo, although crossing national borders in many parts of the world remains for many an exhausting, insecure and highly dangerous act.

5.2.3 The crisis of the Empire – Joseph Conrad's *Heart of Darkness* (1902)

Conquests which restructure the hierarchy of power are a decisive precondition for the geopolitical redistribution of centre and periphery. However, it is not only the military confrontation that erodes the relationship – **crises of legitimation and of values** emanating from the centre itself can also lead to upheaval. The British Empire pursued its colonial policies both inside and outside Europe. Among the colonized European countries is Ireland, whose Catholic south achieved political independence in 1922. The Anglo-Irish dramatist Brian Friel is the author of a play entitled *Translations* (1980), in which he vividly depicts colonial practices by means of maps and the politics of language.

However, the text that we are now going to look at as an illustration of the colonial relationship between centre and periphery describes the situation of the colonizers outside Europe. Joseph Conrad's novel *Heart of Darkness*, written in 1899 and published in 1902, i.e. on the threshold of the new century and a new era, is regarded as a landmark of world literature and is almost uniquely suited to a discussion of basic questions concerning centre and periphery.

Conrad came from a Polish family in Russian-dominated Ukraine. His parents were self-proclaimed Polish patriots whom the Russian occupying forces exiled to the northernmost province of Vologda. As a result of the strains and stresses and deprivations of life there, they both died young, leaving their 11-year-old son an orphan. From this extreme edge of the periphery, the boy gradually worked his way back into a new centre. He spent many years at sea, and forged a career

31 Binder (1993); Goldberg (1994); Ostendorf (1983); Sollers (1986).
32 Rushdie (2002).

for himself in the British merchant navy. In 1886, at the age of 30, he became a naturalized British citizen, and so had now arrived at the centre of the worldwide colonial power known as the British Empire. His books reflect the glories of this empire as well as its **loss of legitimacy**, bound up with profound self-doubt and a crisis of identity as seen by the **frontier crosser** Józef Teodor Konrad Korzeniowski.

Heart of Darkness begins on an anchored ship at sunset. On board is a small crew of men, and a mood of contemplative melancholy spreads over them. Then one member of the crew tells them the long story that is to become the content of the book. The scene of his tale is the Thames, described as the "beginning of an interminable waterway" which leads "to the uttermost ends of the earth".[33] For the sailors, the **Thames** as the portal to this worldwide waterway becomes a central symbol of the colonial project that began with the merchant adventurers of the sixteenth and seventeenth centuries. The national heroes are recalled as 'knights of the sea' together with the names of their ships:

> Hunters for gold or pursuers of fame, they all had gone out on that stream, bearing the sword, and often the torch, messengers of the might within the land, bearers of spark from the sacred fire. What greatness had not floated on the ebb of that river into the mystery of an unknown earth! ... The dreams of men, the seed of commonwealths, the germs of empires. (19)

The narrator breaks into this reverently heroic memory with a sentence that suddenly throws into question the coordinates of history and geography: "'And this also,' said Marlow suddenly, 'has been one of the dark places of the earth.'" (19)

No-one contradicts him, because they are used to his paradoxes, and then he explains his viewpoint to his silent listeners. He makes it clear to them that no historic moment has the potential for permanence, and all historic achievements are as fleeting as the lightning in the sky: "We live in the flicker – may it last as long as the old earth keeps rolling! But darkness was here yesterday." (20) This vision, encompassing thousands of years, brings together all the extremes. The torch of British colonialism has not shone for ever, and so at this melancholy sunset hour we may assume with Marlow that it will not continue to shine for ever. In his imagination, he can see the Roman commander who was once ordered to go to the darkest province in the north. What today is central was then on the outermost periphery:

> [T]he very end of the world, a sea the colour of lead, a sky the colour of smoke [...] precious little to eat fit for a civilized man, nothing but Thames water to drink. [...] Here and there a military camp lost in a wilderness, like a needle in a bundle of hay – cold, fog, tempests, disease, exile, and death – death skulking in the air, in the water, in the bush. (20)

33 Conrad (1996), 17.

Unexpectedly, the heroic memory with its shining names and its talk of honour and fame gives way to a different history. Now the narrator invokes the other, dark side of the colonial project, with terms like 'death', 'savagery', 'wilderness', 'jungles', 'mysteries', and 'the fascination of the abomination'. This is the side that remains hidden from language and consciousness. Just as you must not describe to soldiers the physical pain, the probability that they will die and the futility of the whole enterprise when you send them into battle and wish to keep their morale high, so too must those who are engaged in the colonial project be kept unaware of the dark and demoralizing abyss ahead of them if they are to fulfil their mission. However, that is exactly what Marlow does with his story this evening as the sun sets over Gravesend; author and narrator create a hiatus during which, under sheltered conditions, that which must normally be excluded from the social framework of communication can exceptionally be given expression. Herein lies the privileged role of literature: it can create spaces for the articulation of things which must otherwise remain below the threshold of consciousness and beyond the range of social intercourse.

In Marlow's imaginary experiment, centre and periphery change places: the ship on the Thames, where at sunset a group of men agree to go on an adventure of story-telling, is described as the centre of the world, from where since the dawn of the modern age all waterways have begun their journey to the uttermost ends of the earth, and to which flow back all the proceeds of those journeys. Even so, this centre was itself once the remotest periphery, to which at one time a few brave men had to travel, facing doubts and dangers similar to those confronting the seafarers of today. The colonial project of the British, however, is in one particular way quite different from the Romans' project of conquest. The Romans brought nothing but the sword, whereas the British bore both **sword** and **torch**.

> The conquest of the earth, which mostly means the taking it away from those who have a different complexion or slightly flatter noses than ourselves, is not a pretty thing when you look into it too much. What redeems it is the idea only. An idea at the back of it; not a sentimental pretence but an idea; and an unselfish belief in the idea – something you can set up, and bow down before, and offer a sacrifice to ... (21)

To be precise, there are two things that distinguish the British from the Romans: devotion to the 'principle of effectiveness' and devotion to a meaningful idea which sanctifies the project and justifies total commitment even to the point of sacrificing one's own life.

Marlow's differentiation between (Roman) conquest and (British) colonialism can also be seen as a criticism of Belgian colonial rule as it was practised in the Congo, as well as being a defence of the British system. In its explicitness, however, this defence goes far beyond everything that serves for legitimation. The sword, whose sole purpose is to carve out an expansion of power, must be accompanied – as had been the case ever since the crusades – by the torch of an enlightening religious or civilizing mission that will justify the project in one's own eyes as well as in those of others. Laying bare the fabric of this **rhetorical legitimation** is the first step towards undermining its foundations; the second step is to demonstrate the impracticability, futility and absurdity of the colonial project itself. Conrad endows his narrator with a cynical view of the world, which is devoid of all the rhetoric of honour and meaning. The devastating insights of his vision, which he has acquired at the periphery of the Empire, are what he brings back in place of material goods to the centre. Thus almost subversively the spark of missionary light turns into depressing darkness, which spreads wider and wider as the tale unfolds.

The question of centre and periphery is also given expression in the narrator's description of his aims, which reflect Conrad's own autobiographical reminiscences. He tells his listeners that as a boy he would spend hours dreaming over maps on which there were still many **white areas**. South America, Africa and Australia were places that had an irresistible attraction for him. All of them held out the shining promise of heroic exploration of the unknown, with the prospect of a potential contribution to the progress of human knowledge. As he grew older, however, the white spots on the map disappeared one after the other, to be replaced with a network of rivers and place names. This also applied to the Belgian Congo, the last and biggest of the white spots. The mystery of this place had by no means disappeared for him – it had only changed its nature: in Conrad's tale, the white mark of the unknown gradually changes into the black mark of that which cannot be colonized, the failure of western rationality, the triumph of wilderness over will.

The journey from the centre to the furthest periphery, as described in Conrad's novel, is measurable not only in spatial coordinates; it is also a journey along the axis of time, from the present back into an unknown prehistoric world. In the middle of the nineteenth century, Darwin's Theory of Evolution had had its impact on modern man's complacent myth of human progress, offering him instead an image of himself as not just genetically related to apes but also continuing this relationship in the form of certain rudimentary shared characteristics. From here it was only a small step to a theory of **atavism**, which stated that the pre-civilization beginnings of humankind had never been fully overcome, and the way back to these origins always remained open. Marlow describes his expedition as a journey through both space and time back into the darkness of primeval times:

> Going up that river was like travelling back to the earliest beginnings of the world, when vegetation rioted on the earth and the big trees were kings. An empty stream, a great silence, an impenetrable forest. [...] We penetrated deeper and deeper into the heart of darkness. [...] We were wanderers on a prehistoric earth, on an earth that wore the aspect of an unknown planet. [...] The prehistoric man was cursing us, praying to us, welcoming us – who could tell? We were cut off from the comprehension of our surroundings [...] We could not understand because we

> were too far and could not remember, because we were travelling in the night of first ages, of those ages that are gone, leaving hardly a sign – and no memories. (49 ff)

The black natives are not the embodiment of the culturally unfamiliar, but they represent an **early stage of humanity**, the distant ancestors of Marlow's own evolution and of an earlier state which he senses he can never completely get away from. What has therefore shocked him most deeply is the fact that he cannot dismiss these black people as representatives of a different species. For all their savage strangeness, there is one thing they are not: "Well, you know, that was the worst of it – this suspicion of their not being inhuman. [...] They howled and leaped, and spun, and made horrid faces; but what thrilled you was just the thought of their humanity – like yours – the thought of your remote kinship with this wild and passionate uproar." (51) For the modern traveller, their language is incomprehensible not because it is exotic and culturally alien, but because it is a lost, pre-conscious, preliminary stage of his own. It is a shock to see that one cannot draw a line here to protect one's own identity, but that this strangeness must be acknowledged as an integral element of that identity, even though one has no direct communicative access to it. There are no memories that go back to this primeval time, and so it is the innermost depths of the colonizer, his own origins, that lie in darkness and remain the subject of an insoluble mystery.

The journey through space and time into the heart of darkness is also a penetrating exploration of the human soul and the dark regions deep within it. One might describe this self-examination and self-confrontation as a **project of inner colonization**, in which – as with Conrad's contemporary Sigmund Freud – the periphery is to be brought out of the shadows of forgetfulness and suppression, and placed at the centre of consciousness. Freud saw this as a project of enlightenment; he spoke of 'progress in intellectuality', and compared it to the reclamation of land, for instance the polders of the Zuider Zee in the Netherlands. But in Conrad there is no such enlightening perspective. The mood of the narrator is not one of heroism but of disenchantment and a cynical disillusionment. In Conrad's image of man, the alien self which St George, the mythical colonizer of England (or Russia), overcame in the form of the dragon, can no longer be pushed aside, externalized and demonized. For modern man these old myths now take on a new and immediate dimension: "We are accustomed to look upon the shackled form of a conquered monster, but there – there you could look at a thing monstrous and free." (51) The project of inner colonization consists in recognizing this alien element as part of oneself and so creating a new relationship between the periphery and the centre. With Conrad, the uncompromising commandment of 'Know thyself!' leads to the unflattering awareness that there are regions of the human soul that respond to the primeval screams which Marlow hears all around him. Although, as we have already noted, there is no bridge of communication or memory to take one back into these basic strata of human existence, nevertheless there are mysterious reflections and echoes – rudimentary traces that make their presence felt independently of one's conscious mind and one's normative self-image:

> [I]f you were man enough you would admit to yourself that there was in you just the faintest trace of a response to the terrible frankness of that noise, a dim suspicion of there being a meaning to it which you – you so remote from the night of first ages – could comprehend. And why not? The mind of man is capable of anything – because everything is in it, all the past as well as all the future. (51 f)

"The disintegration of great orders has as a consequence not only the fact that the margins come to life and look into different worlds, but it also implies that old-established forms are shattered from within", writes Bernhard Waldenfels in his book *Der Stachel des Fremden*[34] [The Sting of the Unfamiliar]. This description fits in very well with the developments that took place in the period between Conrad and the postcolonial present. "Things fall apart; the centre cannot hold", as we learn from a famous poem by the Irish poet W. B. Yeats, a contemporary of Conrad's.[35] The first three words of this line were used by the Nigerian writer Chinua Achebe as the title of a novel.[36] Yeats' line describes from the central perspective the decline of a metaphysical order and the threat of chaos and anarchy. From the perspective of the modern African writer, however, the words take on a positive meaning, as they refer to the process of **decolonization** which, after the Second World War, saw the former British colonies unshackled from the motherland and awarded their longed-for political independence and cultural self-determination. Achebe is also the author who, from the perspective of one who had been colonized, wrote a scathing critique of *Heart of Darkness*, in which he accuses Conrad of racism and questions the literary value of the novel. "**The Empire writes back** with a vengeance" – Rushdie's aphorism chimes in perfectly with the tone of Achebe's revenge on the now canonical Conrad.[37]

"Things fall apart; the centre cannot hold" – the words already apply, of course, to Conrad's pitiless analysis of the British Empire at the turn of the twentieth century. His novel is a relentless account of the erosion of British colonialism from its margins inwards. He gives its full medical history, going right through the evolution and vision of the colonial project, and concluding with its profoundly disillusioning futility. The periphery initially exerts a deep fascination on the narrator, but in this anti-*bildungsroman*, as his journey of initiation into the depths of the human soul gathers pace, the fascination dissolves into repulsion. The periphery is revalued: at first it is an area of secrets waiting to be discovered, but then it turns into a region of the soul which, if confronted and acknowledged, brings only depression and moral apathy.

34 Waldenfels (1990), 257.
35 Yeats (1999b).
36 Achebe (1973).
37 Achebe (1977, 1988); Rushdie (1982).

5.3 The mythical landscape – Leslie Marmon Silko's *Ceremony* (1977)

So far we have used the term *space* to denote geographical and political regions which have been marked out by natural and artificial boundaries, and whose area is represented on maps. Space as territory is the subject of national, colonial and geopolitical discourse, in the context of war, planning, construction, administration, trade. **Places**, however, are always individualized by their names and their histories. They are associated with real-life experiences, the senses, and the memory. We shall now extend this contrast through a third category which is important for intercultural comparisons. Along with 'space' and 'place', there is also **'land'**. Our literary example for this concept will take us away from the western sphere of culture: it is the novel *Ceremony* by the female Native American writer Leslie Marmon Silko.[38] The novel represents a cultural movement in the USA which in post-industrial society develops a new approach to space, its essence being drawn from the spiritual dimension of the land in Native American tradition.[39] Voices which have long been condemned to silence now articulate new perspectives and values. Native American literature has taken up elements of tribal cultures that had been broken up or suppressed by the white settlers and which F. J. Turner knew nothing about. The fact that the pioneers of the western frontier took the land away from the natives had long fallen victim to a collective amnesia, and it returned only gradually to America's cultural memory. Through the tabula rasa of the mythical wilderness, the conquest of which marked the beginnings of American culture, the traditions of old local cultures now began to shine through. Over the last few decades, the **voices of the victims** have once more been heard in discourses on space, and as a result there has been a profound change in the American identity and its cultural values. This process is one of increasing attentiveness, expansion of the memory, and a new sensitivity towards the 'periphery'.

Silko's novel *Ceremony* has played an important part in this new awareness; its key term is neither space nor place, but 'land'. The specific meaning of this common word will not be immediately apparent to readers brought up in western cultures, for it requires long and deep immersion in Native American myths, rit-

38 Silko (1977).

39 The dialectical connection between exclusion and 'back to Nature' has been analysed by Heinz Tschachler (1990). He draws a revealing comparison between the ways in which the subject of space is handled by American and Canadian authors, whose work he discusses together with Silko's novel, which also stems from the 1970s. In the tradition of White America, depicted by Charles Reich in *The Greening of America* (1995), space is associated with Nature and Nature with Utopia, but since Utopia plays scarcely any part in the postmodern age, the way becomes clear for a new hedonism. See Schmitt (1969), Turner (1963).

uals and imagery. In western cultural language, land is governed, bought, developed; in Silko's novel one not only lives on the land, but also from it and with it; the land is, in a certain sense, the most important protagonist in the book.[40] It is evoked in sensual images, mythical tales, and cosmic meditations. In cultures without writing, the land takes on the meaning of a 'sacred text', or rather a **'mythical matrix'**. It is inhabited by gods, spirits, ancestors, and it is filled with traces of their appearances, powers, actions and histories.[41]

The novel describes the difficult and roundabout spiritual healing process undergone by a traumatized veteran of the Second World War. The main character Tayo is an illegitimate son of mixed ethnicity, his mother being a Navaho and his father a white man. The most important stage in Tayo's 'cure' is his reconnection with the land. At one and the same time the process is therapeutic, educational and initiatory, and it entails the search for and discovery of an identity, which in turn means the search for **roots** and for lost traditional bonds. Reconnecting with these roots requires a radical change of values – a complete break from those of the white man which his comrades – also young soldiers from the Navaho reservation – have adopted as their own. Their pent-up resentment is reinforced by alcohol:

> "You know," he said, slurring the words, "us Indians deserve something better than this goddam dried-up country around here. Blowing away, every day. [...] What we need is what they got. I'll take San Diego. [...] We fought their war for them. [...] But they've got everything. And we don't got shit, do we? Huh? [...] They took our land, they took everything! So let's get our hands on white women!"[42]

As the drunken group applauds enthusiastically, Tayo's eyes fall on the label of a beer bottle depicting a sparkling spring with the caption: "COORS BEER brewed from pure Rocky Mountain spring water, Adolph Coors, Co., Golden, Colorado." (55 f) He has never seen such a large spring, and it makes him wonder: "Maybe

---

40 Nelson (1993), who analyses three Native American novels, comes to the conclusion that the geophysical landscapes "serve not only as the 'settings' of these fictions but also as principal 'characters' in them." (8) Garcia (1983) writes: "In *Ceremony* the feeling of being at home and of belonging to the land realized by Tayo derives from a special sense of place that is also participation in culture and community" (40). Silko wrote her Laguna novel – like Joyce and his *Dubliners* – a long way from the place itself, and again like Joyce was trying to recreate it. "When I was writing *Ceremony* I was so terribly devastated by being away from the Laguna country that the writing was my way of re-making that place, the Laguna country, for myself." Silko/Wright (1986), 27 f.

41 The close connection between land and myth exists in many oral cultures. In *Songlines* (1988) Bruce Chatwin describes Australia from the perspective of the Aboriginals as a mythical landscape and a cultural text.

42 Silko (1977), 55.

Emo was wrong: maybe white people didn't have everything. Only Indians had droughts." (56)

Laguna, the reservation on the Mexican border with Arizona, is plagued with droughts. It is a fact that the distribution of fertile land for the whites and parched desert for the Indians is hugely unfair. But the novel shows that this way of looking at the problem cannot lead to its solution, because it is fed by white greed which makes a fair evaluation of the land impossible. Step by step, Silko breaks down the polarized thinking that creates unbridgeable gaps between whites and Native Americans, old and new, tradition and modernity, 'us' and 'them'. **Dichotomous thinking** inevitably leads to a sharpening of distinctions, hatred and aggression; it is part of a malignant process which is referred to in the novel as 'witchery' – a mechanism that leads ultimately to total destruction.

Tayo is led away from these destructive contrasts by 'tricksters'. These are **frontier-crossers** between ethnic groups, cultures and different areas of existence, and they embody the principle of 'as well as'. The task of bringing back a herd of particularly resistant spotted cattle, of helping them survive the dry season, and of letting them follow their own instincts regardless of fences and barriers, assumes symbolic significance for Tayo. It takes him to a hill in the north of the reservation, "where there was no sign the white people had ever come to this land" (184). There he discovers something that transcends dryness or fertility, and that is the living quality of the land – alive with animals, feelings and above all stories. Reclaiming the land is not a political or economic project, but especially a **mythical quest**. For Tayo and for the reader the task is to reclaim Indian history, the stories that are rooted in the land, and also to recognize that each individual life is part of those mythical tales and songs that run through the novel itself. This is reflected in the form of the book, which is not divided into the usual chapters, but is held together by a web of interspersed Native American traditions.

There are other ways of resuming cultural contact with the land besides going to places untouched by the white man. This is demonstrated by one of the 'tricksters', the medicine man Old Betonie, who lives and practises his shamanism on the outskirts of a wretched town, where he looks out over a rubbish tip.

> "People ask me why I live here," he said, in good English, "I tell them I want to keep track of the people. [...] They keep us on the north side of the railroad tracks, next to the river and their dump. Where none of them want to live. [...] It strikes me funny," the medicine man said, shaking his head, "people wondering why I live so close to this filthy town. But see, this hogan was here first. Built long before the white people ever came. It is that town down there which is out of place. Not this old medicine man." (117 f)

The novel shows that the healing process is not just a matter of practical action – cattle droving instead of soldiering, or the ritual ceremony with its open ending – but also of changing one's perspective. The new perspective develops in proportion to the degree in which the war-traumatized soul is gradually overwritten by the **cultural memory** of the Navaho. Reconnection with the land, which is filled with mythical stories, also entails building up an identity through reconnection with a cultural memory. This enables the old, self-destructive resentments that had been fed by feelings of inferiority to be replaced by a new, or more accurately an old superiority. Betonie, the medicine man, may well laugh:

> "They don't understand. We know these hills, and we are comfortable here." There was something about the way the old man said the word "comfortable". It had a different meaning – not the comfort of big houses or rich food or even clean streets, but the comfort of belonging with the land, and the peace of being with these hills. (117)

The theme of this novel, though, is not so much a change as an expansion of perspective. The most important requirement is the ability to cross the boundaries that restrict human life, whether spatial, ethnic, cultural or linguistic. Like Silko herself, Tayo has Indian, Mexican and white ancestors. Such border-crossing people are especially well equipped to expand their perspective, opening up new contexts and connections. Thus Tayo's personal war trauma cannot be treated without reference to other **traumas**; family, historical and not least cosmic. The latter has been set off by the dropping of the first atomic bomb, which was developed in this region. The blinding flash of the first nuclear test seared its way deep into the bones of the Indian inhabitants. Suddenly, because of the bomb, the total destruction of the Earth and everyone on it became a real technical possibility. With this peak of destructive power, cultural distinctions disappeared and the whole **human family** emerged as a single species threatened with extinction. The destructiveness of the ever-expanding mechanism of 'witchery' must be matched in scale by the all-embracing therapy of the 'ceremony'. I shall end this chapter with a passage from Silko's novel which gives vivid expression to this inclusive perspective, bridging the differences and rediscovering the human family as revealed in the light of its destructibility:

> Trinity Site, where they exploded the first atomic bomb, was only three hundred miles to the southeast, at White Sands. And the top-secret laboratories where the bomb had been created were deep in the Jemez Mountains, on land the Government took from Cochiti Pueblo: Los Alamos, only a hundred miles northeast of him now, still surrounded by electric fences and the ponderosa pine and tawny sandrock of the Jemez mountain canyon where the shrine of the twin mountain lions had always been. There was no end to it; it knew no boundaries; and he had arrived at the point of convergence where the fate of all living things, and even the earth, had been laid. [...] From that time on, human beings were one clan again, united by the fate the destroyers planned for all of them, for all living things; united by a circle of death that devoured people in cities twelve thousand miles away, victims who had never known these mesas, who had never seen the delicate colors of the rocks which boiled up their slaughter. [...] He cried the relief he felt at finally seeing the pattern, the way all the stories fit together – the old stories, the war stories, their stories – to become the story that was still being told. (246)

Summary

With the 'spatial turn' of the postmodern age, space has assumed the same degree of significance as time in the modern age. Against the background of globalization, the individual identity of places ('glocalization') has become increasingly important, while at the same time the opening up of geographical spaces has been accompanied by that of new virtual spaces.

The basic categories of spatial perception are anthropological, and their starting point is the human body. Above and below, in front and behind, right and left are universal spatial metaphors that help to structure our ways of thinking. Like time, space is by no means a purely mental coordinate, but is also both a precondition and a product of social, political and cultural activity. In addition to distinguishing between 'space' (as the subject of conquest, planning, colonization), 'place' (as a crystallization of history and memory), and 'land' (as a mystic foundation for life), there is also interstitial space, in which fixed attributes intersect or dissolve.

Exemplary literary places are illustrated through various texts. London, the great 19th-century metropolis and hub of the British Empire, with its labyrinthine topography, is described by the romantic *flâneur* De Quincey as a 'wilderness' and 'terra incognita'. His portrait of the city is quite different from those of earlier and later authors: John Gay sees it as a modern, anonymous social space in which people must learn to be considerate towards one another and to allow one another to pass by unhindered; for Poe and Woolf, it has lost its quality as a romantic space of experience, and is now a sometimes impermeable space of perception.

The dialectic of centre and periphery forms the focal point of two more texts. One deals with the expansion of American frontiers towards the west. During this process, in which the wilderness is transformed into civilization, heterogeneous immigrants are also transformed into a unified American nation. A journey from the Thames as centre to the African jungle as periphery is traced in Conrad's *Heart of Darkness*, not simply as a matter of spatial coordinates but also as a voyage through time into the prehistory of the human soul.

In memory cultures without writing, the land takes on the significance of a 'sacred text': mountains, rivers, springs and trees are all crystallized settings – 'landmarks' of mythical narratives which establish contact between the inhabitants and their gods, and which become fixed points of reference for their traditions. Cultural identity is only possible through the adoption and absorption of this predominantly female narrative tradition. In Leslie Silko's novel *Ceremony*, the search for individual identity is also a search for the land and for the roots of buried and forgotten traditions.

Select bibliography

Bakhtin, Michail (1981) "Forms of Time and of the Chronotope in the Novel". In: *The Dialogic Imagination. Four Essays.* Ed. Michael Holquist. Austin (et al.): Texas UP, 84–258.

Baucom, Ian (2005) *Specters of the Atlantic.* Durham/London: Duke UP.

Hubbard, Phil/Kitchin, Rob (2011) *Key Thinkers on Space and Place.* 2nd ed. London: Sage.

Low, Setha M./Lawrence-Zunigais, Denise, eds. (2003) *The Anthropology of Space and Place: Locating Culture.* Malden/Oxford: Blackwell.

Sarkowsky, Katja (2007) *AlterNative spaces: Constructions of Space in Native American and First Nations' literatures.* Heidelberg: Winter.

Warf, Barney, ed. (2009) *The Spatial Turn. Interdisciplinary Perspectives.* London (et al.): Routledge.

6. MEMORY

In recent years, memory has become a major new area of cultural studies, and indeed is now a **paradigm** that links up with a wide **variety of disciplines**. Each one of these approaches it from a different angle and defines it in different ways. *Neurologists* study the neuronal basis, which is so to speak the hardware of the memory in the context of the living organism. *Psychologists* look into the cognitive and emotional thought processes of individuals in concrete, real-life situations. *Psychoanalysts* and *psychotherapists* try to stimulate memory processes in order to deal with people's personal problems. *Sociologists* are interested in communal memories and narratives within their social contexts, such as one finds in groups with a similar background of experience, or in intergenerational exchanges within families. *Historians* investigate the reliability or otherwise of human memory as captured by written sources, and in more recent times they have increasingly linked up with *political scientists* to study the ways in which societies (re-)construct their past in symbolic forms such as monuments and festivals, according to their present needs and current plans for the future. Scholars of *art* and *literature* have also joined in the discourse, their particular focus being the **'cultural memory'** that has built up a long-term cultural heritage through books and paintings, ideas and practices.

The list of activities on this vast building site of scientific study could easily be extended. The important thing to note is that each discipline tackles the subject differently, adding its own particular stone to the great mosaic. The subject of memory is also transdisciplinary in the sense that it transcends every individual approach and can only be studied in interlinking sections. This division of labour actually works very well, but what is not so easy to organize is a productive exchange of knowledge that goes beyond the boundaries of each discipline. Such an exchange has to begin with the realization that from each particular standpoint one can only grasp a part of the complexity, and so every discipline has to develop a sense for what has remained out of its focus and therefore requires information from other sources.

To begin with, we shall briefly survey the wide-ranging territory of cultural memory with the aid of a few basic conceptual distinctions, before illustrating different forms of memory by means of a literary text, Shakespeare's *Hamlet*.

6.1 Basic concepts of memory research

6.1.1 'Gedächtnis' and 'Erinnerung'

In German there are two words for 'memory' which are often used synonymously but can sometimes have virtually opposite meanings.[1] The noun *Erinnerung* is derived from the verb *erinnern* [to remember], whereas the verbal derivation of *Gedächtnis* (*denken* and *gedenken* [to think, to commemorate]) is not quite so obvious. When these words are contrasted with one another, *Erinnerung* generally means the process of looking back on past events, while *Gedächtnis* relates to the precondition for this activity, and is anchored in the brain and the nervous system. Without an organic memory (*Gedächtnis*) there can be no act of remembering (*Erinnerung*). And so *Gedächtnis* stands for the actual faculty (as in the expression 'a good/bad memory'), and *Erinnerung* relates to the concrete, discontinuous act of remembering (as in 'I have a clear/vague memory of such and such an event').

Gedächtnis, however, is not only a precondition for remembering but is also the product of and the collective term for memories that are collected and objectified as *Erinnerungen*. With this meaning, the word can be used metaphorically, in the same way as the word 'memory' is used in external data storage, which takes information out of its temporal context and stores it indefinitely. *Erinnerung*, on the other hand, is always embodied, i. e. bound to a living consciousness; it takes place only in the present and immediately disintegrates into fragments. It cannot be stored indefinitely, but must always be reproduced anew by means of repetition. The two forms are therefore also distinguished by their time structure. This point was particularly important to the philosopher Georg F. W. Hegel, who distinguished between *Gedächtnis*, as the sum of the once thought, expressed and dead (he used the dramatic image of the 'Golgotha of the mind'), and the liveliness, authenticity and inwardness of *Erinnerung*.

In English the word 'memory' has no equal partner, but the word covers a whole range of concepts: remembrance, recall, recollection, reminiscence, souvenir, commemoration and memorization. These words are by no means synonymous. The various meanings relate partly to distinctions between individual and collective memories, or between formal and informal acts of memory, and we shall return later to some of these distinctions. The lexical field is far from fixed, and it is constantly being extended particularly by literary neologisms. Two examples may suffice. In a long poem by the Irish poet Austin Clarke entitled 'Mnemosyne Lay in the Dust', the last verse reads:

---

1 Pethes/Ruchaz (2001). On the conceptualization of remembering and forgetting, see also Weinrich (1998).

> Rememorized, Maurice Devane
> Went out, his future in every vein,
> The Gate had opened.[2]

The gate is that of a psychiatric institution in which the fictional protagonist (like the poet himself) has spent a year, following a mental breakdown. He had lost his memory, identity and all his mental faculties, which had to be regained step by step in a laborious process which he describes as a 'rebirth'. Thus 're-memorized' in this case means having his memory and identity restored, so that he can return to life and also to a future. Another new creation is the word 're-memory' in the novel *Beloved* by the African-American author Toni Morrison; here the term denotes both the static recurrence of traumatic images and the need to renew these images by handing them down to succeeding generations. For Morrison there is not only the contrast between 'remembering' and 'forgetting', but also something in between, which describes the **status of the trauma**: "Disremembered and unaccounted for".[3]

6.1.2 Active and passive memory

Our memories, we are assured by psychologists, are anything but reliable. They are not an exact reflection of a past event but are always distorted by the limitations of our perspective, our perception, our needs and our emotions. As if that wasn't enough, they also change in the course of time through new **reconstructions** which adapt our self-image to the requirements of the present. "My children never quarrelled!" my grandmother used to say when she came to see us five children, who were often at one another's throats. We were delighted to hear that my mother had a different recollection. Her childhood memories included those that had long disappeared from my peace-loving grandmother's collection.

In English we say, 'I remember something', with the object transitively related to the subject. The German, however, begins with a reflexive: 'ich erinnere mich', which makes the person both the sender and the receiver of the memory. In French, people now say, 'je me souviens' (again reflexive), but the old form was 'il me souvient' (literally it comes down to me). These linguistic formulae already show that there are first person memories in which we ourselves are the subject, and there are third person memories that make us the object. "Ich erinnere mich" marks the beginning of a text by Günter Grass, which continues:

> ... or am reminded by something that bothers me, has left its scent behind, or in long overdue letters with treacherous headings has been waiting to be remembered. These and other snares make us stumble. From somewhere remote something turns up that you can't immediately give a name to. Wordless objects give us

2 Clarke (1977), 351.
3 Morrison (1988), 274; van Alphen (1997).

> a nudge, things which for years were around us playing no part – or so we thought – blurt out our secrets: painful, painful![4]

The *I*-memory is the product of a deliberate (re-) construction of the past, which is brought into line with the self-image of the person concerned. The *me*-memory, on the other hand, is inaccessible, unstructured, and uncontrollable; its content can never be captured in its entirety, and its dynamic movements can never be steered. Underlying the conscious memory of the will, which gives us meaning and identity, there is always this dimly lit, unconscious memory that makes its presence felt by sending us unexpected signals. Generally these come through objects that emit remembered sensual impulses. Marcel Proust was the great discoverer and reporter of the passive me-memory, which is not so much concentrated in the head as scattered around the body. His episode with the madeleine in *A La Recherche du Temps Perdu* has become the embodiment of the *mémoire involontaire*. The episode is about his experience when he dips a little cake into his lime blossom tea, and the taste suddenly releases a flood of memories which had remained shut off from his voluntary memory, i.e. the memory that consciously reconstructs the past.

6.1.3 Episodic and semantic memory

The memories that have long been the most common subject of discussion are **autobiographical**, i.e. those in which one's own past experiences have been preserved with a greater or lesser degree of accuracy. However, contrary to the ideas most of us have about their reliability, we are assured by neurologists that what we have stored up and then bring out again later is by no means stable but is liable to major fluctuations, variations and reinterpretations. This scientific insight has already made its mark on art: since the 1990s, flashbacks, distortions and false memories have featured prominently in literature and films. Instead of the 'unreliable narrator' we now have what one might call the 'unreliable rememberer'.[5] Salman Rushdie, Julian Barnes and other postmodern authors offer interesting examples of this psychological and aesthetic premise. Margaret Atwood quotes a passage from a novel by Javier Marías in which he emphasizes this postmodern **principle of unreliability** of memory, adding her own critical view of this position:

> I don't believe that the faculty of memory done is any guarantee that a person remains the same in different times and different places. The person recounting here and now what he saw and what happened to him is not the same person who saw those things and to whom those things happened; neither is he a prolongation of that person, his shadow, his heir or his usurper.

4 Grass (2001), 27.
5 Barnes (2000), Rushdie (1991a).

> End of quote. Fine and dandy, we say, with our streetwise postmodern consciousness. Problems do arise, however. If the 'I' of now has nothing to do with the 'I' of then, where did the 'I' of now come from? Nothing is made of nothing, or so we used to believe.[6]

Autobiographical memories, however, are not the only contents of our personal storehouse. Besides what psychologists call the **'episodic memory'**, referring to our autobiographical memory, we also have a **'semantic memory'**. This is the sum of what we have absorbed not through our own experience but through targeted learning. Whatever we have retained in the way of learning material is exempt from the psychological principle of unreliability and the need for permanent reconstruction. Once you have been taught that 7 x 8 = 56, it will remain so throughout your life, and you will not at any time change it to 55 or 57. Cognitive knowledge, which is stored in our semantic memory, remains just as it was, so long as it does not partly or completely disappear. If this degree of reliability were not attainable, we could never teach our students anything precise, let alone set them exams. The conventional, commonplace distinction between unreliable, changing human memory and the stable data bank of the computer is therefore inaccurate. Both forms are present in the human brain: the dynamic but unstable episodic memory and the reliable semantic memory, which stores whatever we have learned (sometimes by heart).

No matter how reliable or unreliable the episodic memory may be, it is the foundation of our **living identity**. Alzheimer patients who suffer from memory loss (retrograde amnesia) also lose their image of themselves as individuals with their own personal history. They live exclusively in the present, on the basis of their short-term memory – "tethered by the short leash [...] to the stake of the moment"[7], as Nietzsche put it. Our insight into the close connection between episodic, autobiographical memory and identity goes back to the English philosopher John Locke, who recognized the fact that a person's awareness of his own earlier experiences formed the backbone of his being. Only someone with memory, he argued, can take responsibility and be a person in the social and legal sense of the word.[8] Thus identity, which we shall deal with in more detail in our next chapter, is not something that is there for us to find, or that is given to us, but something we have to work out for ourselves. The possibility to construct it may be inhibited if particular memories deform or block a person's development. 'We are the stories that we can tell about ourselves', is the motto of a form of therapy that has as its basis the relationship between identity and memory; its aim is to help patients overcome disturbances to their identity-building process

6 Atwood (1996), 12 f.
7 Nietzsche (1874), 125.
8 Locke (1972). On the moral person, see also Nietzsche (2008).

by talking about things that have been repressed and by re-evaluating things that have been shut out.[9]

While the episodic memory is inevitably restricted, the semantic memory can be systematically extended: it can actually be trained in much the same way as our muscles. This was the aim of Roman **mnemonics**, which have gone through many variations right through to the present day.[10] As knowledge is said to be power, it was always man's dream to increase the capacity of his memory. Hermann Ebbinghaus' empirical, psychological research into memory began in the nineteenth century by examining the extent of this capacity; Ebbinghaus experimented on himself to see how many meaningless syllables he could store for how long in his memory. In the field of the semantic memory, extraordinary feats have not infrequently been achieved by psychopaths. In the film *Rain Man* an autistic character named Raymond Babbitt can remember the astronomical combinations of numbers involved in playing blackjack; there is also a famous story by J. L. Borges about the 'inexorable memory' of a 'mnemopath' named Schereschewski.[11] The semantic memory is trained differently in different cultures. In those without writing, impressive feats are performed by rhapsodists, bards, shamans and griots or whatever other names are given to these **memory specialists** who embody and pass on the fixed traditions of their people. Their task consists in preserving the cultural memory of the group, i. e. their vital myths of origin and their epics, and performing them effectively in public during ceremonies and festivals. The situation is quite different in cultures that use writing and also prioritize individual inspiration: very little prestige is attached to rote learning. Memorizing words is, however, a vital professional qualification for actors, and memorizing facts and figures, data and formulae, rules and regulations is an automatic requirement at school and training college. Learning does not depend just on experience and intellect but also on the memory. This general store of knowledge collected by the semantic memory is a vital supplement to our biographically based episodic memory.

6.1.4 Embodied and disembodied memory

Apart from episodic and semantic memory, psychologists have identified a third system which they call the **'procedural memory'**. This is a form that is situated in the body. Examples of such **'embodied memory'** are cycling, swimming and, on a different level, playing the piano. This category applies to skills that we have mastered once and for all and can continue to exercise relatively independently of the conscious mind. Even everyday actions like making breakfast or taking the dog for a walk can become so automatic through repetition that we can perform

9 Randall (1995).
10 Yates (2001); Herrmann (2000).
11 Borges (2000); cf. Haverkamp (1991).

them without even thinking about them, In this case we call these actions 'habitualized', and they too are part of our 'embodied' memory. As they lack salience, we may find it difficult later to remember them individually.

Since the procedural memory can never be categorized as a completely conscious act or as cognitive knowledge, it cannot be 'disembodied'. Impressions encoded in the semantic and episodic memory, however, can be stored by external carriers. All they need is to be translated into semiotic codes like language, or into images. In the film *Memento* the hero, who has had an accident and 'can't make new memories', tries to use writing in order to prevent the loss of internal short-term memory through external semantic memory: he puts up signs all over his flat, and even has important directions tattooed on his body. This domestic and body writing is supposed to make up for what is missing internally, but of course the task is hopeless.

Although fixing memory in **writing** cannot replace the human memory, it can extend the range considerably. This is how cultures expand the scope of human rote learning. The external storage of knowledge expands the memory and at the same time relieves it, so that inevitably there is a growing imbalance between the embodied memory and the **external archive**. This problem had already come to the attention of Plato, who cast a sceptical eye on the early written culture because he concluded that instead of the human memory being strengthened, it would disintegrate. For Plato writing was not a remedy but a poison.[12] Libraries and archives are gigantic data banks that can be used to create all kinds of things, but they do not guarantee the survival of living, embodied knowledge, which becomes increasingly endangered in a written culture and even more so in a culture of electronic media. Today we rely on our Google memory; in a world where information is out-of-date almost as soon as it reaches us, swift access to data has become more important than the possession of knowledge.

On the basis of what has been said so far, it might seem as if the route from embodied to disembodied knowledge is a one-way street. Of course that is not the case, because externalized knowledge can always be relearned, memorized, subjectively appropriated and hence once more embodied. Even our western culture of writing and media, which has gone so far now in the art of externalizing and storing information in ever faster and more complex databases, cannot quite do without the dimension of embodied knowledge. And so society's cultural memory is made up of two realms, which interact like background and foreground: **storage memory** and **functional memory**. In storage memory sources, objects and data are collected and preserved, independently of whether they are to be used in the immediate present; we might call this society's passive memory. Functional memory, on the other hand, is the active memory of a we-group. Just as the autobiographical memory underpins the identity of an individual, so the

12 Plato (2009).

functional cultural memory provides the foundation for the collective identity. It contains a small selection from the abundance of inherited things that are relevant to that identity. It also requires situations and motivations for this knowledge to be translated into a form of collectively shared memory through actualization, participation, confrontation or appropriation. The German word for this embodied, identity-building treasure trove of cultural knowledge is *Bildung*, which combines elements of culture, education and formation. It depends on the institution of canonization, which at one time referred only to the sanctification of religious texts and revered people. Since the birth of the modern age, however, this form of selection and evaluation has been extended to the products of the art world. Works that are canonized to the status of classics include books, films and musical compositions. These are distinct from the vast numbers of items stored in libraries and archives because they lay claim to being repeatedly read, seen, heard, recognized, bought, sold, learned by heart – in short, re-embodied (see the chapter on 'Media').

6.1.5 Individual and collective memory

Although no-one would question that there is such a thing as individual memory, many people are puzzled by the concept of **'collective memory'**. In her book *Regarding the Pain of Others*, Susan Sontag writes:

> Photographs that everyone recognizes are now a constituent part of what a society chooses to think about, or declares that it has chosen to think about. It calls these ideas "memories", and that is, over the long run, a fiction. Strictly speaking, there is no such thing as collective memory – part of the same family of spurious notions as collective guilt. But there is collective instruction. All memory is individual, unreproducible – it dies with each person. What is called collective memory is not a remembering but a stipulating: that *this* is important, and this is the story about how it happened, with the pictures that lock the story in our minds. Ideologies create substantiating archives of images, representative images, which encapsulate common ideas of significance and trigger predictable thoughts, feelings.[13]

Susan Sontag assumes that a society can 'choose', 'think' 'declare' and 'call', but there is one thing it cannot do, and that is remember. Evidently it can choose without a will, it can think without a mind, and it can call without a tongue, but it cannot remember without a memory. The freedoms of metaphorical speech that she allows to other capabilities do not apply to the concept of memory, which she finds impossible to think of without its organic basis. Her argument ignores the fact that unlike other animals humans are able to extend their memory to things they have not experienced but have nevertheless absorbed into themselves.

13 Sontag (2003), 85 f.

Maurice Halbwachs, the pioneer of research into social memory, was also exposed to scepticism and criticism when he first introduced this concept back in 1925.[14] He studied forms of **social group memory** in which the participants could link back to a common store of experience that had been stabilized by communication – e. g. family members, school classes, military regiments, travel groups. Halbwachs was also able to show that memories are anchored socially, and form the communicative and emotional cement of a group. His radical thesis was that people do not build up an individual memory but are always enclosed in memory communities. Memory, like language, is shaped by processes of communication, i. e. through narrating, absorbing and acquiring memories. A completely isolated human being, according to Halbwachs, therefore could not build up a memory at all.

Nowadays, the term 'collective memory' is used not only in connection with small social groups but also very often ethnic groups, nations and states. However, it needs to be stressed that such units do not *have* a collective memory, but *make* one with the aid of various **symbolic media** such as texts, images, monuments, anniversaries and commemorative festivals. Such common and for each community binding links to the past and to cultural tradition are what give these collectives their **identity as 'we'**. This is not a matter of individual origins but something acquired through learning, participation in the rituals, and all the other practical ways in which people integrate into a community. Until recently, the rules governing selection of these past points of reference followed what Nietzsche called 'monumental historiography'.[15] This was concerned with constructing a heroic self-image of the political 'we'-group, and mythically enhancing it through negative images of the enemy. During the 1990s a turning-point occured in the politics of the past, when different states began to reflect on their historic guilt, and through public confessions to incorporate a **'negative memory'** into their self-image.

6.1.6 Trauma

I began this section, my survey of memory forms, by distinguishing between active and passive memory, and I would like to end it with a few observations on the subject of trauma.

Unlike the pre-conscious but potentially conscious passive memory, trauma is related to an experience that is so incomprehensible, humiliating, painful or life-threatening, that perception automatically closes its gates to such an intruder. For the sake of self-protection, it has been **excluded** and **shut off** in a separate compartment from the conscious mind because it destroys the framework within which the person constructs his identity. This experience becomes diffi-

14 Halbwachs (1992).
15 Nietzsche (1980).

cult to remember and talk about later. What has been locked away in a capsule or in a cellar is not, however, forgotten but is conserved in the shadows and, after a certain amount of time, makes itself felt by way of particular symptoms. The aim of therapy is to bring the buried trauma into conscious memory and to integrate it into the person's identity. In this way, although it cannot be healed, it can lose its destructive force.

The beginnings of trauma research go back to the early twentieth century, but as a recognized diagnosis the concept did not make its way into the handbooks of American psychiatry until the 1980s. A specific feature of trauma is its long-term effects on victims of sexual abuse or torture, which is why the statute of limitations on such crimes has now been lifted. With the collective historical trauma of the **Holocaust**, the **after-effects** play a vital role; it took until the 1980s before some victims could talk about the pain and humiliation they suffered and before people in general were even prepared to listen to them. In this context, the new ethical concept of **'moral witness'**, which gives a voice to those who died, is part of the social recognition of historical traumas.[16] Since then, other acts of genocide besides the Holocaust have entered the world's consciousness, and they too demand symbolic recognition as well as – in a certain measure – material restitution. These include the genocide perpetrated by colonialists on the original inhabitants in different continents – the so-called 'middle passage' of slaves deported from Africa, the slaughter of the Armenians in the First World War, and in the violent final decade of the twentieth century the massacres in the Balkans and in Ruanda. Another aftershock from such historical traumas is that the effects are 'inherited' by subsequent generations. Looking back on the Holocaust, there are reports of the second and third generations of the perpetrators suffering the late consequences of their parents' and grandparents' guilt in the form of psychic disturbances, or in the case of the victims, some people consciously identify with the fate of their family in the sense that they form a kind of family or ethnic 'co-operative' of fellow-sufferers.

It is not only in the fields of psychiatry and history that the concept of trauma has gained in importance over the last twenty years; it has become increasingly prominent in literature and the cinema. Both media have developed new ways of presenting it, which can give a recognizable form to its destructive power and can open it up to being viewed, at least to a degree, from an inner perspective. One example is the novel *Beloved* by Toni Morrison, whose original narrative technique is no longer covered by the old category of the 'unreliable narrator'. Trauma novels are now recognized as a new genre,[17] though this does not mean that there is any sort of uniformity or that the subject has suddenly come from nowhere. There were important trauma novels prior to the 1980s, and they made

16 Felman/Laub (1992); Margalit (2003); Caruth (1996a, 1996b).
17 Granofsky (1995); Erll (2005).

their mark without the new concepts and theories: famous examples are Leslie Silko's *Ceremony* (1977) and Kurt Vonnegut's *Slaughterhouse Five* (1969), both of which deal with traumas from the Second World War against the pacifist background of the Vietnam War; Virginia Woolf's *Mrs Dalloway* (1923) also figures a traumatized hero from the First World War.

We might summarize these introductory observations as follows: the memory does not develop in isolation but always relates socially to other individuals and (in a political context) to other groups, when it reacts and relates to other collective memories. Memory in general has after-effects, of which trauma is the extreme form. That is why what we remember is not shaped by what actually happened, but by whatever can be put in the story that we shall later narrate. What is and is not recalled from the past therefore depends not least on the person, the purpose and the situation for whom and for which this story is *needed*.

6.2 Forms of memory in Shakespeare's *Hamlet*

Shakespeare's *Hamlet* is a play in which memory plays a leading role. On stage it presents a wide variety of the basic forms of memory. The following interpretation focuses on these and because their general significance reaches far beyond Shakespeare's time right through to the present day, we shall therefore not be delving into historical aspects of the play, but only into the general relevance and timeless validity of its various types of memory.

The fact that memory plays such an important part in *Hamlet* does not mean that its role is in any way uniform. If we look closely at certain scenes, we find something like a phenomenology of forms, and so we shall identify and describe these in the sequence in which they occur:

1. **historical memory**, which entails an official representation of the past
2. melancholic **counter memory**, with which Hamlet opposes the court's current desire to forget
3. **traumatic memory** which Hamlet must confront when he meets the ghost of his murdered father
4. mnemotechnical **semantic memory** and the (dis)order of Hamlet's store of knowledge
5. **episodic memory**, which brings forth spontaneous recollections of childhood
6. **memento mori** as memory of death
7. **witness memory**, which includes public commemoration and an appeal to future generations.

6.2.1 Historical memory – (incomplete) knowledge of the past

Every story has a **prehistory** which can't be shown within the restricted framework of the plot. Whatever important events may have happened before the curtain goes up have to be explained by one or more of the characters during the opening scenes in order to give the audience the necessary information. In *Hamlet* this prehistory – the exposition – is never fully revealed. In this respect, the play resembles a detective story, in so far as we are kept in the dark about certain aspects of the background. The difference here, though, is that in contrast to the detective story, the final unravelling of the plot does not in fact solve the many mysteries thrown up by the tragedy. In this play we actually have two prehistories: one concerns the **recent past** (the death of Hamlet's father), and the other the **distant past** (the death of Fortinbras Senior 30 years earlier). Both intersect with the appearance of the ghost, and to a certain degree remain enigmatic.[18]

In Act I, 1, the audience witness the Ghost's third appearance. This is commented on by the initially sceptical Horatio, which adds to the credibility of the scene. The Ghost's disappearance triggers Horatio's historical memory:

> Such was the very armour he had on
> When he the ambitious Norway combated.
> So frowned he once when, in an angry parle,
> He smote the sledded Polacks on the ice.[19]

One of the guards then asks a number of questions, which gives Horatio the chance to describe the whole episode in detail. Marcellus' suggestion: "Good now, sit down, and tell me he that knows ..." (I, 1, 69) prepares us for an epic situation in which historic memory will be given expression, while the drama's plot itself remains at a temporary standstill. What we hear now is not an authorized report but unofficial oral history told on the basis of rumour or "whisper" (I, 1, 79): it is the story of a duel between the dead King Hamlet and Fortinbras, King of Norway, in which the latter lost both his life and all the land in his possession. In addition we are told that now, after thirty years, Fortinbras' son is preparing for a new campaign in order to win back the land that had been lost.

For the horrified witnesses, however, the appearance of the Ghost is not only a reminder of the past, but it also points towards the future. They speak of it as a gloomy omen, "a portentous figure" and fear that it is the precursor to "feared events" (I, 1, 106). And so right from the start it is clear that there is no closure

18 *Hamlet* as a mystery is a topos that runs right through Shakespearian criticism. The play is regarded as Shakespeare's 'Mona Lisa' or 'Sphinx'. The inexhaustibility of this text – what Harold Bloom calls 'Poem Unlimited' – lies in its indeterminacy, due partly to overdetermination and partly to underdetermination.

19 Shakespeare (1997a), I, 1, 59–62.

of the past, which is throwing the dark shadow of unfinished business over the present and future.

6.2.2 Remembering versus forgetting – grief and melancholy

Before Hamlet makes contact with the spirit of his father, the audience sees him first in a scene that takes place at the court of his father's successor, his uncle Claudius. He makes his appearance as a grieving son, whose mind is totally preoccupied with the past and with mourning the death of his father. In the middle of his first monologue, he cries out in despair: "Heaven and earth, must I remember?" (I, 2, 142 f). And remember he must, while all around him court society has banished the dead king from memory and is devoting itself to the daily affairs of the new era. He insists on his human right to mourn at a court which has just been celebrating a royal wedding. His black clothes and his isolation indicate his **melancholic disposition**, which in the Renaissance would have been attributed to a surfeit of black bile and a pathological form of anti-sociality. What distinguishes him from all the other characters in the play is his stubborn devotion to the past, which all of them are so eager to forget. He is totally unwilling to adjust to the new present and to replace the image of his dead father with that of his live uncle Claudius. The persistence with which Hamlet clings to the memory of his father is the complete reverse of the speed with which the rest wish to forget him. The grief expressed by the new king Claudius is as fleeting as it could be – in one and the same breath he moves from the dead Hamlet to his own requirements:

> Yet so far hath discretion fought with nature
> That we with wisest sorrow think on him,
> Together with remembrance of ourselves. (I, 2, 5–7)

Hamlet's mourning is very much in line with Freud's description of melancholy.[20] It is a form of grief that will not let go, refuses to say farewell, and stubbornly seeks to hold onto what has been lost. While grief is an immediate affect, melancholy is a condition and a general approach to life. Hamlet does not in fact show his grief on the stage, but instead delivers a detailed analysis of the indescribability of true grief, which has become famous as an early example of the new discourse of **authenticity**.[21] In a world where anyone can pretend anything, true grief is something internal which cannot be expressed by any outer signs. And so Hamlet does not display his emotions, and utters nothing but words with which he articulates his protest against unwanted family and social ties.

In the first scene at court, Hamlet's remembering is in sharp contrast to everyone else's desire to forget. In their case, forgetting is one of the laws of Nature. These

20 Freud (2005).
21 Trilling (1972).

laws put a seal on the all-inclusive and invariable fate of individual death and the onward movement of generations. A gulf opens up between their acceptance of mortality and his obstinate prolongation of mourning and melancholy. This is a clash between two views of death: Nature versus culture. One might describe Hamlet's grief for his father as the naturally pious response of a loving son, and there are formal means of expressing such respect – observing periods of mourning, and carrying out the appropriate rituals. This is not just a matter of emotion but also part of an implicit **contract between generations**, which guarantees the bond between past and future and the continuity of tradition and culture. Any neglect of these conventions can have disastrous effects: if the mourning and the rituals have not been properly performed, dead people may return to haunt the living and bring misery into their lives.

Hamlet's grief also has a more profound **ethical** dimension. It shows itself in his ability to build up a **counter-memory** through which binding values of the past must be upheld against the demands of the present. The norms of this counter-memory forbid any opportunistic adaptation to the changing circumstances of the here and now. They undermine the predominance of the present by confronting it with a counter image, and thus they turn Hamlet into an out-and-out spoilsport who refuses to join in the celebrations. He wears black as an admonishment to all those who wish to rid themselves of the burden of the past. In the next scene, however, when Hamlet meets the ghost of his father, and grief turns to trauma, his own powers of subversion turn against himself.

6.2.3 Traumatic memory – the Ghost's confusing messages

The ghost of Hamlet's father embodies the uncertain prehistory of the play, which we have already discussed under the heading 'historical memory'. With the apparition, the prehistory abruptly intrudes on the present, **bringing back a past** which evidently contains 'unfinished business'. Because of this, the destinies of the old and the young Hamlet are inextricably entwined – the duel that was fought thirty years ago, when Hamlet was born, has returned to haunt the second generation. The plot of this play does not in any way begin on virgin soil, so to speak, but it unfolds in the shadows of a past full of open wounds and unpaid reckonings. Unlike conventional prehistories that are swiftly dealt with in a passage of exposition, this past does not lie behind the protagonists but is in a certain sense buried beneath their feet, and its disturbing signs will shake the very ground they step on. And so this dominant past continues to exercise its destructive effects across generations and even across the frontiers of life.

The pathological time structure that characterizes the play can be described quite explicitly in psychoanalytical terms. The psychoanalyst Nicholas Abraham, for instance, attributes the injurious and threatening effects of the past to a malign complex of guilt, concealment and ignorance which does not end with the death of the perpetrator but is passed on unconsciously to succeeding generations. This complex makes its presence felt as a gap in the knowledge of the successor, into which he projects his own fantasies. To describe this gap, Abraham has coined the metaphorical term **'crypt'** – the concealed and enclosed burial chamber that lies beneath the altar in medieval churches. Another concept that he introduces to describe the unconscious transfer of trauma is the **'phantom'**.[22] Abraham's thesis is that what we have in *Hamlet* is a family secret of unarticulated and harmful experiences that is passed down tacitly to the younger generation with damaging effects on the formation of identity. He sees the appearance of the ghost of Hamlet's father as a paradigmatic literary example of the transgenerational transfer of trauma. The relationship between the father, whose life contains episodes that have resulted in long-term feelings of guilt, and a son who has no explicit knowledge of these events is typical of this phenomenon. The son has nothing but the **gap** for his own fantasies, which include the mythical greatness of his father. Power and impotence merge seamlessly into one another here. It is this very ignorance or, at most, half-knowledge that allows the trauma to pass from father to son, creating a unity between them which prevents the son from developing his own individual identity.[23]

One might then ask, for instance, whether it is in fact the father's voice coming from the outside, or perhaps Hamlet's inner voice articulating his own dark doubts and fears. How much of this meeting is father and how much son is not altogether certain in a scene that borders on the psychedelic. But one thing that is clear beyond doubt is that now the son knows what the father knows, and this seals the already strong bond between the living and the dead.

The transgenerational trauma can also be called a **'memoria negativa'**, with the negative element being transferred unarticulated from parents to children. Nicholas Abraham reinterprets Shakespeare's revenge tragedy into a mystery play, and he solves the mystery in a sixth act of his own that unties all the knots of the play's dark prehistory. Taking the example of the Ghost, he explains his concept of the 'phantom': "it is not the dead that haunt us, but the gaps that remain in us because of the secrets of others."[24] Abraham is not trying to fix or distort

22 Abraham (1988); Rand (1991).

23 As a professional analyst and puzzle-solver, Nicholas Abraham could not bear to leave unresolved the many indeterminacies that the play preserves till the very end. In order to release himself and the audience from this 'traumatic' effect, he proceeded to write a new ending (in iambic pentameters) which he tacked on as Act VI, and in which he solved all the mysteries of the play's prehistory and compelled Hamlet to face up to the phantoms in his soul. Almost like a criminologist, he draws the material for his Act VI exclusively from details in Shakespeare's text, on which he sheds new light. He treats the play like a patient from whom he extracts information that had hitherto been unconsciously repressed. However, in untying all the knots, the psychoanalyst not only solves the problems, but he also dissolves the play.

24 Abraham (1988), 3; on 'memoria negativa' see Rand (1991), 689 f.

the literary text to fit in with a modern, psychoanalytical interpretation. What he sets out to do is to make particular contexts clearer by relating them to much more general experiences, i. e. he reveals the various potential connections offered by an historical text to illuminate problems that are extremely relevant to the modern human psyche.

There are at least three elements of the Ghost's message that can be linked to the modern concept of the trauma. First, there is its contradictory character. It is extremely **ambivalent**. The source itself is too mysterious to be totally trustworthy, and Hamlet's own reaction hovers between extremes:

> Be thou a spirit of health or goblin damned,
> Bring with thee airs from heaven or blasts from hell,
> Be thy intents wicked or charitable. (I, 4, 21–23)

During their encounter, the over-idealized father initially becomes the innocent victim of a foul murder, then a guilt-ridden soul longing to be relieved and cleansed of its sins. As an innocent victim, it demands that Hamlet "[r]evenge[s] his foul and most unnatural murder" (I, 5, 25). But as a sinner that has come straight from the flames of purgatory, it also begs for Hamlet's help in the purification of its heavily burdened soul. When Shakespeare wrote this play, both forms of action were already deemed old-fashioned. The feudal institution of revenge was regarded as a criminal act, and the religious institution of purgatory had been abandoned in England by the preceding generation.[25] It is not easy for Hamlet, regarded by many as an emphatically modern dramatic hero, to respond to these archaic demands. At the end of the Ghost's final speech, the demand for revenge changes into an appeal to be remembered.

The second aspect is the **secretiveness** of the message. The Ghost shares his knowledge only with Hamlet, who is strictly forbidden to impart it even to his best friend. Communication is further blocked by various oaths that the subterranean spirit makes his son swear, and again this ensures that the trauma remains fixed in Hamlet's own soul. To keep the secret, he feels obliged to seek refuge in acting different roles, which means that he must become a 'trickster', permanently disguising his true self.

A third feature of the trauma, in addition to its ambivalence and its secretiveness, is its overflow of **emotion**. It strikes with such force that it overtaxes the psychic and cognitive faculties of the person concerned, thereby distorting the structure of identity. Hamlet shows just how powerfully the words of the Ghost have affected him: he fears for his reason. Such an experience not only generates "thoughts beyond the reaches of our souls" (I, 4, 37), but as Horatio indicates, it can also lead to madness. Thanks to the Ghost's revelations, Hamlet's body and soul are now both at risk, and so it is little wonder that immediately afterwards

25 Greenblatt (2001).

he is scarcely recognizable. The trauma is an arrow that has split him in two, and now he is not only detached from others in the court of Denmark, but also from his best friend and from himself.

6.2.4 Semantic memory – mnemonics

What we referred to earlier as an 'overflow of emotion' is vividly displayed in the final phase of the meeting between Hamlet and the Ghost. The latter departs with the words: "Adieu. Adieu. Adieu. Remember me." (I, 5, 91) For Hamlet this is a moment of extreme confusion and utter helplessness. He does not know if he should ask for help from heaven or hell:

> O all you host of heaven! O earth! What else?
> And shall I couple hell? O, fie! Hold, hold, my heart,
> And you, my sinews, grow not instant old,
> But bear me stiffly up. (I, 5, 92–95)

In his first soliloquy he had expressed a wish: "O that this too too sallied flesh would melt" (I, 2, 129), whereas now he needs his heart to be strong enough to bear this message. Keeping something in the heart is another expression for remembering it, and this is a problem which, as his senses threaten to give way under the impact of the terrible encounter, he seeks to solve with the aid of reliable mnemotechnology:

> Remember thee?
> Ay, thou poor ghost, whiles memory holds a seat
> In this distracted globe. Remember thee?
> Yea, from the table of my memory
> I'll wipe away all trivial fond records,
> All saws of books, all forms, all pressures past
> That youth and observation copied there,
> And thy commandment all alone shall live
> Within the book and volume of my brain,
> Unmixed with baser matter. (I, 5, 95–104)

The student from Wittenberg does not turn to the rules of oral memory, but takes his writing tablets ('my tables') from his pocket in order to record the words spoken by the Ghost. His memory is described as a 'table' which has been copiously inscribed. In order to do justice to the weight and importance of his father's words, the son believes that he must wipe the slate clean and start afresh with a **tabula rasa**. How much must he forget in order to remember this one all-important message? There can be no doubt that there is something compulsive about his reaction, and as he feverishly writes down the Ghost's commandment that he be remembered, Hamlet shows clear signs of confusion and distraction. The writing is meant to give a fixed order to something that is now swirling around in his head. This moment, at such an important juncture of the play, not only describes an **externalization** of the memory, but also symbolically represents the disturbance taking place in the actual process of memorizing. Hamlet's mind is now constantly switching from one thought to another: "O most pernicious woman! / O villain, villain, smiling, damned villain!" and: "That one may smile, and smile, and be a villain." (I, 5, 105–108) On the one side is the exaggerated emphasis he lays on the task of memorizing, and on the other we can see that the determination to remember is being undermined right from the start. For while Hamlet is absurdly writing down the actual words "Adieu, adieu. Remember me", his mind is already being diverted by other associations arising from his father's speech. The psychologist Daniel Schacter calls this 'absent-mindedness', and categorizes it as one of the "seven deadly sins of memory".[26]

While Hamlet uses writing as a prop for memory, other characters rely on oral memory. The first act of the play contains a scene in which Laertes, who is leaving for Paris, bids farewell to his sister and father. The scene contains many words of warning, first from Laertes to Ophelia, and then from Polonius to Laertes. The brother's strict admonishments to his sister concerning her relationship with Hamlet end: "Farewell, Ophelia, and remember well / What I have said to you." (I, 3, 83 f) She responds: "'Tis in my memory locked and you yourself / Shall keep the key of it." (85 f) In the second part of the scene, roles are reversed, and it is now Laertes who is on the receiving end of his father's instructions, which he must take to heart while he is away. The paternal lecture begins with the words: "my blessing with thee / And these few precepts in thy memory / See thou character" (I, 3, 57 f). Both the father's and the brother's words are formulated in such a way as to make a lasting impression on the memory of the listener. In this first act, then, Shakespeare not only contrasts **written and oral forms of mnemonics**, but also two different forms of paternal instructions. Polonius's solid imperatives are aimed at achieving success in life, whereas the contradictory messages of the Ghost are a destructive force that affects his son's sense of reality, his social relationships, and ultimately his life.

6.2.5 Episodic memory – the lightning flash of a childhood memory

One example of activated **episodic memory** is to be found in the gravediggers' scene in Act V, when Hamlet meditates on human fate, fame, and death. He talks about the cyclical laws of nature and the universality of death – a subject which had already been broached by his mother in Act I: "Thou know'st 'tis common – all that lives must die / Passing through nature to eternity." (I, 2, 72 f) The rebellious powers of his melancholy memory had resisted the idea of this levelling-out process, but by the end of the play he has discovered for himself what he calls "a fine revolution" (V, 1, 82 f), which transforms all human life, all wit and all glory into eternal dust.

26 Schacter (2001).

In the course of his conversation with the gravediggers, Hamlet picks up a skull which has lain in the earth for 23 years. He is told that it is the skull of a man named Yorick, who was his father's court jester and had borne Hamlet on his back many times.[27] Here once again we have a moment of the play's prehistory. This time it is not a public or collective experience but a purely **private reminiscence**. What has come back into memory has absolutely no relevance to the development of the plot. But as a fragment of contingent memory, it serves to give the figure of Hamlet a new specific psychological depth, as suddenly he is confronted with the child he used to be.[28] The image of the entertainer Yorick that is now conjured up in his mind has the typical features of an episodic I-memory: it is vibrant and sensual, relates to an isolated scene with no narrative coherence, and is permeated with nostalgic emotions. It is not the product of conscious reflection, but has lain dormant all this time, and is now **involuntarily** evoked as a passive memory by a particular object that Hamlet has come upon by chance.

6.2.6 Memento Mori – the emblematic memory of death

The conversation with the gravediggers opens up two very different forms of memory in Hamlet: an autobiographical reminiscence, and a meditation about life after death. The personal, sensual one is followed by a reflection on the general insignificance of human life, and ends in a moral insight. In this scene he is hit by two contrasting memories, one episodic, the other semantic: the sensuous flash of an autobiographical reminiscence of his youth and the universal insight into the futility of human aspirations. The latter insight has the quality of an abstract **warning**. In a world oriented towards another transcendent world, we must 'remember' that we have no permanent place here, and all earthly desires and ambitions are relative in the eyes of God.

Shakespeare was the first to present on stage a theme which in his own time was a common subject in media such as books, paintings and sculpture: the **pious contemplation of the skull**. 'Emblem books', which combined a picture with a religious commentary, were particularly fond of this subject, and set out explicitly the line of thought that was to be followed: one must remember one's own mortality, and the vanity and futility of all earthly deeds. The difference between these very general images and the skull that Hamlet holds in his hand lies in its concreteness. We are told that this particular skull has been in the ground for 23

27 Harold Bloom makes the following comment on this scene: "Hamlet always has had nothing in common with his father, his mother, and his uncle. He is a kind of changeling, nurtured by Yorick, yet fathered by himself." Bloom (2003), 9.

28 Bloom (1999), 279; 313 f, regards Falstaff and Hamlet as outstanding exceptions among literary characters, in so far as they give the illusion of being real people because their personal charisma shatters the framework of given roles.

years and belonged to an individual man with an individual name. Hamlet's meditations thus become all the more real and direct in their impact.

Skeleton and skull are the remains of people from whom (except in the field of forensic science) everything personal and individual has been erased. What is left is a universal framework that eliminates all the differences that are so visible and so important in this life. That is why during the Middle Ages and the early modern age death was always talked of as the Great Leveller – a democratic force, even if it only came into effect when it was too late for the living.

Initially, Hamlet is critical of the gravedigger's cheerfulness, which he takes for a form of disrespect:

> HAMLET: Has this fellow no feeling of his business, that 'a sings in grave-making?
> HORATIO: Custom hath made it in him a property of easiness. (V, 1, 61 f)

There follows the traditional meditation on the decay of the flesh and the grave being the final destination, where even the greatest of men are reduced to worthless matter. Hamlet shows great virtuosity in imagining himself as the bones of various characters, but his whole attitude changes when he is told whose skull this once was. However, the moment of personal involvement swiftly passes, and gives way to the **memento mori** meditation. Women should hold this skull before their eyes when they are sitting at the mirror putting on their make-up, but so too should great men when they dream of ruling the world. With this sudden change of mood, from personal reminiscence to emblematic reflection, the nature of the skull also changes. What was the subject of nostalgic memory now becomes a repulsive object. Hamlet discards it with an exclamation of 'Pah!' Underlying this theatrical gesture is the traditional biblical concept of **Vanitas**, the futility of human life and endeavour, which Hamlet carries to macabre extremes. The skull, having just been viewed as the surviving image and monument of a much loved man, suddenly turns into a mere object which must return to the dust from whence it came. Replacing the spiritual cycle whereby the soul of the creature returns to its creator, we have the material cycle of consumer goods: the dust once called Alexander the Great has turned to loam with which one could "stop a bung-hole" (V, 1, 189).

6.2.7 Witness memory – ethics and therapy

In the graveyard scene, Hamlet pours scorn on the possibility of fame and glory as being a human illusion, but in the last scene of the play he directs his gaze towards his own future reputation. The first form of memory that we dealt with in this chapter was historical, i. e. concerning knowledge of the past. The final form we are going to cover is that of the **witness**, and it concerns knowledge to be imparted later. At the beginning it was Horatio who bore the historical memory, and at the end once more it is he who must provide the witness memory.

The relationship between Hamlet and Horatio corresponds to the Renaissance ideal of friendship, which Francis Bacon described in one of his essays: "A principal fruit of friendship is the ease and discharge of the fullness and swellings of the heart, which passions of all kinds do cause and induce."[29] Having had to shut away his innermost thoughts throughout the first four acts, Hamlet can finally yield to the internal pressure and – even though the process is interrupted by death – pass them over to his friend. Another of the 'fruits of friendship', and perhaps even more important for the relationship between the two men, according to Bacon is the friend's support: "aid and bearing a part in all actions and occasions." (117) One needs a friend not only to help carry out actions but also, if an action has been prematurely broken off, to help complete it. That is why the poisoned Hamlet prevents Horatio from drinking out of the same cup. His friend must not die, because he has a vital task to perform: he must tell Hamlet's story.

> O God, Horatio, what a wounded name,
> Things standing thus unknown, shall live behind me! (V, 2, 286 f)

By telling his friend's story, Horatio will do more than perform a ritual: he will enable Hamlet to be remembered for posterity. The role he plays is rather like that of the South African 'Truth and Reconciliation Commission', which in 1994 was concerned less with crime and atonement than with **narration and memory**. The injustice done to Hamlet, the confusing mysteries and unanswered questions – all of this should, when these tragic events have passed, be unravelled and explained in a story. The play, which itself offers no metaphysical consolation for the terrible chain of chaotic and destructive events, nevertheless allows Hamlet the secular compensation of witness memory. At the moment when his voice falls silent, Horatio's takes up the cause of healing his 'wounded name'. His testimony is part of Hamlet's testament. In the absence of any progeny or heir, only Horatio's evidence will be able to preserve the good name and memory of his friend. But it is not only for Hamlet that Horatio must bear witness, because there are others whom Hamlet himself has wronged: primarily Ophelia, but also her father Polonius. Hamlet's instruction to Horatio is: "report me and my cause aright / To the unsatisfied." (V, 2, 281 f) Whereas monumental memory serves to immortalize the name with glory, witness memory is concerned with **guilt** – both its acknowledgement and its reparation. To the degree in which it includes confession and recognition of the wrong done to others, witness memory can help to prevent the dead from rising out of their graves and causing bewilderment and harm to the living with their demands. Horatio's witness memory is therefore vital to keep Hamlet from becoming a 'perturbed spirit' like his father.

This closes the memory circle of the drama. It began in Act I, with the Ghost commanding Hamlet to "Remember me!" and in the final act it is Hamlet himself who asks to be remembered. The difference between the two, however, is unmis-

29 Bacon (1942), 110.

takable: the first injects a trauma into Hamlet that makes him the holder of someone else's secret. The 'crypt' – to use Nicholas Abraham's psychoanalytical term – leads to a split in his personality which robs him of the ability to think and act as an integrated self. On the other hand, the intention of the final command is to integrate the fragments into a story which the friend, as survivor and witness, is to narrate to the world. There is both a **legal** and a **therapeutic** side to this witness memory. As we have already mentioned, the witness will not only speak of the injustice done to Hamlet, but also of the harm he did to others, and this will break the vicious circle of violence and revenge that had drawn the Danish kingdom into a fatal vortex. At the end of the play, the destructive force of the trauma is to be calmed by the tale Horatio will tell. It is he who is entrusted with the project Hamlet could not carry out – to transform the divisive call for revenge into a unified and peace-making memory.

In the end, Horatio promises to deliver a complete account of all these confusing events, for he alone is in a position to "truly deliver" (V, 2, 329) the tale of "how these things came about." (324) We ourselves, however, do not see the fulfilment of this promise. Instead we hear only a generalized list that includes "carnal, bloody and unnatural acts" (325). The details will be left until later, and instead the play ends with the all-conquering Fortinbras making arrangements for the funeral of the fallen Hamlet. These formalities serve to legitimize his seizure of power, along with his claim that he has "some rights of memory in this kingdom" (V, 2, 333). As his name indicates – it means 'strong in arm' – he stands for an unscrupulous dedication to his own cause, and the only language he speaks and understands is that of military action. That is why Hamlet's burial is to be accompanied by "soldiers' music and the rites of war" (343). The play ends, not with the story promised by Horatio but with a "peal of ordnance".

This means that the mysteries which permeate the play from beginning to end are never solved, despite the many bodies littered around the stage. The uncertainties surrounding all the main characters remain, and the question 'What happens in *Hamlet*?' has continued to intrigue audiences, readers and critics down through the ages.[30]

30 Wilson (1966).

Summary

Human memory is an inexhaustible subject which no single discipline can possibly cover with any degree of adequacy. During the last decade, memory discourse has evolved into a transdisciplinary paradigm of cultural studies. Alongside neuroscientists, psychologists and historians, scholars in the fields of literature and culture have made their own important contributions. They not only explore ways in which art thematizes and reflects on remembering and forgetting, but they also investigate the mechanisms and structures of a 'cultural memory' which builds up over a long period of time through the media of texts and pictures, monuments and places, formal ceremonies and everyday practices.

Our memories change over the course of time through a process of constant reconstruction. They can be divided into '*I*-memories', in which we appear as the subject, and '*me*-memories', which make us into the object. The I-memory is the product of a conscious, deliberate construction of the past, whereas the me-memory is scattered over the neuronal associative cortex, and its activity is uncontrollable.

There are many systems of memory. Episodic memory comprises the store of memories accumulated during the life of an individual, and it provides the basis for that person's identity. Semantic memory is the sum total of what we have absorbed through targeted learning. Procedural memory resides in the body, which stores habitualized actions and trained skills. Abilities such as cycling or piano-playing cannot be passed on in the manner of spoken messages. Pictures and texts, on the other hand, can be recorded and stored externally. These modes of storage allow us to relieve and also extend the memory, and prolong it over generations; however, this may lead to a growing discrepancy between the embodied memory and the external archive.

Cultural memory can be divided into two areas: one storage and one functional. The storage memory collects and preserves information which has lost its immediate importance. We might call it society's passive memory. By contrast, functional memory is the active memory of a we-group. It provides a foundation for collectives ranging from small social groups to large units such as nations and states. It is created with the aid of different symbolic media (e. g. texts, pictures, buildings, rituals). Through common points of reference in the past and a shared fund of cultural traditions, such collectives establish their own we-identity.

Over the last few decades, particular attention has been focused on individual and collective trauma, which one may situate in the regions between remembering and forgetting. Trauma relates to an experience which is so painful that it exceeds the processing abilities of the psyche and, in a form of self-defence, is withdrawn and separated from consciousness. The aim of therapy is to transform the isolated, dormant experience – which may have been preserved for decades or even centuries – into conscious memories. The lasting potency of historical traumas arises from the fact that harmful experiences can be transferred unconsciously from one generation to another. In literature and film, new experimental forms of representation are currently being developed which make traumas accessible to the imagination through an internal perspective.

Shakespeare's *Hamlet* stages a wide variety of memory forms. These are explained in the context of the play, and are categorized within a more basic theoretical framework as historical, grief and melancholy, trauma, semantic, episodic, memento mori and witness memory.

Select bibliography

Bal, Mieke/Crewe, Jonathan/Spitzer, Leo, eds. (1999) *Acts of Memory. Cultural Recall in the Present.* Hanover: New England UP.

Erll, Astrid/Nünning, Ansgar, eds. (2005) *Cultural Memory Studies. An International and Interdisciplinary Handbook.* Berlin/New York: de Gruyter.

Landsberg, Alison (2004) *Prosthetic Memory. The Transformation of American Remembrance in the Age of Mass Culture.* New York: Columbia UP.

Radstone, Susannah/Schwarz, Bill, eds. (2010) *Memory. Histories, Theories, Debates.* New York: Fordham UP.

Schacter, Daniel L. (1996) *Searching for Memory. The Brain, the Mind, and the Past.* New York: HarperCollins.

7. IDENTITY

We are all individuals by nature. It is only machines and cloning that can produce identical copies. An 'individual' is marked out through differences between one person and everyone else. Interest in personal identity developed during the early modern age through two approaches – externally in the form of state **control** and **surveillance**, and internally with techniques of **self-examination**. External cultural practices of differentiation that serve to fix the individual's identity changed with the establishment of police forces within the framework of the modern state. Previously, identity had been recorded with the dates of births and deaths in church registers, but until the sixteenth and seventeenth centuries even these – the first objective forms of individuality – were more the exception than the rule. Even so states devised ever more precise ways of individualizing their citizens, and pin-pointed their uniqueness with the introduction of identity papers: in the case of criminal acts, military service, or crossing borders, there is a legal and political obligation to prove who you are. The relevant information includes figures (date of birth, passport number), photographs, address, and unalterable physical features such as the colour of the eyes. These can be refined by the addition of fingerprints and DNA. All this information serves to identify the individual in the context of state bureaucracy.[1] Such external registration and recognition also guarantees a degree of security as well as certain civil rights. Anyone who does not have valid papers will be unable to travel or to vote. Against a background of global migration because of wars and poverty, together with the resultant increase in the number of asylum-seekers, the problem has become more and more urgent, giving rise once more to the question of 'global citizenship'.[2]

Individual identity is not, however, purely an external matter; it is also produced internally, and then it is part of a process involving forms of self-analysis, self-awareness and self-staging.[3] In contrast to descriptive police or state identification, **social identity** is connected with the internalization of values. The uniqueness is then not one of statistics but of qualities. An inner awareness of individual difference was nourished, for instance, by the Protestant practice of examining and writing about the self (cf. Chapter 4). Complete openness with oneself and with a personal God from whom nothing can be kept hidden led to

1 Groebner (2004).
2 Benhabib (2002).
3 Cf. Greenblatt (1980).

a colonization of inner, spiritual regions which had as much influence on the evolution of western history as the colonization of overseas territories.[4]

The identity either attributed to or chosen by a person is a precondition of communal life, in which reliable **forms of recognition** are essential. We shall now consider aspects of individual and collective identity, together with the various concepts they entail. Here too we shall illustrate and develop the theoretical premises by way of literary examples.

7.1 Individual identity

7.1.1 Person

Individual identity can be elucidated with the aid of four categories which at the same time illustrate the historical development of identity concepts. We shall begin with that of the person, which historically covers the widest range and goes right back to the earliest tribal cultures. The French sociologist Marcel Mauss formed a theory about personality that is still relevant today if we wish to describe concepts of identity as they existed before the modern age.[5] According to Mauss, a group has at its disposal a limited number of names which remains constant while the individual bearers of those names move from one generation to another. The members of archaic societies, as individual persons, not only bore the names but were also **bearers of roles and status**. Their recognition by society was commensurate with the degree to which they fitted into the place allotted to them. Becoming a person meant inclusion, acceptance and integration within the group, which was established by the necessary rituals – above all, those of initiation. The word 'person' is derived from the Latin verb *personare*, which refers to the mask through which the live voice of the actor used to speak. In this sense, individual members of pre-modern societies were persons who found their identity by constantly renewing themselves through the adoption of modes of behaviour and the impersonation of different roles. Any detachment from mask and role, as the acting metaphor indicates, is impossible in such a system. In this cultural context, then, becoming a person means at one and the same time embodying given roles and fitting into a hierarchical network of social relations.

Shakespeare wrote at a time that preceded bourgeois constructions of identity. His *dramatis personae* act on a stage where hierarchical connections and social role models dictate the norms of conduct, so that action and identity always stand (or should stand) in clear correspondence to one another. Of course the real drama begins whenever persons depart from their roles and instead of con-

4 Landmarks in the literature of self-examination are the confessions of St Augustine (2008), Rousseau (2005) and De Quincey (2008).

5 Mauss (1979).

forming to the social pattern give way to the asocial forces of vice and passion. The individual is the exception to the rule, which in dramatic terms becomes as interesting as it is morally reprehensible. The identity of persons in Shakespeare's plays is determined by their **status**, their **sex** and their **age**. For each of these categories there are clear prescriptions, and these may and indeed must be violated to a certain degree through the vagaries of the plot if there is to be any development of dramatic interest. The women, for instance, may sometimes put on men's clothing so that for a while they can break out of their narrow confines. On the other hand, men scarcely ever dress up as women. It should be pointed out that in the Elizabethan theatre all the women's roles were played by males, so that the cross-over of sexes always had homoerotic associations. Disguises on stage produce a kind of meta-theatre, enhancing the theatrical pleasure, but of course they also help the villains to execute their dastardly plans (e.g. *Richard III*) just as they enable the good characters to preserve their integrity in a corrupt world (e.g. Kent and Edgar in *King Lear*). The game of identities in Shakespeare, however, is always played within strict parameters: in the end, the social roles and the concomitant norms of conduct are restored and confirmed.

The most important feature of middle-class identity formation, the **autonomy of the individual**, is still clearly a negative quality in Shakespeare. In a pre-modern world of 'vertical solidarity' (Jan Assmann), where class distinctions are affirmed and kept in place by the social obligations that the strong impose upon the weak, independence is not viewed as a positive value. The concept of 'autonomy', which in the modern age is seen as praiseworthy self-determination, was previously associated with negative values such as unbridled egotism and unscrupulous ambition. The autonomous characters in Shakespeare are the so-called Machiavellians who, like Edmund in *King Lear*, think only of what might be advantageous to themselves, and have no concern for the values and feelings of others. Cultural concepts like self-determination and autonomy as positive, critical detachment from social norms still had no place in Shakespeare's world.

An exception to this, or at least a borderline case, is once again Hamlet.[6] From his very first utterance we see him **opposed to the fixing of identities**. Against that which his stepfather wishes to impose on him will soon come that demanded by his dead father – for whom he is to play the role of avenger and restorer of honour. The many identities ascribed to him ("courtier", "soldier", "scholar"; III, 1, 153) run parallel to the many theatrical roles of lovesick melancholic, jester and madman[7] that he slips into as a defensive mechanism; these enable him to do what he wants amid the confusion of activity at court, and to

6 Belsey (1985) says of Hamlet: "[He] has begun to define an interiority as the origin of meaning and action, a human subject as agent" (67). Elsewhere, however, he stresses that "Hamlet is precisely not a unified subject" (42).

7 The Scandinavian word 'Amleth' means Fool. See Barrie (2004).

avoid being entangled in the fine web of intrigue that surrounds him.[8] In this kaleidoscope of falsely attributed and self-chosen identities, which one is the real Hamlet? This question, which he continually asks himself in a number of soliloquies, is never definitively answered in the play. What he himself recognizes in these speeches are the dissonances in himself, irreconcilable with the values and virtues spontaneously practised by his counterparts in the play: Laertes and Fortinbras are model sons, who are untroubled by any inner conflict as they fully embody their social identities and base all their actions on discharging their singular duty. In the dramatic figure of Hamlet we have, for the first time in literature, a revolt against such fixed identities, their blindness, their restrictedness, and the accompanying deprivation of personal freedom that lies at the heart of all social roles. Hamlet, who moves from one identity to another, is simultaneously detached from himself and from the other characters through the inferiority and superiority of his scepticism.

7.1.2 Subject

A very modern concept of the 'person' is the self-determined, so-called **'subject'**, who is guided by internal impulses that run counter to exclusively external norms. We use the term when social identity is not a matter of external attribution but of inner striving. This social model, which has enjoyed great success in the history of identity construction, goes back to a cultural creation of bourgeois liberalism. A hundred years before the important contribution made by German Idealism to this approach (through philosophers such as Kant, Fichte, Hegel and Schelling)[9], the basis had already been laid in England. The beginnings of the bourgeois subject came about with the rise of the middle classes around 1700, and their increasing influence on political, economic and cultural developments. After the so-called 'Glorious' (because it was bloodless) Revolution of 1689, which brought about the still operational rules governing the parliamentary monarchy, not only was there a stable political compromise between the aristocracy and the bourgeoisie, but the religious civil war came to an end and a secular society was finally and firmly established. Intellectual history at this turning-point of the modern age also saw the beginnings of the Natural sciences through Isaac Newton, and the rise of the literary genre which is most closely associated with the new concept of a central, middle-class subject: the **novel**. The fact that identity was no longer to be defined by origin or class, but had become the constructional task of the individual, is given exemplary expression by Daniel Defoe's *Robinson Crusoe*. With the novel there developed a literary discourse of identity which, in a secular and increasingly complex world, varied the pattern of individual self-assurance and self-orientation.

8 Assmann, A. (1999b).
9 Frank (1991).

Underlying the concept of the modern subject were two traditions of theory that came to the fore around 1700: the Enlightenment philosophy of John Locke, and the social philosophy of Shaftesbury. Locke's concept of identity, which has determined our "discussion of the idea of identity to this day"[10], would have been almost unimaginable without the earlier Puritan practice during the sixteenth and seventeenth centuries of writing autobiographies, and it would also have had little cultural resonance had it not been for the prolific success of the middle-class novel during the eighteenth and nineteenth centuries. In his essay *Concerning Human Understanding*, Locke included a chapter headed 'Of Identity and Diversity'.[11] He extended the concept of 'identity' far beyond its earlier definition by adding to the **'idem-identity'** of substantial sameness the **'ipse-identity'** of the self over time.[12] Idem-identity is possessed by two objects that are exactly the same as one another, e. g. two copies of a book. The concept of ipse-identity, however, cannot be applied to objects but only to people, who have consciousness of the self. This form of identity gives precedence to the faculty of self-awareness and self-analysis. Locke stated that in the course of time, individuals might undergo radical changes, but despite these manifest variations they could still recognize themselves as the same person. He established a connection between these obvious changes in a person and the social task of ensuring continuity. His question was: how can people be brought up to be responsible and reliable citizens, and in what is the inner unity of a person anchored?

Locke defined personal identity as a **self-reflexive relationship** which the person had to establish for himself and be answerable for. Consciousness is primarily awareness of the self, and this does not mean solely in the present but can also be extended back into the past in the sense of a retrospective projection. Personal identity emerges from the fact that a person recognizes himself throughout the changes of time. For Locke the concept relates to:

> a thinking intelligent Being, that has reason and reflection, and can consider it self as it self, the same thinking thing in different times and places; which it does only by that consciousness, which is inseparable from thinking, and it seems to me essential to it. [...]
>
> And as far as this consciousness can be extended backwards to any past Action or Thought, so far reaches the Identity of that *Person*; it is the same *self* now it was then; and 'tis by the same *self* with this present one that now reflects on it, that that Action was done. (§ 9, 335)

Locke regards 'person' as a 'forensic concept' which concerns the aims and effects of actions. He defines people as "intelligent Agents capable of Law, and

10 Teichert (2000), 152.

11 Locke (1972). Locke's essay was published in 1689, but the chapter on identity was added to the second edition in 1694. For an excellent commentary on this text, see Teichert (2000).

12 Ricoeur (1992).

Happiness and Misery" (§25, 346). Thus a precondition for citizenship is legal accountability. This is the foundation of the human quest for happiness and for successful thinking, because only someone capable of debt can make a profit, and only someone capable of suffering can search for happiness. For all this, Locke emphasizes, we need one thing more than any other: a reliable memory. **Consciousness** and **memory** occupy the place formerly taken by external norms and powers. From now on, the self is in full charge and so takes full responsibility for its life. All reckonings must be paid on this Earth, in the course of one's own lifetime, and solely before the authority of this earthly court and of public approbation.

If we may acknowledge Locke as the theorist of modern, personal identity who makes the individual legally and morally into a **citizen**, we may regard his contemporary, the Earl of Shaftesbury as the theorist who makes the modern subject a **social being**. His basic quest for social identity also hinges on the problem of consistency despite change: "'tis to gain him a Will, and ensure him a certain resolution, own meaning and design; and as to all his desires, opinions and inclinations, be warranted one and the same person to-day as yesterday, and to-morrow as to-day."[13] The problem concerns the psychology and sociology of urban man, who must develop his identity not by setting himself against society but by integrating into it. Shaftesbury does not argue – like Defoe, for instance – on behalf of an upward-striving middle class as emerged from Puritan dissent, but for the economically and politically dominant gentry, who followed the Whig equation of freedom with liberalism. His image for an increasingly complex society is the port as the intersecting point of a widespread trading network. In a situation based on the free self-development of powers, nothing is so harmful as rigid direction from outside, and that applies as much to the formation of character as it does to trade: "The only danger is, the laying an embargo. The same happens here, as in the case of trade. Impositions and restrictions reduce it to a low ebb. Nothing is so advantageous to it as a free port."[14]

All forms of authoritarian interference should therefore give way to self-regulating trade. Shaftesbury extended the economic principle of liberal self-regulation to all other areas of social communication, and that applied not least to forms of human conduct, including politeness:

> All politeness is owing to liberty. We polish one another, rub off our corners and rough sides by a sort of amicable collision. To restrain this, is inevitably to bring a rust upon men's understandings. 'Tis a destroying of civility, good breeding, and even charity itself, under pretence of maintaining it. (46)

What Shaftesbury calls "amicable collision" is the principle of a 'soft' social control. The norm that controls social control is civility. After the traumatic experi-

13 Shaftesbury (1964a), 123.
14 Shaftesbury (1964b).

ence of a Puritan theocracy, Shaftesbury discovers the 'value of sociality' (Niklas Luhmann), with the central norm of good versus evil being replaced by **civil versus crude**. Civility stands for the dialogic person who has internalized the social norm and removed everything that is not capable of generalization – in short, who has formed a **generalized self**. Crudity stands for the monologic person, who closes his ears to the voices of others and brazenly puts his own special self on show. The monologic type is to be found in Shakespeare in various roles – as dictator, fanatic, sectarian, dogmatist, teacher, pedant and eccentric. What they all have in common is the fact that they do not conform to, articulate or put into practice the social norm, and so their conduct cannot be generalized. Shaftesbury's plea for sociality goes hand in glove with a "farewell to absolute principles"[15].

Shaftesbury is the philosopher of a secular liberalism that advocates the consistent dismantling of hierarchical structures. The norm of sociality which he imposes on people from the outside finds its ideal in the dialogic subject. While Locke's subject gains his identity through his self-reflexive consciousness, Shaftesbury's does so through a dialogic coupling with the norms of society. Anyone who has learned to double and converse with himself, and can thus deal with differences within himself, will avoid being a social nuisance and will not threaten society's democratic multi-sidedness with authoritarian conduct. Shaftesbury therefore considered the perfect literary form to be the Platonic dialogue, which he put into practice himself.

The cultural norm of the middle-class subject as someone capable of action, self-determined, self-aware and of self-made individuality may still be regarded as valid today, but since the 1970s its foundations have been **violently shaken** by the discourse of literary theory. Marxist critics unmasked the middle-class subject as an ideological formation;[16] psychoanalysts demonstrated the fragility of an ego that is not master of its own house; postcolonialists argued from the perspective of the outsiders, the exploited and the subaltern to raise new questions about the problem of agency. Added to these were deconstructive approaches that took up the anti-norm of the fragmented personality and the counter-aesthetic of the 'schizophrenic' text to throw into doubt every ideal of unity and totality.

15 The expression comes from Marquard (1984).

16 One example among many is Jameson (1981), 153 f: "The concept of reification which has been developed in these pages conveys the historical situation in which the emergence of the ego or centred subject can be understood; the dissolution of the older organic or hierarchical social groups, the universal commodification of the labour-power of individuals and their confrontation as equivalent units within the framework of the market, the anomie of these now 'free' and isolated individual subjects to which the protective development of a monadic armature alone comes as something of a compensation."

7.1.3 Sex and Gender

A significant objection to the concept of the middle-class subject came during the nineteenth and early twentieth centuries from women, who experienced for themselves the fact that the subject liberated by the Glorious Revolution and the French Revolution was exclusively male. The emancipation of the male citizen did not include that of the female, nor that of the blacks (which only happened in the civil rights movements in the 1960s). As before, they still had to go on fighting against the basic patriarchal (and white) structures of modern society.

The repression of women also has a literary side which should not be underestimated. Literary models in which the **norms of gender identity** are firmly fixed insinuate their way into the learning process of the (female) reader, confirming the gendered self-image of the sexes, with all the attendant hierarchical values. The Puritan John Milton's epic *Paradise Lost* (1667–1672) was canonized during the Victorian era and thus made compulsory reading for young people. Generations of readers male and female were marked by the binding gender patterns of sexual behaviour embodied by Adam and Eve. The following passage from Book IV gives a very clear account of the external and internal differences, as seen through the eyes of a deeply impressed Satan:

> [...] though both
> Not equal, as their sex not equal seemed;
> For contemplation he and valour formed,
> For softness she and sweet attractive grace;
> He for God only, she for God in him.
> His fair large front and eye sublime declared
> Absolute rule; and hyacinthine locks
> Round from his parted forelock manly hung
> Clustering, but not beneath his shoulders broad:
> She, as a veil down to the slender waist,
> Her unadorned golden tresses wore
> Dishevelled, but in wanton ringlets waved
> As the vine curls her tendrils, which implied
> Subjection, but required with gentle sway,
> And by her yielded, by him best received,
> Yielded with coy submission, modest pride,
> And sweet, reluctant, amorous delay. (IV, 295-331)[17]

The male and female role models are drawn here in every detail, from mentality through outer appearance to the dynamics of sexual relationships. The detailed description of the hair is particularly striking, with Adam's being reminiscent of Adonis, who after his death was changed into a hyacinth. The comparison of Eve's hair with vine tendrils contains an indirect gender-specific message. In sixteenth- and seventeenth-century emblem books, which were illustrated with

17 Milton (1968).

scenes from nature and mythology that were linked to a moral lesson, a common image was that of a vine wound round an elm tree. This symbolizes the female, who is dependent on the strong support of the male. It is not possible for a woman to stand upright on her own. Milton's description of the gender relation is determined by two opposed **hierarchies**: against the intellectual and physical dominance of the man ("absolute rule" – "subjection") is the erotic power of the woman – here indicated by Eve's seductive radiance ("Yielded [...] with sweet, reluctant, amorous delay").

It needs to be stressed that Milton's Eve is not depicted simply as an ideal vision of female virtues; this literary figure also has negative qualities that include vanity, egotism and a desire for power which will ultimately lead to her fall. These unpleasant characteristics are part of a long Christian misogynist tradition that had been passed down through the centuries. For a highly idealized image of woman one must turn to the Victorian poet Coventry Patmore, whose volume of poems *The Angel in the House* draws a lyrical portrait of his wife, which also sums up the wishful thinking of the Victorian husband:

> Man must be pleased: but him to please
> Is woman's pleasure.[18]

A woman's first duty and prime quality was therefore her selflessness, which right from the start obviously put a few obstacles in the way of her developing her own independent identity. From a man's point of view, the perfect woman was a dead woman, especially if her corpse was beautiful.[19] No self, no projects of their own, and no history – that was the lot of the many nineteenth-century women who suffered a painful, not to say unbearable denial of their wishes and waste of their talents. In due course the image of women became more differentiated, and their desires and frustrations more explicit, as they gradually succeeded in making themselves heard in public and taking an active part in **feminine discourse**, instead of leaving it exclusively to men. In this context, women such as the political activist Mary Woolstonecraft and the novelist George Eliot played a major part in the radical change to the image of women in the nineteenth century, thus paving the way for the modern feminist movement. A milestone in this development was Virginia Woolf's fictional essay *A Room of One's Own*[20], in which she reflects on the economic, social and historical conditions of female creativity. A guaranteed income, a room of one's own, and an ancestral gallery of literary forebears would appear to be the necessities for a woman's creativity to be freed from its patriarchal bonds.

18 Patmore (1884), 73.
19 Bronfen (1994).
20 Woolf (2008a).

Since the 1970s, **feminism** has established its own branch of literary studies, with its own methodology. Initially, the main aim was to break free from male domination, to rediscover neglected and forgotten women writers, and to bring their work back into circulation.[21] Discussions on a new image for women led to new norms and ideals, and these in turn threatened to impose their own patterns of behaviour, lifestyles and fantasies. Any answer to the question of what constitutes femininity or female identity will always bring with it the danger of unspoken but fundamental ('essentializing') assumptions. The problematical field between normative determinacy and anarchic indeterminacy has led to deconstructive and performative discourses which increasingly are less concerned with features and concepts of femininity than with performative strategies and different ways of crossing borders.[22]

7.1.4 Inclusive and exclusive identity

Individual identity arises out of both inclusive and exclusive identity. **Inclusive identity** consists of conformity with, or outstanding performance of, roles that prescribe particular expectations and norms of conduct. These roles serve as directives for individual lifestyles and self-images, and they also delimit the range of possible options for action in different situations. What a man or woman is, and can or cannot become, is largely determined by these social role patterns. **Exclusive identity**, on the other hand, is mainly whatever distinguishes one person from another. The differences lead to values such as authenticity and autonomy, so that the individual discovers that he or she is not only different from others, but also to a degree independent of them, with a need to assert his or her uniqueness against theirs.

Inclusive identity comes from **opting in**, i. e. accepting a social position and acquiring identity by belonging. Exclusive identity means **opting out**, i. e. emphasizing distinctions between the self and all preformulated social roles.[23] This form of identity is not the opposite of a social role but involves a new one. At the dawn of the modern age, this was being tried as an affirmation of the individual's uniqueness. With exclusive identity, the unmistakability of the individual, in natural or even trivial matters, was elevated to a marker of his or her singularity, and connected to the new cultural value of authenticity.

This concept was developed in *Hamlet* before it became the object of philosophical discourse. We encounter it during Hamlet's first appearance, in the very first speech in which he makes himself known to the audience. This is the scene that we already discussed in the first chapter, when his mother asks him to cast off his "nightly colour" and, at the same time, to put an end to his melancholy at-

21 Gilbert/Gubar (1979); Mergenthal (1997); Rippl (1993); Weigel (1990).
22 Butler (1990, 1993); Vinken (1992).
23 Assmann, A. (1986); Assmann, A./Friese (1998); Von Moos (2004).

tachment to the past and join in the present life of the court. Death is "common", she says, and so "Why seems it so particular to thee?" (I, 2, 72; 75) As he so often does in the course of the play, Hamlet seizes on one particular word: "Seems, madam? Nay, it is. I know not 'seems'". (I, 2, 76) His grief, he insists, is a feeling over which he has no control. He defends the authenticity of this feeling by negating all the outward shows of appearance. His black clothes, his groans, his tears and his downcast expression are only the surface:

> These indeed seem,
> For they are actions that a man might play.
> But I have that within which passes show (I, 2, 83–85)

This famous speech on appearance and reality makes it clear that what we take for symptoms or outer expressions of grief are in reality nothing but modes of presentation, gestures, and stagings. In the eighteenth century, the age of authenticity, such doubts were common knowledge.[24] Nevertheless, there were differing assumptions about what could be acted and what could not. One can change clothes, and practise gestures, but what about physical reflexes like tears and blushing? Such somatic reactions were then regarded as signs of authenticity, and were taken seriously. For Hamlet, however, tears alone – "the fruitful river in the eye" (I, 2, 80) – are no markers of authenticity but represent the skills of a talented actor. Whoever wishes to speak the Hecuba monologue with the requisite amount of pathos must be able to produce the requisite number of tears. He tests the first player and ends the audition when the first tears appear. One can employ this actor – he is expert at the art of arousing emotions, for as recommended by Roman rhetoric, he is the first to be moved by the words he speaks. Hamlet's critique of signs is therefore far more radical than that of the eighteenth century. He acknowledges no positive signs of **authenticity**, because authenticity is the exact opposite of *all* forms of signification. There need be no connection whatsoever between the genuineness of a feeling and its expression. The exterior does not mirror the interior, and there is not one reliable proof of sincerity because all manifestations can be acted, faked and falsified. For Hamlet, true feeling comes from the innermost depths, over which the will has no control, and this inner core cannot be captured positively, but can only be defined negatively as something that defies all pretence and all description.

The cultural value of authenticity, which enjoyed a spectacular career during the second half of the eighteenth century, was based among other things on precisely the premise that the inner workings of the soul could not be translated. Communication and sociality – as discussed by Hamlet and his mother in their conversation about the manifestation of grief – were of lesser importance once the focus had shifted to the unmistakability and *je ne sais quoi* of the true and unfathomable inner processes. The genius is the prototype of the exclusive identity.

24 Trilling (1972).

A culture that sets great store by originality also prioritizes difference and non-conformity. In the late eighteenth and nineteenth centuries, when the considerable increase in and distribution of written matter produced more popular forms of culture, the exclusive identity came more and more into play. Suddenly it was important to be an original and not a copy.

7.1.5 Doppelganger and multiple identities

The fact that identity is not a given but a cultural, biographical construction is never more clear than when it goes wrong. An especially dramatic and vivid example is the genre of the doppelganger-novel. A doppelganger in this context is a person who has two separate identities. In a different sense, Shaftesbury had already demanded just such a division with his advocacy of the democratic, dialogic being. In the case of the doppelganger the doubling does not lead to inner complexity and flexibility; instead, the person is divided into two completely irreconcilable halves. The decisive factor here is that the two halves are unable to communicate with each other – there is not one stepping stone to bridge the gap between the two warring worlds. Furthermore, the switch from one to the other personality may come without warning and without apparent cause. With R. L. Stevenson's fictional **split personality** of Dr Jekyll/Mr Hyde, the change is brought about initially by means of a drug which Dr Jekyll ingests voluntarily, but gradually it is his alter ego who assumes control. The doppelganger embodies the great dichotomies of western cultural semantics: good and evil, reason and instinct, conscious and unconscious. These are the poles between which the change takes place from one extreme to the other. As he oscillates between them, he lives out the logic of either/or which constitutes the boundaries of all societies and cultures.

In Mary Shelley's *Frankenstein*, the boundary is between reason and emotion, which was redrawn at the beginning of the nineteenth century with the increasing dominance of the Natural sciences. The obtrusive one-sidedness of technological and scientific reason led to the byproduct of violent, uninhibited aggression, which no psychological or cultural training could domesticate. In this novel, the disastrous split comes about because there is a total lack of common ground and understanding between the scientific creator and the being he has created. By making the monster, Victor Frankenstein has blasphemously crossed a forbidden frontier and broken the rules of Nature, which alone has the right to give life. However, this tale focuses on the border not only between humans and Nature (or God), but also on that between the sexes. The male scientist can bring ideas and products into the world, but he is lacking in the female, maternal side that can nurture them, integrate them socially and give them moral support. They therefore split off from their creator and develop a destructive existence of their own that can no longer be brought back under control. While Shelley's doppelganger novel deals with the return of the split and repressed part of the male scientist's mind, Stevenson's is more concerned with social and moral questions.

Here it is the stifling, repressive corset of Victorian respectability that Dr Jekyll seeks to shake off. He wants to give free rein to the instincts he is supposed to 'hide', and to live without any social inhibitions. All the pent-up energy is to be periodically released from the control of the conscience or the super-ego. In a story clearly marked by the Scottish Calvinism of its author, the main focus is on the unbridgeable gap between good and evil. Victorian double standards, in which the norms of social respectability were preached in public, while often in private a blind eye was turned to men's moral excesses, are here dazzlingly broken down and exposed in all their hypocrisy.

In Stevenson's tale there is an important observation which far transcends the doppelganger motif:

> Man is not truly one, but truly two. I say two, because the state of my own knowledge does not pass beyond that point. Others will follow, others will outstrip me on the same lines; and I hazard a guess that man will be ultimately known for a mere polity of multifarious, incongruous and independent citizens.[25]

Two generations later, this was precisely the line followed by Virginia Woolf, who finally put paid to the concept of a consistent, unified identity and replaced it with that of a **multiple identity**. She used the image of a pile of plates, each of which represented a different manifestation of the self but could only be made to appear under particular circumstances. The weaker our conscious control becomes, and the more fragile the façade of our self-staging, the more space is created for the experience of otherness and non-identity.

> For if there are (at a venture) seventy-six different times all ticking in the mind at once, how many different people are there not – Heaven help us – all having lodgement at one time or another in the human spirit? Some say two thousand and fifty-two.[26]

From this it is only a small step to current discussions on identity. Nowadays it is therefore common practice to talk of identity in the plural in order to lay emphasis on its flexibility and diversity.[27]

25 Stevenson (2008), 52 f.
26 Woolf (2008b), 293 f.
27 Here it is important to distinguish between postmodern liberal licence on the one hand and well substantiated psycho-pathological findings on the other. The term 'multiple personality' relates to a new diagnosis arising out of the delayed effects of childhood traumatization through sexual abuse. The symptoms of this are the division of the self into several selves, each of which has remained at a certain stage of development, thus destroying the integrity of the personality, which can no longer be brought together in a unified life history.

7.2 Collective identity – race, nation, culture

For a long time, the central identity question in the western world was 'Who am I?', but now – and especially outside Europe – an immeasurably more important question is: 'Who are we?' While the search for a personal identity is plausible enough, that for a collective one is far more problematic and difficult to grasp. From the eighteenth until well into the twentieth century, **collective identity** was established through factors such as territory, race, language, religion or a numinous 'national spirit', which Herder considered responsible for the formation of a 'national character'.[28] Nowadays, we tend to strip collective identities of all such substantive elements (they are 'de-essentialized') and we categorize them as discursive formations. We recognize them as cultural constructs and concepts that are never given but are produced by systems of symbols and values. Cultures create **options for identity**: they develop programmes which allow individuals to feel that they belong to a group and to demonstrate their membership externally.[29]

Such 'programmes' do not necessarily have to be like Orwell's *1984*, with the demands of the totalitarian state for conformity. **Homogenization** already takes place through the adoption of largely unconscious modes of behaviour. On a higher level come the discursive formations which are communicated through symbolization and are a matter of conscious understanding and appropriation. Here too one can distinguish between inclusive and exclusive identities: in the case of the inclusive, the symbolic element is weaker and remains general enough to absorb the heterogeneous; access to the symbolic storehouse of such a culture is structured hierarchically, but still basically leaves the way open for the less privileged to join in and climb the ladder. The exclusive identity, on the other hand, is typical of groups which draw their identity principally by cutting themselves off from other collectives and so leaving little or no space for inner multiplicity. Their strength lies not in an ability to integrate, but in their clear-cut lines, which make it possible for them to survive and resist assimilation even under conditions of exile and diaspora.

In the nineteenth and twentieth centuries, **national identities** were based on cultural uniqueness; **mythologized history** (e. g. Frederick Jackson Turner's myth of

28 Cf. Assmann, A. (1993a).

29 Niethammer (2000) points out that discussions of identity that shift the emphasis from the individual to the collective have more than doubled. However, he is and has always been a vehement critic of the whole concept of identity, particularly the collective variety. In his renunciation of it, he expresses a typically German mindset, according to which collective identities are not needed and are to be condemned as dangerous ideologies. In view of the new and increasing relevance of this whole subject, both outside and more recently also within Europe, such an approach is oversimplified.

the western 'frontier') was an important instrument for forging national identity. America is a land, however, which in the twentieth century drew its national identity less from its (mythologized) history than from its vision. Being American meant being part of the 'American dream', which painted a picture in which every individual, regardless of his origin or his background, had the chance to rise to the top of the social or economic tree. The dream of equal opportunities concealed not only the different histories but also the profound inequalities engendered by **skin colour**. From the 1940s on, there were white and African-American protests that the American nation was still split into different groups that had not come together to form a common 'we'. The claims of black people for representation in the national identity were clearly articulated by the African-American writer Richard Wright, in a passage which ends with an interweaving of the pronouns 'we' and 'you', thus expressing the problem of identity:

> We black folk, our history and our present being, are a mirror of all the manifold experiences of America. What we want, what we represent, what we endure is what America is. If we black folk perish, America will perish. If America has forgotten her past, then let her look into the mirror of our consciousness and she will see the living past living in the present, for our memories go back, through our black folk of today, through the recollections of our black parents, and through the tales of slavery told by our black grandparents, to the time when none of us, black or white, lived in this fertile land. The differences between black folk and white folk are not blood or color, and the ties that bind us are stronger than those that separate us. The common road of hope which we all have traveled has brought us into a stronger kinship than any words, laws, or legal claims. Look at us and know us and you will know yourselves, for we are you, looking back at you from the dark mirror of our lives![30]

White Americans are called on not to deny their alter ego, or they will lose their own identity. This entails facing up to their history, and remembering the suppressed part of themselves. Both sides are interwoven in an identity that inextricably binds the fate of one to that of the other. James Baldwin is another African-American writer who sees the path to inner integration and to a shared national 'we' being blocked by the whites' suppression of black history:

> It is only in his music, which Americans are able to admire because a protective sentimentality limits their understanding of it, that the Negro in America has been able to tell his story. It is a story which otherwise has yet to be told and which no American is prepared to hear. As is the inevitable result of things unsaid, we find ourselves until today oppressed with a dangerous and reverberating silence.[31]

For Baldwin too, the suppression of black people and of their history throws a shadow over the country which stands in the way of any truly integrated na-

30 Wright/Rosskam (1988), 146. For the references to Wright and Baldwin I am grateful to Barbara Röckl (2006).

31 Baldwin (1998), 19.

tional identity. Ralph Waldo Ellison, the third great African-American author of the immediate postwar period, also expressed his views on the problem of an American identity. In his novel *Invisible Man*, he links up with James Joyce and his bildungsroman *The Portrait of the Artist as a Young Man*. Referring to a famous line in Joyce's novel, he makes an interesting change: 'race' becomes 'face', showing that Ellison is only prepared to consider identity in terms of the individual:

> Stephen's problem, like ours, was not actually one of creating the uncreated conscience of his race, but of creating the *uncreated features of his face*. Our task is that of making ourselves individuals. The conscience of a race is the gift of its individuals who see, evaluate, record [...]. We create the race by creating ourselves and then to our great astonishment we will have created something far more important: We will have created a culture. Why waste time creating a conscience for something that doesn't exist? For you see, blood and skin do not think.[32]

Ellison wrote these lines towards the end of the 1940s, in an individualistic age. Individuals were distinguishable only by their faces. Apart from this difference, nothing separated them – or, to be more precise, nothing was allowed to separate them. Instead of race, Ellison wanted to see a democratic national culture which would unite individuals.

"Blood and skin do not think." Ellison's credo has been massively contradicted over the last twenty years. In the place of individual and nation there is now an intermediate dimension of **ethnic identity**, which is celebrating an explosive comeback. In contrast to biological race, ethnic identity has always been founded on culture, and so its revival has brought about the powerful re-emergence of those suppressed traditions that Wright and Baldwin had already wished to bring back into the public conscience of white Americans.

At this point, I should like to return to Leslie Fiedler's slogan "Cross the border – close the gap!"[33] His euphoric, late 1970s image of multicultural variety and joyful togetherness glossed over a profound national crisis, which made democratic consensus extremely vulnerable and shook America's social values to their foundations. The myth of unity encapsulated by the words *E Pluribus Unum* on the dollar bill, and the image of the melting pot which made the immigrants – at least after the third generation – into harmlessly conformist Americans of different origins and skin colours, lost all conviction. At the same time these immigrants increasingly embraced their own traditions, while minorities (such as the African-Americans and Native Americans, but also people of Jewish and Chinese origin) rediscovered the roots of their own cultures. Those who behind the backs, so to speak, of these minorities had claimed American culture for themselves were the so-called WASPs (White Anglo-Saxon Protestants). Cultural studies

32 Ellison (1994), 347.
33 Fiedler (1971).

played an important part in questioning and reshaping the **politics of identity** as developed since the 1980s in the institutions and value systems of the United States. Such studies provide a discursive platform on which concepts, values and strategies can be discussed and formulated. The emergence of new branches of research within literature departments – African-American, Native-American and Jewish-American Studies – is a sign of the widening range and awareness of what we now call hyphenated identities.

7.3 Contesting the canon – identity politics in the medium of literature

In American universities, identity politics have been particularly controversial in the battle of the literary **canon**. By this, let us repeat, we mean a list of texts that underlie individual and cultural identity-forming. The canon is characterized by three elements: **selection**, **value**, and **duration**. Selection obviously entails omission, and so what the memory is not compelled to preserve can be forgotten.[34] As for evaluation, canonization means **'sanctification'**, whether of persons, religious texts or works of art. The third feature is perhaps the most important: The work must have a durable reputation. The canon is not a pop chart that can be changed from one day to the next according to the taste of the moment. Nor is it constructed generation by generation to meet the prevailing criteria of the age. It is already there, pre-selected, and people must adapt themselves to it, because it confronts them with given norms. The superiority of a canonical text over one that is merely literary consists in the fact that it represents the historical experiences or values of a cultural group and it brings these back to life with every reading. Just like history and myth, it is a vital cog in the wheel of collective identity.

The subject of the canon is today being broached principally by those who find that they have been excluded. This is less a question of access than of representation. Many people feel that it is not a true reflection of their world – particularly women and members of social and cultural minorities. Thus the discussion has been radically decentralized; increasingly it is being approached from standpoints far away from the European centre and from prevailing cultures and social strata. This decentralization of the canon debate has led to a clash of cultures.

The problem of establishing traditions, along with side effects of inclusion and exclusion, has become all the more complex through a growing awareness of three factors:

34 Assmann, A./Frank (2004).

1. the vital link between cultural tradition and collective identity
2. the multiplicity, variety and mutual exclusiveness of cultural identities
3. the downgrading of female cultural potential through male dominance, and the destruction of indigenous traditions by colonial rule

These factors have led to the problem of the canon extending to an ongoing, worldwide struggle for cultural self-determination.[35] As an example we shall now discuss two novels by a female Caribbean author, in which cultural socialization in a colony of the British Empire is depicted from the perspective of an indigenous girl.

7.3.1 Caribbean experiences with the western canon – Jamaica Kincaid

Jamaica Kincaid grew up on the Caribbean island of Antigua, which she left when she was 17. In her autobiographical novel *Annie John* (1983), she describes her childhood and adolescence on the little island, and in *Lucy* (1990) she tells the story of her first year of self-imposed exile in the USA. These books deal with the search for identity on two levels: one of family and the other of culture. On the family level, which we shall cover only briefly, the problem is presented as a symbiotic mother-daughter relationship, in which the borderlines of individual identity become blurred. It requires an enormous effort from the author to break free from her identification with her mother: "I was not like my mother – I was my mother."[36] Earlier she has told us: "I had come to feel that my mother's love for me was designed solely to make me into an echo of her, and I didn't know why, but I felt that I would rather be dead than just an echo of someone." (36)

Awareness of identity begins both in the family and in culture with awareness of difference. In *Annie John* we hear about the experiences of the heroine in an English colonial school. In another text Kincaid succinctly sums up the essence of British colonial education: "You [the British] distorted or erased my history and glorified your own."[37] Annie's key experience takes up the whole of Chapter 5, under the heading "Columbus in Chains". This refers to the caption accompanying a colour picture in her history book, in which one sees the conqueror chained hand and foot on his ship, having been ordered to return to Spain. Annie is fascinated by this picture, and stops paying attention to the teacher. In looking at it, she experiences a similar feeling of triumph to that which her mother had had when she heard about the increasing immobility of her tyrannical father. Her reaction had been: "So the great man can no longer get up and go."[38] The same

35 See Bronfen/Marius/Steffen (1997).
36 Kincaid (1991), 90.
37 Kincaid (1988).
38 Kincaid (1986), 78.

words come into Annie's head, and she cannot resist writing them in thick letters below the picture of the chained Columbus. The deed arouses the wrath of the teacher:

> I had gone too far this time, defaming one of the great men in history, Christopher Columbus, discoverer of the island that was my home. And now look at me. I was not even hanging my head in remorse. Had my peers ever seen anyone so arrogant, so blasphemous?
>
> I was sent to the headmistress, Miss Moore. As punishment, I was removed from my position as prefect, and my place was taken by the odious Hilarene. As an added punishment, I was ordered to copy Books I and II of Paradise Lost, by John Milton, and to have it done a week from that day. (82)

The first two books of *Paradise Lost* are full of guilt and punishment, so they were regarded as a suitable imposition. With the time-consuming task of copying out 1855 archaic lines, the Puritan culture of guilt was thus transplanted into a remote British colony. What takes place in this classroom is a battle – not with weapons but with cultural **symbols**. The insult to the emblematic colonial figure of Columbus is punished by the drudgery of writing out a hegemonic text. However, the affair becomes rather more complex than the simple process of crime and punishment might suggest. The canonized text chosen as a disciplinary measure not only deals with hierarchy, authority and insubordination, but it also offers a model for revolt. "I was not even hanging my head in remorse. Had my peers ever seen anyone so arrogant, so blasphemous?" This is an attitude that has to be learned, and there could be no finer set of instructions than Books I and II of *Paradise Lost.* Generally, canonical texts are noted for their complex structures which offer a great **number of interpretations**; in this case the colonial canon also includes a republican one, which talks of liberation, autonomy and self-determination (using the example of Satan).

There is an additional way in which Annie John can identify with Milton's Satan. Once again it is a picture that inspires her – this time an illustration in Milton's epic:

> Altogether, I looked old and miserable. Not long before, I had seen a picture of a painting entitled The Young Lucifer. It showed Satan just recently cast out of heaven for all his bad deeds, and he was standing on a black rock all alone and naked. Everything around him was charred and black, as if a great fire had just roared through. [...] Satan was wearing a smile, but it was one of those smiles that you could see through, one of those smiles that make you know the person is just putting up a good front. At heart, you could see he was really lonely and miserable at the way things had turned out. (94 f)

This time it is not the heroic defiance or the mythical guilt that makes the heroine identify with the fallen archangel,[39] but his heroic isolation. The burned-out

39 Kincaid (1991), 139: "I felt like Lucifer, doomed to build wrong upon wrong."

world around him seems to her to illustrate the still unknown and unfathomable emptiness within her own lonely, adolescent soul.

In the novel *Lucy*[40], the intrinsic uncertainty and disunity of the first person narrator's identity is manifested through her various names. In her passport her name is Lucy Josephine Potter; Josephine is a reference to her Uncle Joseph, who became rich and from whom the family hopes to gain an inheritance; Potter is the name of the English slave-owner to whom her ancestors belonged. These official names are joined by others which she chooses for herself and which refer to literary role models: Emily, Charlotte, Jane, Enid. (149) She was given the name Lucy by her mother. When she asked why her mother had chosen this particular name, she was told: "I named you after Satan himself. Lucy, short for Lucifer. What a botheration from the moment you were conceived." (152) This answer strikes the heroine like an epiphany:

> I was transformed from failure to triumph. It was the moment I knew who I was. When I was quite young and just being taught to read, the books I was taught to read from were the Bible, Paradise Lost, and some plays by William Shakespeare. I knew well the Book of Genesis, and from time to time I had been made to memorize parts of Paradise Lost. The stories of the fallen angel were well known to me, but I had not known that my own situation could even distantly be related to them. Lucy, a girl's name for Lucifer. That my mother would have found me devil-like did not surprise me, for I often thought of her as god-like, and are not the children of gods devils? (152 f)

Devils in Milton's mythology have very little in common with the Devil, who in Caribbean folklore is invoked or driven out. Anyone in Antigua who is possessed has to travel overseas in order to get rid of him, "because the Devil cannot walk over water" (21). In contrast to this Devil in the island's folklore, who is a real as well as a latent threat to daily life, Milton's is a highly literary figure with a history and a rich inner life. For Lucy the reader, who has absorbed the colonial literary canon, he is someone she can identify with and through whom she can distance herself from the constraints and expectations of her own native world. The canonized texts she studies at school enable this Caribbean girl to take on a socialized, colonial cultural identity that pays absolutely no attention to local conditions or indigenous traditions. Study of these texts means two things in Kincaid's novels: they are an instrument of governance and discipline, but at the same time they are a medium for self-examination and self-discovery.

7.4 Wanderers between cultures

7.4.1 Mary Antin

Kincaid voluntarily left the place of her Caribbean origin at the age of 17, and has not returned since. Wars, pogroms and economic necessity have contributed to

40 Kincaid (1991).

the fact that during the twentieth century and now at the start of the twenty-first, millions of people have been forced to **migrate** and suffer radical changes to their whole way of life. An early example is that of Mary Antin, who was born in 1881 in White Russian Polotsk, emigrated to the USA with her Jewish parents, and wrote her memoirs in Boston when she was 28. With this autobiography, the author bade farewell to her former self. Concerning the protagonist of her text, she wrote: "her life ended when mine began."[41] She calls the dramatic cultural switch from the White Russian shtetl to the slums of a modern American city a rebirth. The title of her book, *The Promised Land*, has a double meaning: it refers both to the Puritan American myth according to which those who come to this continent have the chance to make a completely new beginning, and to the Jewish tradition of the land that will mark the end of their exile. Antin's 'exile' is thus transformed into a new home. The new culture demands a new identity, and through the act of writing she attempts both to record the old one and to get rid of it. She is the perfect example of the enthusiastic immigrant who with her autobiography stages her own **identity change**. However, the fact that this conversion is not without profound tensions and conflicts is clear from the following observation:

> It is painful to be consciously of two worlds. The Wandering Jew in me seeks forgetfulness, I am not afraid to live on and on, if only I do not have to remember too much. (xiv)

Though she is eager to be assimilated into the new culture, Antin's memory is charged with the world of her former life. A danger for the wanderer between two cultures is that the burden of a dysfunctional memory becomes impracticable and can obstruct the search for a new identity. While Locke saw identity as a matter of remembering earlier phases of life, for Antin **forgetting** is the way to achieve a new identity. Paradoxically she discharges her memory by writing her autobiography. In her writings, she externalizes and offloads the Jewish world of her origins by putting it into a book.

7.4.2 Joseph Conrad

At around the same time, an English author from the Polish Ukraine confessed in Polish to a Polish friend:

> Both at sea and on land my point of view is English, from which the conclusion should not be drawn that I have become an Englishman. That is not the case. Homo duplex has in my case more than one meaning.[42]

This is the author whose novel *Heart of Darkness* we discussed in the chapter on 'Space', and who in 1895 at the age of 38 translated his name, Józef Teodor Konrad Korzeniowski, to Joseph Conrad. Unlike Mary Antin, he wrote novels, not au-

41 Antin (1942), xi.
42 Najder (1964), 240.

tobiographies. He himself declared: "I am not a personage for an orderly biography, either auto or otherwise." His biographers have complained that he carefully erased the details of his life, and sometimes left false trails for them to follow. Antin's openness is in stark contrast to the art of disguise which Conrad practised all his life and to which he alludes in the confidential lines quoted above. Although he too crossed the border from East to West, he sees no possibility of an integral identity for himself. An immigrant automatically becomes a **'homo duplex'**. While Antin sought to overcome the problem of double identity chronologically, by calling her second life a rebirth and by discarding her first life through writing – much as a snake discards its old skin – Conrad's crossing of cultural borders took on the form of constitutional concealment. For him there was no simple personal division into the before and after, but a twilight doubling of appearance and reality that allowed no reliable conclusion as to what was and what wasn't his true identity. In an interview, a Polish reporter said to him: "I would like to find in the English writer the immortality of Poland." His reply was:

> "The immortality of Poland? You – we. No one doubts it. English critics – and after all I am an English writer – whenever they speak of me they add that there is in me something incomprehensible, inconceivable, elusive. Only you can grasp this elusiveness, and comprehend what is incomprehensible. That is Polishness. Polishness which I took from Mickiewicz and Slowacki. [...]"
>
> After a pause, his cigarette goes out. "What the devil's the matter with this cigarette? Because, you see, strictly speaking I'm a sailor. C'est mon métier."[43]

As the wanderer between cultures can never undergo a complete conversion of identity, all that is left to him is the masking of his inner other self, the Englishman and Pole expressing himself in French phrases. Conrad's formula for this hybrid identity, 'homo duplex', links up with the Romantic motif of the doppelganger on which he focuses in his novel.[44]

7.4.3 Salman Rushdie

At the beginning of his novel *The Satanic Verses*, Rushdie's hero sings a song from a popular film as he falls from heaven. The lyrics are:

> O, my shoes are Japanese, [...]
> These trousers English, if you please.
> On my head, red Russian hat;
> My heart's Indian for all that.[45]

What Salman Rushdie has in common with Antin and Conrad is the fact that he too is one of the **displaced writers** who have left their place of origin and write in a language that is not their mother tongue. In his case, however, the problem

43 Najder (1983), 199.
44 Conrad (1995).
45 Rushdie (1992), 5.

of **intercultural identity** takes a very different line. While Antin reacts to it with conversion and Conrad with disguise, Rushdie puts it playfully on show. This approach has only been made possible because of the fact that national identities are no longer equated with metaphysical qualities – as they were in Conrad's time – but are increasingly defined in the economic terms of consumer goods. The whole focus has shifted from the level of 'essence' to that of **'lifestyle'**. For the Romantics, the qualities of national character were not for sale, whereas lifestyles are not only open to individual choice, but also – like shoes, trousers and hats – available in virtually any combination. However, unlike all these changeable, external attributes, the pop song tells us that the Indian heart remains as an unalterable and authentic personal essence.

Rushdie's situation, though, is more complicated, because his heart is also split. As a Muslim with deep respect for Hindu culture, he already has to balance two souls, each of which relativizes the other. What applies to him as a microcosm he suspects also applies to the macrocosm of his birthplace, the city of Bombay, where the spatial juxtaposition of many different faiths and cultures produces a secularizing effect. This bears witness to an intercultural identity which has become even more complex through migration. The fact that there is more to it than postmodern multiplicity, relativism and eclecticism is clear from the following:

> I am speaking now of those of us who emigrated ... and I suspect that there are times when the move seems wrong to us all, when we seem, to ourselves, post-lapsarian men and women. We are Hindus who have crossed the black water; we are Muslims who eat pork. And as a result – as my use of the Christian notion of the Fall indicates – we are now partly of the West.[46]

Emigration for Rushdie is not just a liberating **crossing of borders**; he also feels it as a **betrayal** and connects it with original sin. This description has little of the postmodern euphoria over the mixture of one and all, unless we take it a step further and interpret the Fall along Christian lines as not being simply a catastrophe but also a blessing in disguise, a *felix culpa*. Melancholy and euphoria condition one another. "If we want to be Orientals, Greeks, Romans, all at the same time, we shall be nothing reliable", wrote Johann Gottfried Herder at the end of the eighteenth century, when he invented the myth of national character.[47] Rushdie would probably reply today: But we have long since been Arabs, Jews and Hindus all at the same time. Races and cultures go all the way through us, and we are all products and embodiments of interculture. At this point, the tone of his *Satanic verses* becomes enthusiastic:

> [It] celebrates hybridity, impurity, intermingling, the transformation that comes of new and unexpected combinations of human beings, cultures, ideas, politics, mov-

46 Rushdie (1992), 15.
47 Herder (1984), 655.

> ies, songs. It rejoices in mongrelization and fears the absolutism of the Pure. *Mélange*, hotchpotch, a bit of this and a bit of that is *how newness enters the world*. It is the great possibility that mass migration gives the world, and I have tried to embrace it. The *Satanic Verses* is for change-by-fusion, change-by-conjoining. It is a love-song to our mongrel selves.[48]

It is a symptom of the complexity of our global world disorder that *Satanic Verses*, a love-song to **hybrid mixtures**, aroused the wrath of the guardians of 'the Pure' and for years put Rushdie's life in acute danger. How much of the self and how much of the other do humans need? Today we hear the voices of *postmodern* authors demanding a new era of the **transcultural**, in which a global mixture of races, cultures, media and lifestyles predominates, and in which there is "no longer a clear borderline between the strange and the familiar"[49]. At the same time we also hear the voices of the fundamentalists, and those of the *postcolonial* authors, who after a long history of suppression and eradication are now in search of their own cultures and traditions. Our world is as fixed on **homogenization** as on **differentiation**: boundaries are constantly being crossed or demolished, but at the same time new ones are being built up.

In contemporary British literature the theme of migration now plays an increasing role and is presented in various ways. While the first generation was primarily confronted with problems of social discrimination and belonging (Sam Selvon, *The Lonely Londoners* (1956); Joan Riley, *The Unbelonging*, 1985), members of the second and third generations born in England have constructed new definitions of 'Englishness'. In the 1990s Islam became a highly politicized issue in the Western world, after the fatwa against Salman Rushdie and the burning of his *Satanic Verses* (1988) in Bradford (1989). There were also less problematic representations of multicultural topics, for example in the genre of popular films such as *East is East* (1999) or *Bend it like Beckham* (2002). The beginning of Hanif Kureishi's debut novel *The Buddha of Suburbia* – "I am an Englishman born and bred, almost." – is often quoted as an example of the problems that a member of the second immigrant generation had to face in British multicultural society. Here, wandering between cultures also meant experimenting with new forms of expression. Since 2000 the relationship between migrants and the host society as represented in films and literature has changed significantly, focusing more and more on the origins of migrants. In her novel *White Teeth* (2000) Zadie Smith marks the transition towards a picture of multi-culti London in a more humorous and ironic tone, while at the same time critically undermining a shallow concept of multiculturalism. Other films and novels focus on the difficulties of social and cultural integration (e. g. the film *Yasmin*, 2004). A new theme is intergenerational family constellations, which introduce the long and violent, deeply em-

48 Rushdie (1991b).
49 Welsch (1994), 158.

bodied legacy of the colonial past into the contemporary present of London society (e.g. Nadeem Aslam's novel *Maps for Lost Lovers,* 2004).[50]

In this situation, where the **boundaries are permanently shifting**, it is well worth drawing on the experiences of the border-crossers and on the sensitivity of artists. The two are closely linked, for the artist takes what is familiar to him and makes something strange out of it. Those who have crossed the frontiers from one state, society and culture to another have a great deal in common with those who have crossed the frontiers of familiarity, tradition and perception. New insights that run counter to cultural traditions are brought to us today especially by those artists who have lived through migration or have consciously dug deep into the complex archaeological layers of their cultural memory. Unlike Antin and Conrad, they no longer seek to bury their intercultural gifts, but they thrive on them. They write all the more freely about their cultural heritages, having eliminated the normative divisions between national states and cultures. Under the banner of globalization, world trade has expanded not just in consumer goods but also in people and in cultural wares. Rushdie deliberately combines the perspective of the border-crosser with the 'stereoscopic' view of the artist[51]:

> Indian writers in these islands, like others who have migrated into the north from the south, are capable of writing from a double perspective: because they, we, are at one and the same time insiders and outsiders in this society. This stereoscopic vision is perhaps what we can offer in place of the 'whole sight'. (19)
>
> Our identity is plural and partial. Sometimes we feel that we straddle two cultures; at other times that we fall between two stools. But however ambiguous and shifting this ground may be, it is not an infertile territory for a writer to occupy. If literature is in part the business of finding new angles at which to enter reality, then once again our distance, our long geographical perspective, may provide us with such angles. (15)

The advantage that such migrants have over others was strikingly summed up by Henry James in his novel *The Ambassadors*, written at the end of the nineteenth century. There it is said of the hero:

> He was burdened, poor Strether, with the oddity of a double consciousness. There was detachment in his zeal and curiosity in his indifference.[52]

From this paradoxical observation one can extrapolate a useful generalization: to find out what it is like to cross borders, and to test identities, the aesthetic experience of literature can provide an important starting point and training ground for the acquisition of intersubjective and intercultural understanding.

50 Cf. Kastendiek/Sturm (2007).
51 Rushdie (1991b).
52 James (1964), 18.

Summary

Every human being is by nature an individual who is distinct from all other individuals in his or her society. However, cultural interest in individual identity did not develop until early in the modern age. Accordingly, the concept of the 'person' has changed over the course of history, from being the bearer of a name, role and status in pre-modern societies to the autonomous, self-determined individual of our own time. The modern subject is a cultural creation of the middle classes, and sees itself as a self-motivated centre of action and experience. However, until the nineteenth century this subject was conceived of mainly as being male. Not until the emancipation of women was the aspect of gender incorporated into the concept of subject and identity.

Individual identity emerges from a combination of the inclusive and the exclusive. Inclusive identity arises from conformity to social roles and the fulfilment of expectations in relation to those roles (opting in), whereas exclusive identity is shaped by emphasizing a difference between the self and the prescribed social roles (opting out).

The doppelganger motif demonstrates the failure of unifying identity structures, and indicates radical conflicts within social structures and cultural semantics. This acid test of identity no longer applies under postmodern conditions in which identity has become pluralized. Now identities are regarded as hybrid, mixed, fragmented, multiple. At the same time, ethnic minorities are rediscovering their roots and are subordinating the values of individualism to those of belonging to a group and sharing a history of suffering.

Literary texts provide examples of identity construction, from early modern times right through to the present. Shakespeare's *Hamlet* dramatizes the transition from a pre-modern inclusive to a modern exclusive identity, which is linked to the new value of authenticity, fed by a Protestant ethic that casts suspicion on any form of 'self-fashioning'.

The protagonists of Jamaica Kincaid's novels provide us with vivid examples of identity construction under the conditions of colonial education and the authority of the canon. Thanks to the complexity of the cultural text (here it is Milton's *Paradise Lost*), it becomes an instrument of power and discipline, but at the same time a medium for rebellion and self-discovery.

Other literary examples provide variations on the theme of cultural border-crossing and its consequences for identity building. *Mary Antin* is a biography in which Jewish pre-history in Eastern Europe is written down, then concluded and expunged by the act of immigration. In the case of Joseph Conrad, who became a Briton by choice, the Polish substrata of his biography remained a virulent element of his (double) identity, although he sought to cover them up. A very different case is that of the British Muslim Salman Rushdie, for whom it is not membership of ethnic and cultural groups but border-crossing itself that constitutes the guiding principle of his identity structure as well as being the inspiration for his literary work.

Select bibliography

Burke, Peter J. (2009) *Cultural Hybridity.* Cambridge: Polity Press.

Burke, Peter J./Stets, Jan E. (2009) *Identity Theory.* Oxford (et al.): Oxford UP.

Král, Françoise (2009) *Critical Identities in Contemporary Anglophone Diasporic Literature.* London/New York: Palgrave Macmillan.

Martín Alcoff, Linda (2006) *Visible Identities: Race, Gender, and the Self.* Oxford (et al.): Oxford UP.

Stein, Mark (2004) *Black British Literature. Novels of Transformation.* Columbus: Ohio State UP.

References

Literature quoted

Primary literature

Achebe, Chinua (1973) *Things Fall Apart.* (1958) London: Heinemann.

Achebe, Chinua (1977, 1988) "An Image of Africa: Racism in Conrad's *Heart of Darkness*". In: P. B. Armstrong, ed. (2006) *Heart of Darkness.* A Norton Critical Edition. 4th ed. London/ New York: Norton, 251–262.

Addison, Joseph (1965) *The Spectator.* No. 411 (1711). Ed. D. F. Bond. Vol. 3. Oxford: Clarendon, 535–539.

Alexie, Sherman (2000) "The Unauthorized Autobiography of Me". In: A. Krupat, B. Swann, eds. *Here First. Autobiographical Essays by Native American Writers.* New York: Modern Library, 3–13.

Antin, Mary (1942) *The Promised Land.* (1912) Boston, MA: Mifflin.

St. Augustine (2008) *Confessions.* Trans. H. Chadwick. 4th ed. Oxford (et al.): Oxford UP.

Bacon, Francis (1942) "Of Friendship". In: Id. *Essays and New Atlantis.* (1625) Roslyn, NY: Walter J. Black, 109–118.

Bacon, Francis (2004) *The Instauratio magna.* Part II: *Novum organum* and Associated Texts. Ed. G. Rees, M. Wakely. Oxford: Clarendon Press.

Baldwin, James (1998) "Many Thousands Gone" (1955). In: Id. *Collected Essays.* New York: Library of America, 19–34.

Barnes, Julian (2000) *England, England.* New York: Random House.

Baudelaire, Charles (1995) *The Painter of Modern Life and Other Essays.* (1859) Trans. J. Mayne. 2nd ed. London (et al.): Phaidon Press.

Beckett, Samuel (1967) *Waiting for Godot. A Tragicomedy in Two Acts.* (1952) London: Faber and Faber.

Borges, Jorge L. (2000) "Funes, His Memory" (1944). In: Id. *Fictions.* Trans. A. Hurley. London: Penguin, 91–99.

Burton, Robert (1972) *The Anatomy of Melancholy.* (1621) London: Dent.

Byatt, Antonia S. (1978) *The Virgin in the Garden.* London: Chatto & Windus.

Chatwin, Bruce (1988) *Songlines.* London: Picador.

Chaucer, Geoffrey (1969a) "Chaucers Wordes unto Adam". In: Id. *Complete Works.* Ed. W. Skeat. Oxford (et al.): Oxford UP, 118.

Chaucer, Geoffrey (1969b) "The Canterbury Tales". In: Id. *Complete Works.* Ed. W. Skeat. Oxford (et al.): Oxford UP, 419-717.

Clarke, Austin (1977) "Mnemosyne Lay in the Dust". In: Id. *Collected Poems.* Ed. L. Miller. Oxford (et al.): Oxford UP, 327–352.

Conrad, Joseph (1995) *The Secret Agent.* (1907) London: Routledge.

Conrad, Joseph (1996) *Heart of Darkness.* (1902) Complete, authoritative text with biographical and historical contexts, critical history, and essays from five contemporary critical perspectives. Ed. R. C. Murfin. 2nd ed. Boston (et. al.): Bedford Books.

Defoe, Daniel (1972) *Robinson Crusoe.* (1719) Oxford (et al.): Oxford UP.

Douglas, Alfred (1894) "Two Loves". In: *The Chameleon* 1/11, 25–28.

Earle, John (1811) *Microcosmography or a Piece of the World discovered; in Essays and Characters.* Ed. Philip Bliss. London: White and Cochrane.

Eliot, George (1996) *Adam Bede.* (1859) Oxford (et al.): Oxford UP.

Eliot, George (1998) *Felix Holt, the Radical.* (1866) Oxford (et al.): Oxford UP.

Eliot, T. S. (1963) *Four Quartets.* (1943) London: Faber and Faber.

Eliot, T. S. (1967) "The Love Song of J. Alfred Prufrock" (1917). In: Id. *Selected Poems.* London: Faber and Faber, 11–16.

Ellison, Ralph Waldo (1994) *Invisible Man.* (1952) New York: The Modern Library.

Emerson, Ralph Waldo (1971) "The American Scholar" (1837). In: Id. *Collected Works of Ralph Waldo Emerson.* Vol. 1: Nature, Adresses, and Lectures. Cambridge, MA: Harvard UP, 49–70.

Emerson, Ralph Waldo (1979) "Circles" (1841). In: Id. *Collected Works of Ralph Waldo Emerson.* Vol. 2: Essays: First Series. Cambridge, MA: Harvard UP, 177–190.

Freud, Siegmund (2005) "Mourning and Melancholia" (1917). In: Id. *On Murder, Mourning and Melancholia.* Trans. S. Whiteside. London: Penguin, 201–218.

Freud, Sigmund (1966) "Project for a Scientific Psychology" (1895) In: *The Standard Edition of the Complete Psychological Works of Sigmund Freud.* Trans. and ed. J. Stratchey. Vol. I (1886-1899). London: Hogarth Press, 295–397.

Freud, Sigmund (2002) *Civilization and Its Discontents.* (1930) London: Penguin.

Friel, Brian (1980) *Translations.* London: Faber and Faber.

Gay, John (1974) "Trivia: or, The Art of Walking the Streets of London" (1716). In: V. Dearing, ed. *Poetry and Prose.* Vol. 1. Oxford: Clarendon, 134–181.

Goethe, Johann Wolfgang von (1981) *Anschauendes Denken. Goethes Schriften zur Naturwissenschaft.* Ed. H. Günther. Frankfurt a. M.: Insel.

Goethe, Johann Wolfgang von (1988) "Zahme Xenien" (1827). In: Id. *Sämtliche Werke. Briefe, Tagebücher und Gespräche.* Vol. 2: Gedichte 1800-1832. Frankfurt a. M.: Klassiker-Verlag, 640–648.

Grass, Günther (2001) "Ich erinnere mich". In: M. Wäldle, ed. *Die Zukunft der Erinnerung.* Göttingen: Steidl, 27–34.

Hartley, Leslie P. (2002) *The Go-Between.* (1953) New York: Review Books.

Heine, Heinrich (1981) "Lutetia". In: Id. *Sämtliche Schriften in 12 Bänden.* Ed. K. Briegleb. Vol. 9. Frankfurt a. M.: Ullstein, 217–548.

Herbert, George (2002a) "Iesu" (1667). In: Id. *The Temple. Sacred Poems and Private Ejaculations.* Berlin: Waxmann, 105 ff.

Herbert, George (2002b) "The Temple" (1633). In: Id. *The Temple. Sacred Poems and Private Ejaculations.* Berlin: Waxmann, 2 f.

Herder, Johann Gottfried (1803) *Outlines of a Philosophy of the History of Man.* (1784) Trans. T. Churchill. Vol. 1. London: Luke Hanfard.

Hobbes, Thomas (1997) *Leviathan.* (1651) New York: Norton.

Hofmannsthal, Hugo von (2005) "A Letter". In: *The Lord Chandos Letter and Other Writings* (1874-1929). Trans. J. Rotenberg. New York: Nyrb, 117–128.

Hulme, Thomas E. (1962) "A Lecture on Modern Poetry" (1913). In: Id. *Further Speculations.* Ed. S. Hynes. Lincoln: Nebraska UP, 67-76.

James, Henry (1946) "The Real Thing" (1893). In: Id. *Henry James.* Fourteen Stories. London: Rupert Hart-Davis, 181-209.

James, Henry (1964) *The Ambassadors.* (1903) Oxford (et al.): Oxford UP.

James, Henry (1986) "The Future of the Novel" (1899). In: id. *Henry James on the Theory and Practice of Fiction.* Eds. W. Veeder et al. Chicago: Chicago UP.

Johnson, Samuel (1992) *The Letters.* Vol. 1: 1731–1772. Oxford: Clarendon.

Joyce, James (1969) *Stephen Hero.* (1944) London: Cape.

Joyce, James (1993) *A Portrait of the Artist as a Young Man.* (1916) London: Macmillan.

Joyce, James (1997) *Ulysses.* (1922) London: Picador.

Kant, Immanuel (2007) *Critique of Judgement.* (1790) Trans. J. C. Meredith. Oxford (et al.): Oxford UP.

Kincaid, Jamaica (1986) *Annie John.* New York: Plume.

Kincaid, Jamaica (1988) *A Small Place.* New York: Plume.

Kincaid, Jamaica (1991) *Lucy.* New York: Plume.

Kureishi, Hanif (2007) *The Buddha of Suburbia.* (1990) London: Faber and Faber.

Lamb, Charles (1964) "Distant Correspondents" (1822). In: Id. *The Essays of Elia and the last Essay of Ella.* Oxford (et al.): Oxford UP, 150–157.

Lawrence, David H. (1994) *Lady Chatterley's Lover.* Harmondsworth: Penguin.

Lawrence, David H. (2003) "Walt Whitman". In: A. Beal, ed. *Selected Literary Criticism.* London: Heinemann, 392–407.

Lessing, Gotthold E. (1984) *Laocoön. An Essay on the Limits of Painting and Poetry.* (1766) Trans. E. A. McCormick. Baltimore: Johns Hopkins UP.

Lévi-Strauss, Claude (1966) *The savage mind.* London: Weidenfeld and Nicolson.

Locke, John (1972) "Of Identity and Diversity" (1690). In: Id. *An Essay Concerning Human Understanding.* Ed. J. Yolton. Vol. 1. London: Dent, 274–293.

Marvell, Andrew (1999) "To His Coy Mistress" (1681). In: H. Meller, R. Sühnel, eds. *British and American Classical Poems.* Heidelberg: C. Winter, 122 f.

Melville, Herman (1968) *Typee. A Peep at Polynesian Life.* (1846) In: Id. *The Writings of Herman Melville.* Vol. 1. Evanston: Northwestern UP.

Melville, Herman (1987) *Bartleby, the Scrivener.* (1856) In: Id. *The Piazza Tales. The Writings of Herman Melville.* Vol. 9. Evanston: Northwestern UP.

Melville, Herman (1988) *Moby Dick; or, The Whale.* (1851) In: Id. *The Writings of Herman Melville.* Vol. 6. Evanston: Northwestern UP.

Milton, John (1968) *The English Poems of John Milton.* Ed. H. C. Beeching. Oxford (et al.): Oxford UP.

Morrison, Toni (1988) *Beloved.* New York: Plume.

Morrison, Toni (1993) *The Bluest Eye.* (1970) London: Picador.

Morrison, Toni (1998) *Song of Solomon.* (1977) London: Vintage.

Nietzsche, Friedrich (1874) "On the Utility and Liability of History for Life". In: K. A. Pearson, D. Large, eds. (2006) *The Nietzsche Reader.* Malden/Oxford: Blackwell, 124–141.

Nietzsche, Friedrich (1980) *On the Advantage and Disadvantage of History for Life* (1874). Trans. P. Preuss. Indianapolis/Cambridge: Hackett.

Nietzsche, Friedrich (2008) *On the Genealogy of Morals: A Polemic.* Trans. Douglas Smith. 3rd ed. Oxford (et al.): Oxford UP.

Orwell, George (1961) *1984.* (1949) New York: Hartcourt.

Patmore, Coventry (1884) *The Angel in the House.* (1854) London: John W. Parker & Son.

Philip, M. NourbeSe (1991) "Discourse on the Logic of Language". In: S. Nasta, ed. *Motherlands. Black Women's Writing from Africa, the Caribbean and South Asia.* London: The Women's Press, xi f.

Pinter, Harold (1971) *The Birthday Party.* (1958) London: Methuen & Co.

Plato (2009) *Phaedros.* Trans. R. Waterfield. 2nd ed. Oxford (et al.): Oxford UP.

Poe, Edgar Allan (1984) "The Man of the Crowd". In: Id. *Complete Stories and Poems of Edgar Allan Poe.* (1840) New York: Doubleday, 215–221.

Pound, Ezra (1963) *Literary Essays.* Ed. T. S. Eliot. London: Faber and Faber.

Pound, Ezra (1968) *Selected Poems.* London: Faber and Faber.

Proust, Marcel (1996) *In Search of Lost Time.* Vol. 6: Time Regained & A Guide to Proust. Ed. S. Moncrieff. London: Vintage.

De Quincey, Thomas (1879) *The Collected Writings.* Ed. D. Masson. London: Black.

De Quincey, Thomas (2008) *Confessions of an English Opium Eater and Other Writings.* (1821) Oxford (et al.): Oxford UP.

Rossetti, Dante G. (1873) *Poems.* Leipzig: Bernhard Tauchnitz.

Rossetti, Dante G. (1970) *The Collected Works. Poems, Prose-tales and Literary Papers.* Vol. 1. St. Claire Shores, MI: Scholarly Press.

Rousseau, Jean-Jacques (2005) *The Confessions.* Trans. J. M. Cohen. London: Penguin.

Rushdie, Salman (1982) "The Empire Writes Back With a Vengeance" (1982). In: *London Times,* 03.07.1982.

Rushdie, Salman (1990) *Haroun and the Sea of Storys.* London: Granta.

Rushdie, Salman (1992) *The Satanic Verses.* (1988) Dover: The Consortium.

Earl of Shaftesbury, Anthony Ashley-Cooper (1964a) "An Essay on Wit and Humour in a Letter to a Friend" (1709). In: J. M. Robertson, ed. *Characteristics of Men, Manners, Opinions, Times.* New York: Bobbs-Merrill Company, 103–212.

Earl of Shaftesbury, Anthony Ashley-Cooper (1964b) "Soliloquy or Advice to an Author" (1710), in: J. M. Robertson, ed. *Characteristics of Men, Manners, Opinions, Times.* New York: Bobbs-Merrill Company, 103–212.

Shakespeare, William (1997a) *Hamlet* (1601). In: Id. The Norton Shakespeare. Based on the Oxford Edition, ed. Stephen Greenblatt. London/New York: W.W. Norton & Company, 1659–1759.

Shakespeare, William (1997b) *Henry IV. Part I* (1598). In: Id. The Norton Shakespeare. Based on the Oxford Edition, ed. Stephen Greenblatt. London/New York: W.W. Norton & Company, 1147–1224.

Shakespeare, William (1997c) *A Midsummer Night's Dream* (1595-96). In: Id. The Norton Shakespeare. Based on the Oxford Edition, ed. Stephen Greenblatt. London/New York: W.W. Norton & Company, 805–863.

Shakespeare, William (1997d) *Richard II* (1595–99). In: Id. The Norton Shakespeare. Based on the Oxford Edition, ed. Stephen Greenblatt. London/New York: W.W. Norton & Company, 943–1014.

Shakespeare, William (1997e) *Romeo and Juliet* (1595). In: Id. The Norton Shakespeare. Based on the Oxford Edition, ed. Stephen Greenblatt. London/New York: W.W. Norton & Company, 865–941.

Shakespeare, William (1997f) "Sonnet 77". In: Id. The Norton Shakespeare. Based on the Oxford Edition, ed. Stephen Greenblatt. London/New York: W.W. Norton & Company, 1949.

Shakespeare, William (1997g) *The Tempest* (1611). In: Id. The Norton Shakespeare. Based on the Oxford Edition, ed. Stephen Greenblatt. London/New York: W.W. Norton & Company, 3047–3107.

Shakespeare, William (1997h) *The Winter's Tale* (1609). In: Id. The Norton Shakespeare. Based on the Oxford Edition, ed. Stephen Greenblatt. London/New York: W.W. Norton & Company, 2873–2953.

Shakespeare, William (1997i) *The Tragedy of Othello the Moor of Venice* (1603-4). In: Id. The Norton Shakespeare. Based on the Oxford Edition, ed. Stephen Greenblatt. London/New York: W.W. Norton & Company, 2100–2174.

Shakespeare, William (1997j) *The Comical History of the Merchant of Venice, or Otherwise Called the Jew of Venice* (1596-98). In: Id. The Norton Shakespeare. Based on the Oxford Edition, ed. Stephen Greenblatt. London/New York: W.W. Norton & Company, 1090–1145.

Shakespeare, William (1997k) *The Tragedy of King Lear* (1604-05). In: Id. The Norton Shakespeare. Based on the Oxford Edition, ed. Stephen Greenblatt. London/New York: W.W. Norton & Company, 2337–2491.

Shelley, Mary (1965) *Frankenstein: or, the Modern Prometheus.* (1818) London: Dent.

Shelley, Percey B. (1968) "A Defence of Poetry". In: D. J. Enright, E. de Chickera, eds. *English Critical Texts.* Oxford (et al.): Oxford UP.

Silko, Leslie M. (1977) *Ceremony.* New York: Viking Press.

Silko, Leslie/Wright, James (1986) *The Delicacy and Strength of Lace.* Ed. A. Wright. Saint Paul: Gragwolf Press.

Stein, Gertrude (1968) *Geography and Plays.* New York: Haskell House.

Sterne, Laurence (2004) *The Life and Opinions of Tristram Shandy, Gentleman.* (1759–67) New York: Modern Library.

Stevenson, Robert L. (2008) "The Strange Case of Dr Jekyll and Mr Hyde". (1886) In: *Strange Case of Dr Jekyll and Mr Hyde and Other Tales.* Oxford (et al.): Oxford UP, 1–66.

Swift, Jonathan (1965) *Gulliver's Travels.* (1726) Malden/Oxford: Blackwell.

Thoreau, Henry D. (1995) "Sounds" (1854). In: Id. *Walden, or: Life in the Woods.* Boston: Houghton Mifflin.

Walker, Alice (1982) *The Color Purple.* London/New York: Harcourt Brace Jovanovich.

Whitman, Walt (1958) *Leaves of Grass.* (1855) Ed. G. Allen. New York: New American Library.

Wilde, Oscar (2003) *The Picture of Dorian Grey.* (1890) London: CRW.

Woolf, Virginia (1993) "Oxford Street Tide" (1932). In: Id. *The Essays of Virginia Woolf. 1929-1932.* Ed. S. Clarke. Vol 5. London: The Hogarth Press, 480–491.

Woolf, Virginia (1994) "Street Haunting. A London Adventure" (1930). In: Id. *Collected Essays.* Vol. 4. London: The Hogarth Press, 480–491.

Woolf, Virginia (2008a) *A Room of One's Own, and Three Guineas.* (1929) Oxford (et al.): Oxford UP.

Woolf, Virginia (2008b) *Orlando. A Biography.* (1928) Oxford (et al.): Oxford UP.

Wordsworth, William (1970) *The Prelude or Growth of a Poet's Mind.* (1850) Oxford (et al.): Oxford UP.

Yeats, William B. (1999a) "The Lake Isle of Innisfree" (1890). In: H. Meller, R. Sühnel, eds. *British and American Classical Poems.* Heidelberg: C. Winter, 128.

Yeats, William B. (1999b) "The Second Coming" (1919). In: H. Meller, R. Sühnel, eds. *British and American Classical Poems.* Heidelberg: C. Winter, 238.

Secondary Literature

Abraham, Nicolas (1988) "The Phantom of Hamlet or the Sixth Act". In: *Diacritics*, Winter 1988, 2–20.

Agamben, Giorgio (2002) *Homo sacer. Die souveräne Macht und das nackte Leben.* Frankfurt a. M.: Suhrkamp.

Albers, Irene (2001) "Das Fotografische in der Literatur". In: K. Barck et al., eds. *Ästhetische Grundbegriffe. Historisches Wörterbuch in sieben Bänden.* Vol. 2. Stuttgart: Metzler, 534–550.

Van Alphen, Ernst (1997) *Caught by History: Holocaust Effects in Contemporary Art, Literature and Theory.* Stanford: Stanford UP.

Ariès, Philippe (1975) *Geschichte der Kindheit.* München: Hanser.

Ariès, Philippe (1980) *Geschichte des Todes.* München: Hanser.

Arnold, Matthew (1960) *On the Classical Tradition.* In: Id. *The Complete Prose Works.* Vol. 1. Ann Arbor: Michigan UP.

Assmann, Aleida (1986) "Opting In und Opting Out. Zum Wandel des Stilbegriffs im England des 18. Jahrhunderts". In: H. Gumbrecht, K. L. Pfeiffer, eds. *Stil. Geschichten und Funktionen eines kulturwissenschaftlichen Diskurselements.* Frankfurt a. M.: Suhrkamp, 127–143.

Assmann, Aleida (1989) „Die Häuslichkeit der Welt. Zu Elaine Scarry's *The Body in Pain*", in: *Delfin* 12, 37–46.

Assmann, Aleida (1991a) „Die Weisheit Adams". In: Id., ed. *Weisheit* (Archäologie der literarischen Kommunikation III). München: Fink, 305–324.

Assmann, Aleida (1991b) "Schriftliche Folklore. Zur Entstehung und Funktion eines Überlieferungstyps". In: Id., J. Assmann, C. Hardmeier, eds. *Schrift und Gedächtnis.* München: Fink, 175–193.

Assmann, Aleida (1993a) „Das Problem der Identität aus kulturwissenschaftlicher Sicht", in: *Leviathan* 3, 238–253.

Assmann, Aleida (1993b) „Exkarnation. Gedanken zur Grenze zwischen Körper und Schrift". In: J. Huber, A. M. Müller, eds. *Raum und Verfahren. Interventionen.* Frankfurt a. M.: Stroemfeld/Roter Stern.

Assmann, Aleida (1995) „Was sind kulturelle Texte?". In: Andreas Poltermann, ed. *Literaturkanon – Medienereignis – kultureller Text.* Berlin: Erich Schmidt, 232–244.

Assmann, Aleida (1999a) *Erinnerungsräume. Formen und Wandlungen des kulturellen Gedächtnisses.* München: C. H. Beck.

Assmann, Aleida (1999b) „An we had the trick to see't. Geheimnis und Neugierde in Shakespears *Hamlet*". In: Id., J. Assmann, eds. *Geheimnis und Neugierde.* (Archäologie der literarischen Kommunikation V). München: Fink, 209–221.

Assmann, Aleida (2004) „Die Unverzichtbarkeit der Kulturwissenschaften". In: *Hildesheimer Universitätsreden*, NF 2, Hildesheim, 29–37.

Assmann, Aleida/Assmann, Jan/Hardmeier, Christof, eds. (1998) *Schrift und Gedächtnis.* 3. Aufl. München: Fink.

Assmann, Aleida/Friese, Heidrun, eds. (1998) *Identitäten. Erinnerung, Geschichte, Identität.* Frankfurt a. M.: Suhrkamp.

Assmann, Aleida et al., eds. (2004) *Positionen der Kulturanthropologie.* Frankfurt a. M.: Suhrkamp.

Assmann, Aleida/Frank, Michael C., eds. (2004) *Vergessene Texte.* Konstanz: Konstanz UP.

Assmann, Jan (1996) *Ägypten. Eine Sinngeschichte.* München: Hanser.

Assmann, Jan (1997) *Das kulturelle Gedächtnis. Schrift, Erinnerung und politische Identität in frühen Hochkulturen.* München: Beck.

Atwood, Margaret (1997) *In Search of Alias Grace. On Writing Canadian Historical Fiction.* Ottawa: Ottawa UP.

Augé, Marc (1995) *Non-Places. Introduction to an Anthropology of Supermodernity.* Trans. J. Howe. London/New York: Verso.

Austin, John L. (1992) *How To Do Things With Words. The William James Lectures delivered at Harvard University in 1955.* London: Oxford UP.

Bachelard, Gaston (1994) *The Poetics of Space.* Trans. M. Jolas. Boston: Beacon Press.

Bakhtin, Michael M. (1968) *Rabelais and His World.* Cambridge, MA: M.I.T. Press.

Bakhtin, Michail M. (1981) "Forms of Time and of the Chronotope in the Novel". In: M. Holquist, ed. *The dialogic imagination: Four essays by M. M. Bakhtin.* Austin and London: Texas UP.

Balász, Bela (1924) "Visible Man, or the Culture of Film". Trans. R. Livingston. In: *Screen* (2007), 48 (1), 91-108.

Barrie, Robert (2004) "Telmahs: Carnival Laughter in Hamlet". In: M. Burnett, J. Manning, ed. *New Essays on Hamlet.* New York: AMS Press, 83–100.

Barthes, Roland (1981) *Camera Lucida: Reflections on Photography.* Trans. R. Howard. New York: Hill and Wang.

Barthes, Roland (1989) *Sade, Fourier, Loyola.* Trans. R. C. Miller. Berkeley (et. al.): California UP.

Barthes, Roland (1990) "The Death of the Author". In: Id. *Image – Music – Text.* Trans. S. Heath. New York: The Noonday Press, 142-148.

Baumann, Gerd, ed. (1986) *The Written Word. Literacy in Transition.* Oxford: Clarendon Press.

Belsey, Catherine (1985) *The Subject of Tragedy: Identity and Difference in Renaissance Drama.* London, New York: Methuen.

Benhabib, Seyla (2002) *The Claims of Culture. Equality and Diversity in the Global Era.* Princeton: Princeton UP.

Benjamin, Walter (1968) "The Work of Art in the Age of Mechanical Reproduction". In: Id. *Illuminations. Essays and Reflections.* Ed. H. Arendt. New York: Schocken Books, 217–252.

Benjamin, Walter (2002) *The Arcades Project.* Ed. Rolf Tiedemann. Trans. H. Eiland, K. McLaughlin. New York: Belknap Harvard UP.

Benjamin, Walter (2006) "On the Concept of History". In: Id. *Selected Writings.* Vol. 4: 1938-1940. Eds. H. Eiland, M. W. Jennings. Cambridge, MA (et al.): Belknap Harvard UP, 389–400.

Bhabha, Homi K. (2008) *The Location of Culture.* London (et al.): Routledge.

Binder, Wolfgang, ed. (1993) *Ethnic Cultures in the 1920s in North America.* Frankfurt a. M.: Peter Lang.

Bloom, Harold (1973) *The Anxiety of Influence.* Oxford (et al.): Oxford UP.

Bloom, Harold (1999) *Shakespeare. The Invention of the Human.* New York: Riverhead Books.

Bloom, Harold (2003) *Hamlet. Poem Unlimited.* New York: Riverhead Books.

Blumenberg, Hans (1981) *Wirklichkeiten, in denen wir leben.* Stuttgart: Reclam.

Bogardus, Ralph (1984) *Pictures and Texts. Henry James, A. L. Coburn and New Ways of Seeing in Literary Culture*. Ann Arbor, MI: UMI Research Press.

Bosse, Heinrich (1981) *Autorschaft ist Werkherrschaft. Über die Entstehung des Urheberrechts aus dem Geist der Goethezeit*. Paderborn: Schöningh.

Bourdieu, Pierre (1974) „Der Habitus als Vermittlung zwischen Struktur und Praxis", in: *Zur Soziologie der symbolischen Formen*. Frankfurt a. M.: Suhrkamp, 125–58.

Bröck, Sabine (1988) *Der entkolonialisierte Körper. Die Protagonistin in der afroamerikanischen weiblichen Erzähltradition der 30er bis 80er-Jahre*. Frankfurt a. M.: Campus.

Bronfen, Elisabeth (1994) *Nur über ihre Leiche: Tod, Weiblichkeit und Ästhetik*. München: Kunstmann.

Bronfen, Elisabeth/Marius, Benjamin/Steffen, Therese, eds. (1997) *Hybride Kulturen. Beiträge zur anglo-amerikanischen Multikulturalismusdebatte*. Tübingen: Stauffenburg.

Buch, Hans C. (1972) *Ut Pictura Poesis. Die Beschreibungsliteratur und ihre Kritiker von Lessing bis Lukács*. München: Hanser.

Bühler, Karl (1982) *Sprachtheorie. Die Darstellungsfunktion der Sprache* (1934). Stuttgart: Fischer.

Burke, Kenneth (1966) "Definition of Man". In: *Language as Symbolic Action. Essays in Life, Literature, and Method*. Berkeley, LA: California UP, 2–24.

Butler, Judith (1990) *Gender Trouble. Feminism and the Subversion of Identity*. New York: Routledge.

Butler, Judith (1993) *Bodies that Matter: On the Discursive Limits of "Sex"*. New York: Routledge.

Caplan, Jane, ed. (2000) *Written on the Body. The Tattoo in European and American History*. London: Reaktion.

Carlyle, Thomas (1926) *On Heroes, Hero-Worship, and the Heroic in History*. London: Everyman.

Caruth, Cathy (1996a) *Trauma. Explorations in Memory*. Baltimore: Johns Hopkins UP.

Caruth, Cathy (1996b) *Unclaimed Experience. Trauma, Narrative and History*. Baltimore: Johns Hopkins UP.

Cassirer, Ernst (1983) *Wesen und Wirkung des Symbolbegriffs*. Darmstadt: WBG.

Cassirer, Ernst (1988) *Philosophie der symbolischen Formen. Die Sprache* (1923). Vol. 1. Darmstadt: WBG.

Cavalli, Alessandro (1991) "Soziale Gedächtnisbildung in der Moderne". In: A. Assmann, D. Harth, eds. *Kultur als Lebenswelt und Monument*. Frankfurt a. M.: Fischer.

De Certeau, Michel (1984) *The Practice of Everyday Life*. Trans. S. Rendall. Berkeley: California UP.

Clifford, James T. (1997) *Routes. Travel and Translation in the Late Twentieth Century*. London: Harvard UP.

Curschmann, Michael (1999) „Wort – Schrift – Bild. Zum Verhältnis von volkssprachigem Schrifttum und bildender Kunst vom 12. bis zum 16. Jahrhundert". In: W. Haug, ed. *Mittelalter und frühe Neuzeit*. Tübingen: Niemeyer, 378–470.

Daniel, Ute (1993) "'Kultur' und 'Gesellschaft'. Überlegungen zum Gegenstandsbereich der Sozialgeschichte." In: *Geschichte und Gesellschaft* 19/1, 68–99.

Derrida, Jacques (1988) *Limited Inc. Two Essays*. Evanston: North Western UP.

Dohrn van Rossum, Gerhard (1992) *Die Geschichte der Stunde. Uhren und die moderne Zeitordnung*. München/Wien: Hanser.

Duden, Barbara (1998) *The Woman Beneath the Skin: A Doctor's Patients in Eighteenth-century Germany.* Cambridge, MA: Harvard UP.

Van Dülmen, Richard (1995) "Historische Kulturforschung zur Frühen Neuzeit. Entwicklung – Probleme – Aufgaben". In: *Geschichte und Gesellschaft* 21, 403–429.

Eagleton, Terry (2000) *The Idea of Culture.* Malden/Oxford: Blackwell.

Ecker, Gisela, ed. (1999) *Trauer tragen, Trauer zeigen. Inszenierungen der Geschlechter.* München: Fink.

Eco, Umberto (1972) *Einführung in die Semiotik.* München: UTB Fink.

Eco, Umberto (1985) *La struttura assente. La ricerca semiotica e il metodo strutturale.* Milano: Bompiani.

Edel, Leon (1974) "Novel and Camera". In: J. Halperin, ed. *The Theory of the Novel. New Essays.* Oxford (et al.): Oxford UP, 177–188.

Ehlich, Konrad (1983) "Text und sprachliches Handeln. Die Entstehung von Texten aus dem Bedürfnis nach Überlieferung". In: A. Assmann, J. Assmann, C. Hardmeier, eds. (1998) *Schrift und Gedächtnis.* (Archäologie der literarischen Kommunikation I). München: Wilhelm Fink, 24–43.

Eisenstein, Elizabeth (1997) *The Printing Press as an Agent of Change. Communications and Cultural Transformations in Early-modern Europe.* Cambridge: Cambridge UP.

Elias, Norbert (1977) *Über den Prozess der Zivilisation. Soziogenetische und psychogenetische Untersuchungen.* Vol. 2: Wandlungen der Gesellschaft. Entwurf zu einer Theorie der Zivilisation. Frankfurt a. M.: Suhrkamp.

Elias, Norbert (1978) *Über den Prozess der Zivilisation. Soziogenetische und psychogenetische Untersuchungen.* Vol. 1: Wandlungen des Verhaltens in den weltlichen Oberschichten des Abendlandes. Frankfurt a. M.: Suhrkamp.

Eliot, T. S. (1962) *Notes Towards the Definition of Culture.* London: Faber and Faber.

Eliot, T. S. (1969) "Tradition and Individual Talent" (1919). In: *The Sacred Wood. Essays on Poetry and Criticism.* London: Methuen, 47–59.

Ellis, Havelock (1918) *The Erotic Rights of Women; and, The Objects of Marriage. Two Essays.* Battersea: Battley Bros.

Erll, Astrid (2005) *Kollektives Gedächtnis und Erinnerungskulturen. Eine Einführung.* Stuttgart/Weimar: Metzler.

Ernst, Wolfgang/Vismann, Cornelia, eds. (1998) *Geschichtskörper. Zur Aktualität von Ernst Kantorowicz.* München: Fink.

Erzgräber, Willi (1998) *James Joyce. Mündlichkeit und Schriftlichkeit im Spiegel experimenteller Erzählkunst.* Tübingen: Narr.

Falk, Julia S. (1995) "Roman Jakobson and North American Linguistics". In: *Historiographia Linguistica,* 23/3, 335–367.

Felman, Shoshana/Laub, Dori (1992) *Testimony. Crises of Witnessing in Literature, Psychoanalysis and History.* New York: Routledge.

Fiedler, Leslie A. (1971) "Cross the Border – Close the Gap". In: *The Collected Essays of Leslie Fiedler.* Vol. 2. New York: Stein and Day, 461–485.

Fisher, Philip (1997) *The Making and Effacing of Art. Modern American Art in a Culture of Museums.* Cambridge, MA: Harvard UP.

Fisher, Philip (2002) *The Vehement Passions.* Princeton: Princeton UP.

Flasch, Kurt (1992) „Historische Arbeit an Zeichen". In: T. Borsche, W. Stegmeier, eds. *Zur Philosophie des Zeichens.* Berlin/New York: de Gruyter, 136–149.

Foucault, Michel (1967) *Madness and Civilization. A History of Insanity in the Age of Reason.* Trans. R. Howard. London: Travistock Publications.

Foucault, Michel (1985) "Freiheit und Selbstsorge". In: H. Becker, ed. *Freiheit und Selbstsorge. Interview 1984 und Vorlesung 1982.* Frankfurt a. M.: Materialis, 7–28.

Foucault, Michel (1994) *The Birth of the Clinic: An Archaeology of Medical Perception.* New York: Vintage Books.

Foucault, Michel (1990) *The History of Sexuality.* New York: Vintage Books.

Frank, Manfred (1991) *Selbstbewußtsein und Selbsterkenntnis. Essays zur analytischen Philosophie der Subjektivität*, Stuttgart: Reclam.

Frank, Michael C. (2006) *Kulturelle Einflussangst. Inszenierungen der Grenze in der Reiseliteratur des 19. Jahrhunderts.* Bielefeld: Transcript, 87–128.

Frank, Michael C. (2011) "'A Mark Indelible': Herman Melville and the Cross-Cultural History of Tattooing in the Nineteenth Century". In: S. Jobs, G. Mackenthun, eds. *Embodiments of Cultural Contact.* Münster (et al.): Waxmann, 41–60.

Frühwald, Wolfgang et al., eds. (1991) *Geisteswissenschaften heute.* Frankfurt a. M.: Suhrkamp.

Gallagher, Jane/Greenblatt, Stephen (2000) *Practising New Historicism.* Chicago: Chicago UP.

Garcia, Reyes (1983) "Senses of Place in Ceremony". In: *Melus – The Journal of the Society for the Study of the Multi-Ethnic Literature of the United States* 10, 37–48.

Gates, Henry L. (1988) *The Signifying Monkey: A Theory of Afro-American Literary Criticism.* Oxford (et al.): Oxford UP.

Geertz, Clifford (1999) *Dichte Beschreibung. Beiträge zum Verstehen kultureller Systeme.* Frankfurt a. M.: Suhrkamp.

Giesecke, Michael (1991) *Der Buchdruck in der frühen Neuzeit. Eine historische Fallstudie über die Durchsetzung neuer Informations- und Kommunikationstechnologien.* Frankfurt a. M.: Suhrkamp.

Gilbert, Sandra M./Gubar, Susan (1979) *The Madwoman in the Attic. The Woman Writer and the Ninetheenth-Century Literary Imagination.* New Haven/London: Yale UP.

Ginzburg, Carlo (1983) *Spurenlesen. Über verborgene Geschichte, Kunst und soziales Gedächtnis.* Berlin: Wagenbach.

Goldberg, David T. (1994) *Multiculturalism: A Critical Reader.* Malden/Oxford: Blackwell.

Granofsky, Ronald (1995) *The Trauma Novel. Contemporary Symbolic Depictions of Collective Disaster.* New York: Lang.

Greenblatt, Stephen (1980) *Renaissance Self-Fashioning: from More to Shakespeare.* Chicago: Chicago UP.

Greenblatt, Stephen (1992) *Learning to Curse. Essays in Early Modern Culture.* New York: Routledge.

Greenblatt, Stephen (2001) *Hamlet in Purgatory.* Princeton: Princeton UP.

Greiner, Walter F./Kemmler, Fritz, eds. (1979) *Realismustheorien in England (1692–1912).* Tübingen: Niemeyer.

Groebner, Valentin (2004) *Der Schein der Person. Steckbrief, Ausweis und Kontrolle im Europa des Mittelalters.* München: Beck.

Grossberg, Lawrence (1996) "The Space of Culture, the Power of Space". In: I. Chambers, L. Curti, eds. *The Post-Colonial Question. Common Skies, Divided Horizons.* London/New York: Routledge, 169–188.

Große Kracht, Klaus (2001) "Rezension zu Terry Eagletons *Was ist Kultur? Eine Einführung.*" In: *Arbitrium 19.* Tübingen: Max Niemeyer, 261 f.

Hagstrum, Jean (1958) *The Sister Arts: The Tradition of Literary Pictorialism and English Poetry from Dryden to Gray.* Chicago: Chicago UP.

Halbwachs, Maurice (1992) *On Collective Memory.* Ed. L. A. Coser. Chicago: Chicago UP.

Hall, Stuart et al. (1980) "'Encoding/Decoding'. In Centre for Contemporary Cultural Studies". In: Id. et al., eds. *Culture, Media, Language: Working Papers in Cultural Studies, 1972-79.* London: Hutchinson, 107–116.

Hall, Stuart (1986) "Cultural Studies: Two Paradigms." In: R. Collins et al., ed. *Media, Culture and Society. A Critical Reader.* London: Sage, 32–48.

Hall, Stuart (1990) "The Emergence of Cultural Studies and the Crisis of the Humanities." In: *October,* Vol. 53, S. 11–23.

Haraway, Donna (1998) *Simians, Cyborgs, and Women.* London: Free Association Books.

Hartley, Leslie P. (2002) *The Go-Between.* New York: Review Books.

Havelock, Eric (1982) *The Literate Revolution in Greece and its Consequences.* Princeton: Princeton UP.

Havelock, Eric (1986) *The Muse learns to Write: Reflections on Orality and Literacy from Antiquity to the Present.* New Haven: Yale UP.

Haverkamp, Anselm (1991) "Auswendigkeit. Das Gedächtnis der Rhetorik". In: Id., R. Lachmann, eds. *Gedächtniskunst. Raum – Bild – Schrift: Studien zur Mnemotechnik.* Frankfurt a. M.: Suhrkamp, 25–52.

Heger, Klaus (1976) *Monem, Wort, Satz und Text.* Tübingen: Niemeyer.

Helgerson, Richard (1976) *The Elizabethan Prodigals.* Berkeley: California UP.

Herrmann, Douglas J. (2000) *Gedächtnis-Training. Über 70 Methoden, das Lernen und Einprägen zu verbessern.* Niedernhausen/Ts: Bassermann Verlag.

Hessel, Franz (1984) *Ein Flaneur in Berlin.* Berlin: Arsenal.

Hill Rigney, Barbara (1978) *Madness and Sexual Politics in the Feminist Novel. Studies in Brontë, Woolf, Lessing and Atwood.* Madison: Wisconsin UP.

Horn, Eva (1998) *Trauer Schreiben. Die Toten im Text der Goethezeit.* München: Fink.

Humm, Maggie (2003) *Modernist Women and Visual Cultures. Virginia Woolf, Vanessa Bell, Photography and Cinema.* New Brunswick, NJ: Rutgers UP.

Jäger, Ludwig (1997) "Die Medialität der Sprachzeichen. Zur Kritik des Repräsentationsbegriffs aus der Sicht des semiologischen Konstruktivismus". In: M. Lieber, W. Hirdt, eds. *Kunst und Kommunikation. Betrachtungen zum Medium Sprache in der Romania.* Tübingen: Stauffenburg, 199–220.

Jakobson, Roman (1960) "Closing Statement: Linguistics and Poetics". In: T. A. Sebeok, ed. *Style in Language.* Cambridge, MA: MIT Press. 350–377.

Jameson, Frederic (1981) *The Political Unconscious. Narrative as a Socially Symbolic Act.* London: Methuen.

Jochum, Uwe (1999) *Kleine Bibliotheksgeschichte.* Stuttgart: Reclam.

Kantorowicz, Ernst (1957) *The King's Two Bodies. A Study in Medieval Political Theology.* Princeton: Princeton UP.

Kany, Roland (1987) *Mnemosyne als Programm. Geschichte, Erinnerung und die Andacht zum Unbedeutenden im Werk von Usener, Warburg und Benjamin.* Tübingen: Niemeyer.

Kastendiek, Hans/Sturm, Roland, eds. (2007) *Länderbericht Großbritannien.* Schriftenreihe Vol. 543 der Bundeszentrale für Politische Bildung, Bonn.

Kittler, Friedrich/Turk, Horst/Nassen, Ulrich, eds. (1980) *Austreibung des Geistes aus den Geisteswissenschaften*. Paderborn: Schoeningh.

Kittler, Friedrich A. (1990) : *Discourse Networks. 1800/1900*. Trans. M. Merteer. Stanford, CA: Stanford UP.

Krämer, Sybille, ed. (1998) *Medien – Computer – Realität: Wirklichkeitsvorstellungen und Neue Medien*. Frankfurt a. M.: Suhrkamp.

Kripke, Saul (1980) *Naming and Necessity*. Cambridge, MA: Harvard UP.

Latour, Bruno (1986) "Visualisation and Cognition: Drawing Things Together." In: H. Kucklick, ed. *Knowledge and Society: Studies in the Sociology of Culture and Present 6*, JAI Press, 1–40.

Laurenson, Diana/Swingewood, Alan (1972) *The Sociology of Literature*. London: MacGibbon & Kee.

Leavis, Frank R. (1948) *The Great Tradition*. London: Chatto & Windus.

Lefebvre, Henri (1991) *The Production of Space*. (1974), Malden/Oxford: Blackwell.

Lippe, Rudolf zur (1987) *Sinnenbewusstsein. Grundlegung einer anthropologischen Ästhetik*. Reinbek: Rowohlt.

Mainberger, Sabine (1995) *Schriftskepsis. Von Philosophen, Mönchen, Buchhaltern und Kalligraphen*. München: Fink.

Marcuse, Herbert (1964) *One-Dimensional Man: Studies in the Ideology of Advanced Industrial Society*. Boston: Beacon.

Margalit, Avishai (2003) *The Ethics of Memory*. Cambridge, MA: Harvard UP.

Marquard, Odo (1981) *Abschied vom Prinzipiellen. Philosophische Studien*. Stuttgart: Reclam.

Matt, Peter von (1983) *... fertig ist das Angesicht. Zur Literaturgeschichte des menschlichen Gesichts*. München/Wien: dtv.

Mauss, Marcel (1979) "Body Techniques". In: Id. *Sociology and Psychology. Essays* (1950). London: Routledge and Kegan Paul, 95–119.

Mayer, Ruth (1999) "Vielbevölkerte Zone". In: Jan Engelmann, ed. *Die kleinen Unterschiede. Der Cultural Studies Reader*. Frankfurt/New York: Campus, 231–243.

Mayer, Ruth (2002) *Artificial Africas. Colonial Images in the Times of Globalization*. Hanover, NH: New England UP.

Mead, George H. (1993) *Geist, Identität und Gesellschaft aus der Sicht des Sozialbehaviorismus*. Frankfurt a. M.: Suhrkamp.

Mergenthal, Silvia (1997) *Erziehung zur Tugend. Frauenrollen und der englische Roman um 1800*. Tübingen: Niemeyer.

Miller, J. Hillis (1995) *Topographies*. Stanford: Stanford UP.

Minnis, Alastair J. (1984) *Medieval Theory of Authorship*. London: Scolar Press.

Mitchell, William J. T. (1994) *Picture Theory*. Chicago: Chicago UP.

Mitchell, William J. T. (2005) *What Do Pictures Want? The Lives and Loves of Images*. Chicago: Chicago UP.

Mittelstraß, Jürgen (1996) "Die unheimlichen Geisteswissenschaften" (Akademievorlesung am 9. Februar 1995). In: *Berlin-Brandenburgische Akademie der Wissenschaften. Berichte und Abhandlungen* 2. Berlin, 215–235.

Moos, Peter von, ed. (2004) *Unverwechselbarkeit. Persönliche Identität und Identifikation in der vormodernen Gesellschaft*. Köln/Weimar: Böhlau.

Morley, David (1992) *Television, Audiences and Cultural Studies.* London/New York: Routledge.

Mukařovský, Jan (1977) "Poetic Designation and the Aesthetic Function of Language." In: Id.: *The Word and Verbal Art: Selected Essays.* Ed. and trans. J. Burbank, P. Steiner. New Haven: Yale UP, 68-73.

Müller, Jan-Dirk, ed. (1996) *,Aufführung' und ,Schrift' in Mittelalter und früher Neuzeit.* DFG-Symposium 1994, Stuttgart: Metzler.

Najder, Zdzislaw, ed. (1964) *Conrad's Polish Background: Letters To and From Polish Friends.* Trans. H. Carroll. Oxford (et al.): Oxford UP.

Najder, Zdzislaw, ed. (1983) *Conrad Under Familial Eyes.* Trans. H. Carroll. Cambridge: Cambridge UP.

Nelson, Robert M. (1993) "Place, Vision, and Identity in Native American Literatures". In: D. Morrison, ed. (1997) *American Indian Studies.* New York: Peter Lang, 265-283.

Neumann, Gerhard (2000) *Lesbarkeit der Kultur: Literaturwissenschaften zwischen Kulturtechnik und Ethnographie.* München: Fink.

Niethammer, Lutz (2000) *Kollektive Identität: Heimliche Quellen einer unheimlichen Konjunktur.* Reinbek: Rowohlt.

Nowotny, Helga (1996) "Die Erfindung der Zwischenwelt. Zwischenräume, Zwischenzeiten, Zwischen Niemand und Jemand". In: B. Felderer, ed. *Wunschmaschine Welterfindung. Eine Geschichte der Technikvisionen seit dem 18. Jahrhundert.* Wien/New York: Springer, 8–23.

Nussbaum, Martha (1999) "'Secret Sewers of Vice': Disgust, Bodies, and the Law". In S. A. Bandes, ed. *The Passions of Law.* Critical America. New York/London: New York UP, 19–62.

Ostendorf, Bernd (1983) *Amerikanische Gettoliteratur. Zur Literatur marginaler und unterdrückter Gruppen in Amerika.* Darmstadt: Wissenschaftliche Buchgesellschaft.

Osterhammel, Jürgen (2003) *Kolonialismus. Geschichte – Formen – Folgen.* München: C.H. Beck.

Pearsall, Derek (1985) "Middle English Romance and its Audiences". In: M.-J. Arn, H. Wirtjes, eds. *Historical and Editorial Studies in Medieval and Early Modern English. For Johan Gerritsen.* Groningen: Welters-Noordhoff, 37–47.

Peirce, Charles S. (1903) "A syllabus of certain topics of logic". In: The Peirce Edition Project, eds. (1998) *The Essential Peirce. Selected philosophical writings.* Vol. 2: 1893-1913. Bloomington/Indianapolis, IN: Indiana UP, 226-241.

Pethes, Nicolas/Ruchatz, Jens, eds. (2001) *Gedächtnis und Erinnerung, Ein interdisziplinäres Lexikon.* Reinbek: Rowohlt.

Pfotenhauer, Helmut (1987) *Literarische Anthropologie. Selbstbiographien und ihre Geschichte – am Leitfaden des Leibes.* Stuttgart: Metzler.

Pinder, Wilhelm (1926) *Das Problem der Generation in der Kunstgeschichte Europas.* Berlin: Frankfurter Verlags-Anstalt.

Plessner, Helmuth (1928) "Die Stufen des Organischen und der Mensch. Einleitung in die philosophische Anthropologie". In: G. Dux, O. Marquardt, E. Ströker, eds. (1981) *Gesammelte Schriften.* Vol. IV. Frankfurt a. M.: Suhrkamp.

Plett, Heinrich F. (1975) *Rhetorik der Affekte. Englische Wirkungsästhetik im Zeitalter der Renaissance.* Tübingen: Niemeyer.

Pöppel, Ernst (1988) *Grenzen des Bewusstseins: über Wirklichkeit und Welterfahrung.* Stuttgart: DVA.

Posner, Roland (1997) *Semiotik. Ein Handbuch zu den zeichentheoretischen Grundlagen von Natur und Kultur.* Berlin/New York: de Gruyter.

Pratt, Mary L. (1986) "Fieldwork in Common Places". In: J. Clifford, G. E. Marcus, eds. *Writing Culture. The Poetics and Politics of Ethnography.* Berkeley: California UP, 27–50.

Rand, Nicholas (1991) "Kann man nach Freud noch Hamlet lesen?". In: *Psyche* 8, 675-690.

Randall, William L. (1995) *The Stories We Are: An Essay on Self-Creation.* Toronto, ON: Toronto UP.

Readings, Bill (1997) *The University in Ruins.* Cambridge: Harvard UP.

Reich, Charles A. (1995) *The Greening of America.* New York: Crown Trade.

Ricoeur, Paul (1992) *Oneself as Another.* Trans. K. Blamey. Chicago: Chicago UP.

Rieger, Stefan (1995) "Autorfunktion und Buchmarkt". In: M. Pechlivanos et al., eds. *Einführung in die Literaturwissenschaft*, Stuttgart: Metzler.

Rippl, Gabriele, ed. (1993) *Unbeschreiblich weiblich. Texte zur feministischen Anthropologie.* Frankfurt a. M.: Fischer.

Rippl, Gabriele (2005) *Beschreibungs-Kunst. Zur intermedialen Poetik angloamerikanischer Ikontexte (1880 - 2000).* München: Fink.

Röckl, Barbara (2006) *Through a Glass, Darkly. The Mirror Metaphor in Texts by Richard Wright, James Baldwin and Ralph Ellison.* Dissertation, Konstanz.

Rosenthal, Caroline (2004) "The Other American Renaissance. Sisam Warmer's 'The Wide, Wide World'". In: A. Assmann, M. Frank, eds. *Vergessene Texte.* Konstanz: Konstanz UP, 83–104.

Rüsen, Jörn (1990) *Zeit und Sinn, Strategien historischen Denkens.* Frankfurt a. M.: Fischer.

Rushdie, Salman (1991a) "'Errata': Or, Unreliable Narration in *Midnights Children*" (1983). In: Id. *Imaginary Homelands. Essays and Criticism 1981-1991.* London: Granta Books.

Rushdie, Salman (1991b) *Imaginary Homelands. Essays and Criticism 1981-1991.* London: Granta Books.

Rushdie, Salman (2002) *Step Across This Line. Collected Nonfiction 1992-2002.* New York: Random House.

Sartre, Jean Paul (1964) *Was ist Literatur? Ein Essay.* Hamburg: Rowohlt.

De Saussure, Ferdinand (1916) *Cours de linguistique générale.* Ed. C. Bally, A. Sechehaye. Lausanne/Paris : Payot.

Scarry, Elaine (1985) *The Body in Pain. The Making and Unmaking of the World.* Oxford (et al.): Oxford UP.

Schacter, Daniel L. (2001) *Seven Sins of Memory. How the Mind Forgets and Remembers.* Boston: Houghton Mifflin.

Schenda, Rudolf (1976) *Die Lesestoffe der Kleinen Leute. Studien zur populären Literatur im 19. und 20. Jahrhundert.* München: Beck.

Scherpe, Klaus (1999) "Kanon – Text – Medium. Kulturwissenschaftliche Motivationen für die Literaturwissenschaft". In: W. Schmidt-Dengler, A. Schwob, eds. *Germanistik im Spannungsfeld zwischen Philologie und Kulturwissenschaft.* Wien: Edition Praesens, 19-35.

Schivelbusch, Wolfgang (1977) *Geschichte der Eisenbahnreise. Zur Industrialisierung von Raum und Zeit im 19. Jahrhundert.* München: Hanser.

Schlögel, Karl (2003) *Im Raume lesen wir die Zeit. Über Zivilisationsgeschichte und Geopolitik.* München: Hanser.

Schmidt, Siegfried J. (2000) *Kalte Faszination: Medien, Kultur, Wissenschaft in der Mediengesellschaft.* Weilerswist: Velbrück Wissenschaft.

Schmitt, Peter J. (1969) *Back to Nature. The Arcadian Myth in Urban America.* Oxford (et al.): Oxford UP.

Schorske, Carl (1999) "Grace and the Word: Austria's Two Cultures and Their Modern Fate". In: Id. *Thinking with History, Explorations in the Passage to Modernism.* Princeton: Princeton UP, 125–140.

Schwab, Gabriele (1994) *Subjects without Selves. Transitional Texts in Modern Fiction.* Cambridge/London: Harvard UP.

Schweizer, Nikolaus R. (1972) *The Ut Pictura Poesis Controversy in Eighteenth-Century England and Germany.* Bern/Frankfurt a. M.: Lang.

Shilling, Chris (1993) *The Body and Social Theory.* London: Sage.

Simon, Josef (1989) *Die Philosophie des Zeichens.* Berlin/New York: de Gruyter.

Soja, Edward W. (1989) *Postmodern Geographies. The Reassertion of Space in Critical Social Theory.* London/New York: Verso.

Sollers, Werner (1986) *Beyond Ethnicity. Consent and Descent in American Culture.* Oxford (et al.): Oxford UP.

Sontag, Susan (2003) *Regarding the Pain of Others.* New York: Farrar, Strauss and Giroux.

Stafford, Barbara M. (1991) *Body Criticism. Imaging the Unseen in Enlightenment Art and Medicine.* Cambridge, MA: MIT.

Stegmeier, Werner (1994) "Weltabkürzungskunst. Orientierung durch Zeichen". In: J. Simon, ed. *Zeichen und Interpretation.* Frankfurt a. M., 119-141.

Steiner, George (1997) *Der Garten des Archimedes.* München: Hanser.

Steiner, Uwe C. (1997) "Können die Kulturwissenschaften eine neue moralische Funktion beanspruchen? Eine Bestandsaufnahme". In: *DVjS* 71/1, March.

Teichert, Dieter (2000) *Personen und Identitäten.* Berlin/New York: de Gruyter.

Todorov, Tzvetan (1995) *Symboltheorien.* Tübingen: Niemeyer.

Trabant, Jürgen (1999a) "Zeichen – Sprache". In: H. Bosse, U. Renner, eds. *Literaturwissenschaft – Einführung in ein Sprachspiel.* Grundkurs, Vol. 3, Freiburg: Rombach, 31–47.

Trabant, Jürgen (1999b) "Wo ist eigentlich die Literatursemiotik geblieben?". In: E. Goebel, W. Klein, eds. *Literaturforschung heute.* Berlin: Akademie Verlag, 269–275.

Trilling, Lionel (1972) *Sincerity and Authenticity.* Oxford (et al.): Oxford UP.

Tschachler, Heinz (1990) *Ökologie und Arkadien. Natur und nordamerikanische Kultur der siebziger Jahre.* Frankfurt a. M./Bern/New York: Lang.

Turner, Frederick J. (1962) *The Frontier in American History.* New York: Holt, Rinehart and Winston.

Turner, Frederick J. (1963) "The Significance of the Frontier". In: Id. *The Significance of the Frontier in American History.* New York: Ungar, 27–58.

Tylor, Edward B. (1958) *Primitive Culture* (1871). New York: Harper & Row.

Vidler, Anthony (1992) *The Architectural Uncanny – Essays in the Modern Unhomely.* Cambridge, MA: MIT Press.

Vinken, Barbara, ed. (1992) *Dekonstruktiver Feminismus. Literaturwissenschaft in Amerika.* Frankfurt a. M.: Suhrkamp.

Waldenfels, Bernhard (1990) *Der Stachel des Fremden*. Frankfurt a. M.: Suhrkamp.

Waldenfels, Bernhard (2000) *Das leibliche Selbst. Vorlesungen zur Phänomenologie des Leibes*. Frankfurt a. M.: Suhrkamp.

Waldenfels, Bernhard (2001) *Verfremdung der Moderne. Phänomenologische Grenzgänge*. Göttingen: Wallenstein.

Warburg, Aby M. (1980) *Ausgewählte Schriften und Würdigungen*. Ed. D. Wuttke. Baden-Baden: Koerner.

Weigel, Sigrid (1990) *Topographien der Geschlechter. Kulturgeschichtliche Studien zur Literatur*. Reinbek: Rowohlt.

Weigel, Sigrid (2004) "Zum 'topographical turn'. Raumkonzepte in den Cultural Studies und den Kulturwissenschaften". In: Id. *Literatur als Voraussetzung der Kulturgeschichte. Schauplätze von Shakespeare bis Benjamin*. München: Fink, 233–247.

Welsch, Wolfgang (1994) "Transkulturalität. Lebensformen nach der Auflösung der Kulturen". In: K. Lugert, R. Renger, eds. *Dialog der Kulturen. Die multikulturelle Gesellschaft und die Medien*. Wien: Österreichischer Kunst- und Kulturverlag, 147–149.

White, Hayden (1973) *Metahistory. The Historical Imagination in Nineteenth Century Europe*. Baltimore: Johns Hopkins UP.

Wierlacher, Alois et al., eds. (1993) *Kulturthema Essen: Ansichten und Problemfelder*. Berlin: Akademie Verlag.

Wilentz, Gay (1992) "English Is a Foreign Anguish: Caribbean Writers and the Disruption of the Colonial Canon". In: Karen R. Lawrence, ed. *Decolonizing Tradition: New Views of Twentieth-Century "British" Literary Canons*. Urbana: Illinois UP, 261–278.

Williams, Raymond (1958) *Culture and Society*. Harmondsworth: Penguin Books.

Williams, Raymond (1976) *Keywords. A Vocabulary of Culture and Society*. Glasgow: Fontana.

Wilson, John D. (1966) *What Happens in 'Hamlet'*. Cambridge: Cambridge UP.

Woodmansee, Martha, ed. (1983) *Erkennen und Deuten. Essays zur Literatur und Literaturtheorie. Edgar Lohner in memoriam*. Berlin: Erich Schmidt.

Wright, Richard/Rosskam, Edwin (1988) *Twelve Million Black Voices*. (1941) New York: Thunder's Mouth Press.

Wulf, Christoph, ed. (1985) *Lust und Liebe. Wandlungen der Sexualität*. München: Piper.

Wulf, Christoph, ed. (1997) *Vom Menschen. Handbuch Historische Anthropologie*. Weinheim: Beltz.

Wulf, Christoph (2004) *Anthropologie – Geschichte, Kultur, Philosophie*. Reinbek: Rowohlt.

Yates, Frances (2001) *The Art of Memory*. Chicago: Chicago UP.

Zumthor, Paul (1983) *Introduction à la Poésie Orale*. Paris: Eds. du Seuil, 245-261.

Further Reading

Abel, Günter (1999) *Sprache, Zeichen, Interpretation*. Frankfurt a. M.: Suhrkamp.

Armstrong, Philip (2008) *What Animals Mean in the Fiction of Modernity*. London (et al.): Routledge.

Bachmann-Medick, Doris (2006) *Cultural Turns. Neuorientierungen in den Kulturwissenschaften*. Reinbeck: Rowohlt.

Bal, Mieke/Crewe, Jonathan/Spitzer, Leo, eds. (1999) *Acts of Memory. Cultural Recall in the Present*. Hanover, NH: New England UP.

Barker, Chris (2008) *Cultural Studies: Theory and Practice.* 3rd ed., London: Sage.

Barthes, Roland (1982) *Empire of Signs.* Trans. R. Howard. New York: Hill & Wang.

Bataille, Georges (1970) *Histoire de l'œil.* Paris: Gallimard.

Baucom, Ian (2005) *Specters of the Atlantic.* Durham/London: Duke UP.

Becker, Barbara/Schneider, Irmela, eds. (2000) *Was vom Körper übrig bleibt. Körperlichkeit – Identität – Medien.* Frankfurt a. M./New York: Campus.

Becker, Sabina (2007) *Literatur- und Kulturwissenschaften: ihre Methoden und Theorien.* Reinbek: Rowohlt.

Bender, John/Wellbery, David, eds. (1991) *Chronotypes. The Construction of Time.* Stanford: Stanford UP.

Bieber, Hans J., ed. (2002) *Die Zeit im Wandel der Zeit.* Kassel: Kassel UP.

Birkenhauer, Theresia, ed. (1998) *Zeitlichkeiten – zur Realität der Künste: Theater, Film, Photographie, Malerei, Literatur.* Berlin: Vorwerk 8.

Bohn, Volker, ed. (1990) *Bildlichkeit.* Frankfurt a. M.: Suhrkamp.

Bohrer, Karl Heinz (2003) *Ekstasen der Zeit: Augenblick, Gegenwart, Erinnerung.* München/Wien: Hanser.

Bohrer, Karl Heinz (2004) *Plötzlichkeit: zum Augenblick des ästhetischen Scheins.* Frankfurt a. M.: Suhrkamp.

Borsche, Tilman/Stegmeier, Werner, eds. (1992) *Zur Philosophie des Zeichens.* Berlin/New York: de Gruyter.

Briggs, Asa/Burke, Peter (2009) *A Social History of the Media. From Gutenberg to the Internet.* Cambridge: Polity Press.

Brocker, Manfred/Nau, Heimo H. (1997) *Ethnozentrismus. Möglichkeiten und Grenzen des interkulturellen Dialogs.* Darmstadt: Primus.

Burke, Peter J. (2009) *Cultural Hybridity.* Cambridge: Polity Press.

Burke, Peter J./Stets, Jan E. (2009) *Identity Theory.* Oxford (et al.): Oxford UP.

Butler, Judith (1997) *Excitable Speech. A Politics of the Performative.* New York (et al.): Routledge.

Carlson, Marvin (2003) *Performance. A Critical Introduction.* London/New York: Routledge.

Christ, Susan/Jordan, John, eds. (1995) *Victorian Literature and the Victorian Visual Imagination.* Berkeley: California UP.

Collins, Richard et al., eds. (1986) *Media, Culture and Society. A Critical Reader.* London: Sage.

Crane, Diana/Kawashima, Nobuko/Kawasaki, Ken'ichi, eds. (1992) *The Production of Culture. Media and the Urban Arts.* London: Sage.

Curschmann, Michael (2007) "Epistemologisches am Schnittpunkt von Wort und Bild". In: Id. *Wort, Bild, Text. Studien zur Medialität des Literarischen in Hochmittelalter und früher Neuzeit.* Tübingen: Niemeyer, 378–470.

Döring, Jörg et al. (2008) *Spatial Turn. Das Raumparadigma in den Kultur- und Sozialwissenschaften.* Bielefeld: Transcript.

Douglas, Mary (1974) *Ritual, Tabu und Körpersymbolik. Sozialanthropologische Studien in Industriegesellschaft und Stammeskultur.* Frankfurt a. M.: Fischer.

During, Simon (2005) *Cultural Studies: A Critical Introduction.* London (et al.): Routledge.

Eco, Umberto (1976) *A Theory of Semiotics.* London: Macmillan.

Edensor, Tim (2002) *National Identity, Popular Culture and Everyday Life.* Oxford: Berg.

Erll, Astrid/Nünning, Ansgar, eds. (2005) *Gedächtniskonzepte der Literaturwissenschaft. Theoretische Grundlegung und Anwendungsperspektiven.* Berlin/New York: de Gruyter.

Erll, Astrid/Nünning, Ansgar, eds. (2008) *Cultural Memory Studies. An International and Interdisciplinary Handbook.* Berlin/New York: de Gruyter.

Ette, Ottmar (2005) *Zwischen Welten schreiben. Literaturen ohne festen Wohnsitz.* Berlin: Kadmos.

Fahlenbach, Kathrin, ed. (2005) *Medien, Macht, Wahrnehmung. Mediale Dispotive des Sehens und Hörens.* Frankfurt a. M.: Lang.

Faulstich, Werner (2000) *Medienkulturen.* München: Fink.

Featherstone, Mike, ed. (1995) *Global Modernities.* London: Sage.

Fischer-Lichte, Erika (2005) *The Semiotics of Theatre.* Trans. J. Gaines, D. L. Jones. Bloomington/Indianapolis: Indiana UP.

Fiske, John (1989) *Understanding Popular Culture.* Boston: Unwin Hyman.

Flusser, Villém (1999) *Medienkultur.* Frankfurt a. M.: Fischer.

Foucault, Michel (1995) *Discipline and Punish. The Birth of the Prison.* Trans. A. Sheridan. New York: Vintage.

Frisby, David (1985) *Fragments of Modernity: Theories of Modernity in the Work of Simmel, Kracauer, and Benjamin.* Cambridge: Polity.

Fröhlich, Melanie (2008) *Zeitkonzeptionen in Erzähltheorie und Kulturwissenschaft. Ein kritischer Vergleich.* Saarbrücken: VDM.

Grossberg, Lawrence et al., eds. (1998) *Mediamaking. Mass Media in a Popular Culture.* Thousand Oaks, CA: Sage.

Großklaus, Götz (1997) *Medien-Zeit, Medien-Raum. Zum Wandel der raumzeitlichen Wahrnehmung in der Moderne.* Frankfurt a. M.: Suhrkamp.

Großklaus, Götz (2004) *Medien-Bilder. Inszenierung der Sichtbarkeit.* Frankfurt a. M.: Suhrkamp.

Gudehus, Christian/Eichenberg, Ariane/Weizer, Harald, eds. (2010) *Gedächtnis und Erinnerung. Ein interdisziplinäres Handbuch.* Stuttgart/Weimar: Metzler.

Günzel, Stephan, ed. (2009) *Raumwissenschaften.* Frankfurt a. M.: Suhrkamp.

Hall, Stuart et al., eds. (1980) *Culture, Media, Language. Working Papers in Cultural Studies.* London: Hutchinson.

Hallet, Wolfgang/Neumann, Birgit, eds. (2009) *Raum und Bewegung in der Literatur. Die Literaturwissenschaften und der Spatial Turn.* Bielefeld: transcript.

Hammersmith, James P. (1978) "Hamlet and the Myth of Memory". In: *English Literary History* 45, 597–605.

Harms, Wolfgang, ed. (1990) *Text und Bild. Bild und Text* (DFG-Symposium 1988). Stuttgart: Metzler.

Haug, Walter, ed. (1999) *Mittelalter und frühe Neuzeit. Übergänge, Umbrüche, Neuansätze.* Tübingen: Niemeyer.

Hayles, Nancy K. (1999) *How We Became Posthuman: Virtual Bodies in Cybernetics, Literature, and Informatics.* Chicago: Chicago UP.

Helbig, Jörg, ed. (1998) *Intermedialität. Theorie und Praxis eines interdisziplinären Forschungsgebiets.* Berlin: Erich Schmidt.

Hepp, Andreas, ed. (1999) *Kultur – Medien – Macht. Cultural Studies und Medienanalyse.* Opladen: Westdeutscher Verlag.

Hess-Lüttich, Ernest W. B./Müller, Jürgen E./Van Zoest, Aart J. A., eds. (1998) *Signs & Space.* Tübingen: Gunter Narr.

Hodkinson, Paul (2011) *Media, Culture and Society. An Introduction.* London: Sage.

Honnefelder, Gottfried, ed. (1989) *Was also ist die Zeit? Erfahrungen der Zeit.* Frankfurt a. M.: Insel.

Hörning, Karl H./Winter, Rainer, eds. (2005) *Widerspenstige Kulturen: Cultural Studies als Herausforderung.* Frankfurt a. M.: Suhrkamp.

Hubbard, Phil/Kitchin, Rob (2011) *Key Thinkers on Space and Place.* 2nd ed. London: Sage.

Jaeger, Friedrich et al., eds. (2004) *Handbuch der Kulturwissenschaften.* Bd. 1–3. Stuttgart: Metzler.

Jahraus, Oliver (2003) *Literatur als Medium. Sinnkonstruktion und Subjekterfahrung zwischen Bewusstsein und Kommunikation.* Weilerswist: Vellbrück.

Kablitz, Andreas, ed. (2003) *Zeit und Text: philosophische, kulturanthropologische, literarhistorische und linguistische Beiträge.* München: Fink.

Kaschuba, Wolfgang (2004) *Die Überwindung der Distanz. Zeit und Raum in der europäischen Moderne.* Frankfurt a. M.: Fischer.

Kern, Stephan (2003) *The Culture of Time and Space: 1880-1918.* London: Harvard UP.

Koselleck, Reinhart (2000) *Zeitschichten. Studien zur Historik.* Frankfurt a. M.: Suhrkamp.

Kosut, Mary/Moore, Lisa J. (2010) *The Body Reader. Essential Social and Cultural Readings.* New York: New York UP.

Král, Françoise (2009) *Critical Identities in Contemporary Anglophone Diasporic Literature.* London/New York: Palgrave Macmillan.

Kümmel, Albert et al., eds. (2004) *Einführung in die Geschichte der Medien.* Paderborn: Fink UTB.

Landsberg, Alison (2004) *Prosthetic Memory. The Transformation of American Remembrance in the Age of Mass Culture.* New York: Columbia UP.

Leistyna, Pepi (2005) *Cultural Studies. From Theory to Action.* Malden/Oxford: Blackwell.

Liebrand, Claudia/Schneider, Irmela, eds. (2002) *Medien in Medien.* Mediologie 6. Köln: Dumont.

List, Elisabeth/Fiala, Erwin, eds. (2004) *Grundlagen der Kulturwissenschaft. Interdisziplinäre Kulturstudien.* Tübingen/Basel: Francke.

Low, Setha M./Lawrence-Zunigais, Denise, eds. (2003) *The Anthropology of Space and Place: Locating Culture.* Malden/Oxford: Blackwell.

Loxley, James (2007) *Performativity.* The New Critical Idiom. New York (et al.): Routledge.

Lull, James (2000) *Media, Communication, Culture. A Global Approach.* Cambridge: Polity Press.

Lüsebrink, Hans-Jürgen (2005) *Interkulturelle Kommunikation. Interaktion, Fremdwahrnehmung, Kulturtransfer.* Stuttgart/Weimar: Metzler.

Martín Alcoff, Linda (2006) *Visible Identities: Race, Gender, and the Self.* Oxford (et al.): Oxford UP.

Maye, Harun/Scholz, Leander, eds. (2011) *Einführung in die Kulturwissenschaft.* München: Fink.

McLuhan, Marshall (1962) *The Gutenberg Galaxy: The Making of Typographic Man.* London: Routledge.

Mersch, Dieter, ed. (1998) *Zeichen über Zeichen. Texte zur Semiotik von Peirce bis Eco und Derrida.* München: dtv.

Middeke, Martin, ed. (2002) *Zeit und Roman: Zeiterfahrung im historischen Wandel und ästhetischer Paradigmenwechsel vom sechzehnten Jahrhundert bis zur Postmoderne.* Würzburg: Königshausen & Neumann.

Miller, Toby, ed. (2001) *A Companion to Cultural Studies* (Blackwell Companions in Cultural Studies 3). Malden/Oxford: Blackwell.

Mitchell, William J. T. (1986) *Iconology. Image, Text, Ideology.* Chicago: Chicago UP.

Nünning, Ansgar, ed. (1998) *Metzler Lexikon Literatur- und Kulturtheorie.* Stuttgart: Metzler.

Nünning, Ansgar/Nünning, Vera, eds. (2003) *Konzepte der Kulturwissenschaften.* Stuttgart: Metzler.

Nünning, Ansgar/Sommer, Roy, eds. (2004) *Kulturwissenschaftliche Literaturwissenschaft.* Tübingen: Narr.

Öhlschläger, Claudia/Wiens, Birgit, eds. (1997) *Körper – Gedächtnis – Schrift. Der Körper als Medium kultureller Erinnerung.* Geschlechterdifferenz & Literatur, Vol. 7. Berlin: Erich Schmidt.

Ong, Walter J. (1982) *Orality and Literacy. The Technologizing of the Word.* London: Methuen.

Pias, Claus et al., eds. (1999) *Kursbuch Medienkultur. Die maßgeblichen Theorien von Brecht bis Baudrillard.* Stuttgart: DVA.

Pirner, Manfred L., ed. (2003) *Homo medialis. Perspektiven und Probleme einer Anthropologie der Medien.* München: kopaed-Verlag.

Poltermann, Andreas, ed. (1995) *Literaturkanon – Medienereignis – kultureller Text.* Berlin: Erich Schmidt.

Rabb, Jane M., ed. (1995) *Literature and Photography. Interactions 1840–1990. A Critical Anthology.* Albuquerque: New Mexico UP.

Radstone, Susannah/Schwarz, Bill, eds. (2010) *Memory. Histories, Theories, Debates.* New York: Fordham UP.

Renner, Ursula (2005) "Schädel-Meditationen. Zur Kulturgeschichte eines Denkmodells". In: W. Hulk, U. Renner, eds. *Biologie, Psychologie, Poetologie.* Würzburg: Königshausen & Neumann, 171-200.

Ricoeur, Paul (1984) *Time and Narrative.* Trans. K. McLaughlin, D. Pellauer. Chicago: Chicago UP.

Riedel, Wolfgang (1996) *‚Homo Natura'. Literarische Anthropologie um 1900.* Berlin: de Gruyter.

Ryan, Michael (2010) *Cultural Studies: A Practical Introduction.* Malden/Oxford: Blackwell.

Sarkowsky, Katja (2007) *AlterNative spaces: Constructions of Space in Native American and First Nations' literatures.* Heidelberg: Winter.

Schacter, Daniel L. (1996) *Searching for Memory. The Brain, the Mind, and the Past.* New York: HarperCollins.

Schapiro, Meyer (1996) *Words, Script and Pictures. Semiotics of Visual Language.* New York: George Braziller Inc.

Schleifer, Ronald (2009) *Modernism and Time: The Logic of Abundance in Literature, Science, and Culture, 1880–1930.* Cambridge (et al.): Cambridge UP.

Schmitz-Emans, Monika/Schmeling, Manfred, eds. (1999) *Das visuelle Gedächtnis der Literatur.* Würzburg: Königshausen & Neumann.

Schnell, Ralf, ed. (2007) *Mediennutzung, Medienwirkung, Medienregulierung.* Stuttgart: Metzler.

Segeberg, Harro (2003) *Literatur im Medienzeitalter. Literatur, Technik und Medien seit 1914.* Darmstadt: Wissenschaftliche Buchgesellschaft.

Simon, Josef (1994) *Zeichen und Interpretation.* Frankfurt a. M.: Suhrkamp.

Simonis, Annette, ed. (2000) *Zeitwahrnehmung und Zeitbewusstsein der Moderne.* Bielefeld: Aisthetis.

Spry, Tami (2011) *Body, Paper, Stage. Writing and Performing Autoethnography.* Walnut Creek, CA: Left Coast Press.

Starobinski, Jean (1991) *Kleine Geschichte des Körpergefühls.* Frankfurt a. M.: Fischer.

Stein, Mark (2004) *Black British Literature. Novels of Transformation.* Columbus, OH: Ohio State UP.

Sternberg, Meir (2009) "The Laokoon Today. Interart Relations, Modern Projects and Projections". In: *Poetics Today* 20/2, 291-379.

Stierstorfer, Klaus/Volkmann, Laurenz, eds. (2005) *Kulturwissenschaft interdisziplinär.* Tübingen: Gunter Narr.

Teske, Doris (2002) *Cultural Studies. GB – Anglistik – Amerikanistik.* Berlin: Cornelsen.

Trabant, Jürgen (1996) *Elemente der Semiotik.* Stuttgart: UTB.

Uricchio, William/Kinnebrock, Susanne, eds. (2006) *Media Cultures.* Heidelberg: Winter.

Waechter, Matthias (1996) *Die Erfindung des amerikanischen Westens. Die Geschichte der Frontier-Debatte.* Freiburg: Rombach.

Warf, Barney, ed. (2009) *The Spatial Turn. Interdisciplinary Perspectives.* London (et al.): Routledge.

Weinrich, Harald (1998) *Lethe. Kunst und Kritik des Vergessens.* München: Beck.

Wende, Waltraud (2004) *Kultur – Medien – Literatur. Literaturwissenschaft als Medienkulturwissenschaft.* Würzburg: Könighausen & Neumann.

Whitrow, Gerald J. (1988) *Time in History. The Evolution of Our General Awareness of Time and Temporal Perspective.* Oxford (et al.): Oxford UP.

Winkels, Hubert (1997) *Leselust und Bildermacht. Über Literatur, Fernsehen und neue Medien.* Köln: Kiepenhauer & Witsch.

Wirth, Uwe, ed. (2002) *Performanz. Zwischen Sprachphilosophie und Kulturwissenschaften.* Frankfurt a. M.: Suhrkamp.

Wischermann, Clemens, ed. (2000) *Körper mit Geschichte. Der menschliche Körper als Ort der Selbst- und Weltdeutung.* Studien zur Geschichte des Alltags, Vol. 17. Stuttgart: Steiner.

Woodward, Kathrin (1977) *Identity and Difference.* London: Sage.

Index of Subjects

Index of Names